Contents

PART 4 INFORMATIONAL READING 95

PART 5 CREATIVE WRITING WITH CHILDREN 125

PART 6 MAKING INFORMATIONAL WRITING FUN 157

Find worksheets and other activities in a workbook available for purchase, expanding on the ideas in this book, at www.365TeacherSecrets.com.

Introduction

How To Make This Book Work for Your Family:

Congratulations! You have just taken the first step in helping your child improve not only his academics in elementary school but also his attitude toward school this year and for years to come. *365 Teacher Secrets for Parents* is jam-packed with fun ways to work with and help your child. No longer does school have to be tough. Who says practicing things at home can't be fun?

We have written this book after years of teaching elementary school and many more years working closely with individual elementary-aged children. We've spent over ten years collecting 365 of the very best ideas, the most helpful activities, and, yes, some secrets teachers have been using successfully for years, to help remediate and/ or enrich young children, so that we could share them with you.

Some of the ideas in this book cover the major subjects in school: reading, writing, math, spelling, science, and social studies. We also have included ideas for getting started, developing critical thinking skills, increasing self-esteem and self-reliance, and creating school-year success.

The elementary school years are very important. They set the tone for your child's entire school career and beyond. On one hand, too many struggles early on can turn kids off to learning, damage self-confidence, and make it difficult to ever catch up. On the other hand, a great, successful experience can help children develop a love of learning and help them do well during all of their schooling years.

So, how can you be sure your child's experience is a good one? Start by creating good habits at home, knowing what is going on in his classroom, keeping up on his progress, and practicing anything that needs work. Inside this book are ways to do all of that!

How to use this book

We have created this book in a busy-parent-friendly way by offering you one simple idea or activity per day. (There are also variations so you can tailor the activity to meet your child's specific needs.) We hope that one idea per day will be easy to stick with and that—one year from now—you will have learned many important ways to work with your child and to make learning fun.

Parts 1 and 2 introduce small ways to get you started down the right track both at home and at school. Parts 3-10 each focus on one area of the elementary school curriculum. The last two Parts concentrate on critical thinking and self-esteem/ self-reliance.

The ideas in this book are not cumulative. In other words, you do not have to read every idea in order to understand a later one. If we do reference something we have discussed at length earlier, we let you know where you can look to find out more. Many ideas also come with original, ready-made worksheets we've created and placed in a workbook available for purchase on our website (www.365teachersecrets.com) to help you get started or to see an example.

One way to use this book would be to begin at the beginning with Part 1, Idea #1. Just commit to one brief idea/activity per day. Maybe your whole family can read it together. Maybe just you and your child will work together. Either way, if the idea seems to fit what your child needs, give it a try. If it doesn't seem applicable to your child at this time, skip it. You can always come back to it later.

Another way to use this book would be to jump right to a particular Part if your child is having trouble in one or more areas. You can browse the whole Part for ideas you want to try or go one day at a time there as well. (Note: Part 1 is full of ways to help get ready and organized at home, so it may be a good idea to read it early on even if you are skipping around.)

Of course, you can do both. Begin with Idea #1, but also jump ahead to a certain Part if your child needs help in a particular subject.

When the year is over, and you have read all 365 ideas, you do not have to stop there. Going through the book again the next year can help refresh your memory and remind you of things you may have passed over the first time. If you have more than one child, reviewing the ideas one day at a time may help you see things in a new light; what might not have seemed a good fit for one child may be perfect for another!

Whether your child is behind and needs some extra help or is right on target, this book will offer you and your family one fun, helpful, easy idea each day for a year. There is something for every child, whether she is just beginning elementary school and needing to get off to a good start or in middle or upper elementary.

You are your child's first and most important teacher. By buying this book, you have shown your commitment to helping her improve. We hope you will enjoy all of the ideas, activities and expert secrets inside its cover. Soon you may realize these ideas really aren't so "secret," after all—they seem commonsense once you become aware of them.

So, congratulations on beginning an exciting journey of helping your child grow, learn, and find success in elementary school! We hope you learn a lot and, of course, have fun.

Website:

You will find 365 terrific ideas inside this book. In addition, we've also created a website, www.365TeacherSecrets.com, to accompany the book. There you will find a workbook you can purchase, full of original worksheets we've created to accompany over 100 of the book's ideas and activities. (Check the end of each activity to see if there is an accompanying workbook page.)

The workbook is full of

- organizers for games;
- detailed explanations of concepts mentioned;
- creative pages on which to compose ideas, plans, etc.;
- poetry frames;
- writing organizers;
- explanations and how-to's of reading, writing, and math concepts;
- book lists;
- word lists;
- science experiments;
- Math Games;
- puzzles;
- and much, much more!

All of the activities in the book stand alone, and the pages in the workbook are not necessary. However, they do a lot of the work for you and give you additional opportunities to practice with your child the many concepts in the book. We think you will find them very helpful.

Part 1
Getting Ready: Building Lasting Work Habits

Part 1 is dedicated to creating the good habits of life-long learners. Unlike most of the remaining Parts, which are devoted to one specific content area, Part 1 contains general information to get your family off to a good start. The 31 ideas and concepts should help put your child on the right track toward academic success.

#1
D.E.A.R.
(Drop Everything and Read)

Take time to read; it is the foundation of wisdom.
~Old English Prayer

Today make it a point to cuddle up and read with your child every day. Research shows that even as little as 15 minutes a day not only enhances your child's love of reading but also contributes to his overall academic success. It doesn't matter if you have a kindergartner or a fifth-grader, children love to be read to. It is intimate, free, and fun. It is perhaps the easiest way to increase your child's academic skills. Experiment and find an uninterrupted time that works well with your family. Try:

- first thing in the morning;

- right after school;

- after dinner; or

- at bedtime.

Check out the American Library Association website for lots of information on good books to read at all reading levels: http://www.ala.org/alsc/booklists.

#2

T.E.A.M. Work!

Snowflakes are one of nature's most fragile things,
but just look what they can do when they stick together.
~Vista M. Kelly

T.E.A.M. is an acronym for Together Everyone Achieves More. Make this a family motto. Obviously, you want to help your child succeed in school. You can do that. So can the rest of the family. In this Part, you will read about specific ways to get the whole family involved in learning. Today, sit down and discuss commitments each family member can make to be aware of and involved in what is going on academically in your child's life.

Many projects at home and at school can involve the entire family. Every person can contribute something. Let your child contribute, too, to *your* endeavors. The more you open up communication for the whole family, the more support everyone receives. Decide today that the success of your child is important and worthy of everyone's effort.

Exercise: On a sheet of paper (or on the corresponding page in the Workbook that accompanies this book, if you have it) work with your child to write down your commitments.

See our workbook available for purchase at www.365TeacherSecrets.com for a sample page for you and your child to write down your commitments.

#3
Defining Success

The only place you'll find success before work is in the dictionary.
~May B. Smith

You want your child to be successful. You bought this book to find ways to help ensure that. You will find many, but keep in mind that success comes in many forms. Often, elementary parents become too focused on *academic* success, wanting to get their child off to a good start. While this is definitely a valid point, don't forget to find other ways your child is successful.

Today, begin an informal discussion (perhaps at the dinner table) about success. How does everyone define it? How does each hope to achieve it? If the discussion starts off slowly or if you just want to add some inspiration, try reading this poem by Harry Emerson Fosdick:

To laugh often and much;

to win the respect of intelligent people and the affection of children;

to earn the appreciation of honest critics and endure the betrayal of false friends;

to appreciate beauty;

to find the best in others;

to leave the world a bit better, whether by a healthy child, a garden patch or a redeemed social condition;

to know even one life has breathed easier because you have lived.

This is to have succeeded.

Your child is already full of wonder and beauty and successes. While on the road to *academic* achievement, try not to lose sight of the many other important things and all of the other ways that people are successful in life. With your child, write down all the talents he already possesses and discuss how they make him special.

See our workbook available for purchase at www.365TeacherSecrets.com for a sample page for you and your child to write down ways your family is successful.

#4
Setting Goals

> *Goals not written down are just wishes.*
> *~Unknown*

To encourage your child to care about her success, have her set goals for herself. Ask her what she'd like to improve upon. For a younger child, encourage her to start with something simple and attainable such as learning her address and phone number so she'll feel successful right away. For older children, the goals could be complex, such as learning the multiplication tables, writing in cursive, or doing long division.

Have your child set new goals each week, month, or whenever the previous goal is achieved. Keep track of her progress in a visible place, such as a refrigerator, so that everyone can be proud of her success. You may even want to have the whole family try this! Wouldn't it be great if *everyone* had a goal they were working to attain? When your child sees that others have goals, too, and that they have to really work at them, she will not only be more motivated to accomplish hers but also will understand that goals can take time.

See our workbook available for purchase at www.365TeacherSecrets.com for a sample page for you and your child to write down your goals.

#5
Personal Journals

> *Nurture your mind with great thoughts.*
> *~Benjamin Disraeli*

Reading aloud with no one around can be a safe way for your child to experiment with and gain command of reading skills. *Writing* only for himself can do the same for his writing skills. One way to accomplish this is to let your child choose a diary or notebook to use as a personal journal. In this journal, he is free to write whatever crosses his mind with no one there to check his spelling or point out punctuation errors.

Some children will love this idea and write in their journal every day with pleasure. For others, it may be helpful to set aside some time (perhaps right after D.E.A.R. time, just before bed, or first thing in the morning) just for the purpose of journaling. If every day seems too much at first, begin with one or two times a week and gradually work up to a comfortable amount of time and frequency. It's better to set smaller, easily attainable goals. Requiring too much too soon can backfire and create a reluctant writer.

#6
The Message Center

Failure to prepare is preparing to fail.
~Anonymous

Creating a Message Center is an easy way for the entire family to get organized and stay on track. It needs to be in a central location that all family members see frequently throughout the day, such as the kitchen. Every family has different needs, so every message center will not look the same. Here are some great ideas to get you started:

- Display a monthly calendar where everyone writes important events for all to see.

- Offer a weekly calendar so that everyone, at a glance, can know what is going on each day. (The wipe-off kind work great because they're reusable, have plenty of room, and are easy to update. Try a different color for each family member!)

- Have a specific and convenient place for communications (e.g., letters to and from school, notices, lunch money) to be dropped off or picked up. This could be a magnetic bin on the side of the fridge, a tray on the desk, or something similar.)

You could try displaying:

- Descriptions of important homework assignments or projects so the whole family is aware of them and may be more apt to help with them.

- Spelling lists. Again, the whole family can be involved in helping your child practice them.

- A word of the day or week. This could be a spelling word, a reading word (for younger children), or even a challenge word (older kids can learn its definition and try using it!)

- Great accomplishments. (Drawings, good spelling tests, a finished report, poetry...)

#7
Be a Role Model

The country clubs, the cars, the boats,
Your assets may be ample,
But the best inheritance you can leave your kids
Is to be a good example.
~Barry Spilchuk

Teachers know the importance of making sure they are also reading during the class' silent reading time. The children are always amazed at this at the beginning of the school year. "*You* like to read, too?" That is one opportunity teachers have to do exactly as the children are doing. *You* have so many others.

Your child can see you using a calculator to balance your checkbook, preparing healthy meals from all of the different food groups, reading maps to prepare for a road trip. Do you take any kind of classes for your job or outside of it? Consider doing some of your homework side-by-side when your child does his. Could you and your child sign up to take a continuing education class together through your school district? How fun to learn something new together!

When your child grows up seeing you doing and enjoying these things, he will know they are a part of life and naturally want to learn to do them himself. Let your child see you doing all of the different things you do during the day. Let him help (even if it's a small job) as often as he wants. Make an effort after dinner to turn off the TV and read the paper, write a letter, or pick up the book your child is reading for school and check it out. You can *say* reading is fun and math is important, but you may never even have to if you actually live it! If your child sees that *you* value these things, chances are that he will, too.

#8
Life is Full of Learning

The work can wait while you show the child the rainbow,
But the rainbow won't wait while you do the work.
~Patricia Clafford

Everywhere you go and everything you do with your child is an opportunity for learning. Of course, you do not want everything you say and do to become a lesson, but just being aware of the endless *opportunities* can broaden your child's view of the world.

A good teacher will bring all of the classroom lessons to life by showing how they apply to the real world. You can do this, too. Here are some examples:

- Ask your child questions about gas when you're filling up the tank.

- Read signs together while driving somewhere.

- Predict and then count the number of cars that drive by your house in a 15-minute span.

- Research and visit the oldest building in your town.

- Discuss the water cycle the next time it rains.

- Lie in the grass together and observe the bugs. (Look up one you don't recognize in a bug book from the library.) Now, roll over and talk about the clouds. (Don't forget to find shapes in them!)

You get the picture! Learning is everywhere! These activities take no preparation at all. Just look around and initiate discussions when you're with your child. Think about what she's learning in school. How does it relate to her life? Point it out. A child will remember so much more if she can see how it fits into the big picture—her world. A good teacher will always do this. *You* can, too!

#9

I Don't Know. Let's Find Out!

> *Obstacles don't have to stop you.*
> *If you run into a wall, don't turn around and give up.*
> *Figure out how to climb it, go through it, or work around it.*
> *~Michael Jordan*

Yes, it is easy and enjoyable to tell your child about things in real-life situations, but what happens when the discussion continues further than your knowledge on that particular subject? It's actually quite simple. Tell your child you just don't know! This may shock him at first if he has never heard you say that before because children tend to think their teachers and parents know everything. However, we all know we *don't* know it all.

Teach your children that smart people don't have all the answers, they just know how and where to find them. Finish your "I don't know" with "but..."

- ...let's go to the library and check out a book on dinosaurs.

- ...let's go home and ask your brother about how pictures are developed.

- ...let's look up the solar system on the Internet.

- ...let's call Aunt Beth; she's been to Africa.

- ...let's write a letter to Grandpa Bill; he used to fly planes.

You're actually teaching your child a wonderful lesson every time you admit you're not sure about something. You're providing him with a new tool, a new life skill: researching.

See our workbook for a worksheet to help organize this activity.

#10
Share and Share Alike

I think the one lesson I have learned is that there is no substitute for paying attention.
~Diane Sawyer

Have you ever asked your child, "So, what did you do in school today?" and received the infamous reply, "Nuthin'"? Next time, try opening up the lines of communication by asking her a more specific question such as:

- What was the best part about today? (Besides lunch and recess!)

- Tell me about one thing that made you happy, sad, frustrated, etc.

- What was one thing you could have done better today?

- What are you most proud of today?

A reluctant talker might be encouraged if *you* go first and begin by discussing your day. (That way you can squeeze your questions about her day into your conversation!) If you are open and willing to share your thoughts and feelings, you can feel confident that soon your child will, too.

#11
Thinking Out Loud

Enthusiasm is contagious. Start an epidemic.
~Unknown

Did you know that talking to yourself not only helps you organize your thoughts but also helps your child? When you are working through a problem, make it a point to say what you are thinking out loud. Look for opportunities to do this. For example:

> "I need to make 100 cupcakes for the bake sale. If each muffin tin makes 12 cupcakes and I have 2 muffin tins I can make 24 at a time. So, let's see... how many batches will I need to bake? I will divide 100 by 24...."

Your child will realize that adults, like children, must go through a series of steps to conquer a problem. If you're enthusiastic about learning and are willing to take the time to really think something through, then chances are your child will be, too!

#12
Language is More Than Reading and Writing

We have two ears and one mouth so that we can listen twice as much as we speak.
~Epictetus

Parents are usually very aware of how well their children are doing in reading and writing. You may set aside time to help them practice and make an effort to show them that they are valued. There are two other components of language that are also very important, and these skills are often overlooked. They are *listening* and *speaking*.

You do not need to set aside time in the day or week to practice listening and speaking to show your child that these are important life skills. Just make an effort to show your child you are really listening to her when she is speaking. She will know she has your attention by your body language, eye contact, and relevant responses. Show her how to do the same when *she* is listening. Try to remember that these, too, are important skills for life.

Try this website for Active Listening Games: http://www.buzzle.com/articles/active-listening-games.html.

#13
Get it Together

Beginnings are always messy.
~John Galsworthy

Is your morning routine chaotic or calm? Do you hear these panicked cries in the morning just as the school bus pulls up: "Mom, where is my backpack?" "I can't find my homework!" Here are a few suggestions if your morning is more hectic than relaxed:

- Have a specific place for your child's backpack that everyone agrees upon. When he comes home from school, help him make it a habit to put it there every day. After homework is completed, practice putting everything back into the backpack and place it in its special spot the night *before* school. Now, even on mornings when everyone is running behind, he can just grab his backpack and know that everything is in it, done, and ready to turn in.

- Buy or create a homework folder or notebook. For younger children, get one with a dual pocket folder. Have him keep his assigned homework in the left pocket. He can transfer the work to the right pocket once it is completed. He should bring home the folder every day whether there is homework in it or not so that it becomes a habit.

- For the older elementary child, an assignment notebook may be best. The notebook can be used to record assignments for the day and whether they were finished. If your child tends to be forgetful about doing his homework or bringing it home, a habit could be made that you check his assignment book every day. At first, it may mean a trip back to school to pick up forgotten books or assignments, but if that extra time needed to go back to school cuts out his play/free time, you may start to see a less forgetful child.

#14

Getting There is Half the Fun

It's good to have an end to journey toward;
but it is the journey that matters in the end.
~Ursula K. LeGuin

When you are working with your child on a project, it is tempting to focus solely on *finishing* it, but that may actually send the wrong message. The steps your child takes in order to complete the project are often equally as important as the project itself.

For instance, if your child needs to write a report, the process involved might include brainstorming, researching, reading, note-taking, drafting, revising, and editing. Each of these skills is important in and of itself and should be emphasized along with the completion of the project.

You could divide the overall project into steps and concentrate on one step a day to emphasize its importance and avoid your child becoming overwhelmed. The steps and effort she contributes toward completing a task are very often more important than the final product because she is learning *how* to do things, not just to get them done.

#15

Just do it!

I hear and I forget,
I see and I remember,
I do and I understand.
~Confucius

Did you ever say to someone, "Could you just write it down for me?" Have you ever been somewhere ten times and yet cannot get there again on your own because you hadn't actually driven the car there yourself? Did you tell your child the fire was hot several times, but it took him burning himself never to touch it again?

As the saying above goes, *telling or showing* someone something may not be enough. When children (and adults, too, for that matter) are told something, they may or may not remember it. If they can see it written down, they may retain more. When they do it, when they are part of the discovery of learning about it, chances are they'll never forget it.

You can take this even one step further by having your child teach learned information to someone else. (He can also write about it for himself in his journal.) You cannot teach something or journal about it without knowing enough about it.

#16
Break it up!

Nothing is particularly hard
if you divide it up into small jobs.
~Henry Ford

Many tasks, from homework assignments to chores, can seem overwhelming to children. No matter what the job is, if your child needs help, perhaps you could help her *before* she even starts. See if you and your child can work together to break the entire task into smaller, more manageable parts.

For a younger child, it may be helpful to write the steps down for her to check off as she accomplishes them. For older children, a verbal discussion may be all that is necessary to get them off to a good start. Your child may be more willing and able to take the whole project on herself once she sees a clear way to get there.

#17
Having a Homework Policy

How doth the little busy bee improve each shining hour
And gather honey all the day from every opening flower!
~Isaac Watts

If your child is like most, he is probably as busy as a bee. Whether he has homework every day or seldom, truckloads or not much, it is important for your family to have a Homework Policy. This may include rules for when homework is to be completed, where, and how.

Many fights stem from kids trying to put homework off until later in the evening or even for another day. If you establish rules that must be obeyed, your child will feel no need to argue. Choose a time when you or another responsible adult will be around to help out if needed. You could try first thing after school, just before or after dinner, before any TV/ video games, etc. Just make sure that he has time to finish before bed.

Your rules may differ for long-term homework projects. Perhaps you could use the idea of breaking the project down into smaller parts here, too, and create a timetable for when certain steps need to be completed.

Having a homework policy will not only alleviate endless requests for postponement, but it will also let both you and your child know that homework doesn't have to be overwhelming.

See our workbook available for purchase at www.365TeacherSecrets.com for a place to record your homework policy.

#18
Creating a Study Area

If you have built castles in the air, your work need not be lost;
that is where they should be.
Now put foundations under them.
~Henry David Thoreau

Giving your child a special, well-equipped study space is a good foundation for quality accomplishments. When your child has a designated spot in which to complete homework, it will not only help her to be better organized, but also will offer her a welcome and ready place that is just right for producing her best work. It should be an area with enough space for her to spread out the things she will need to be working on. It should be a well-lit, relatively quiet area with no distractions (such as the TV, phone, or little siblings) so that she can concentrate. Some things that would be helpful to have in the study area include:

- a dictionary and thesaurus;

- pens, pencils (with erasers), colored pencils, crayons;

- a pencil sharpener;

- a stapler, paper clips;

- a ruler;

- a calculator;

- a globe;

- a comfy chair.

With these supplies readily available to her, your child may be more apt to use them to complete, or even *enhance*, her work.

#19
Creating a Life Long Learner

The important thing is not so much that every child be taught,
as that every child should be given the wish to learn.
~John Lubbock

As your family takes the journey toward academic success together, there is something very important to keep in mind. Try to remember that your goal is not to fill your child up with information. You want to awaken his sense of curiosity, ambition, and desire to learn on his own. It's not so important *what* you teach him but that you teach him to think.

If you can instill in your child a sense of wonder and a love of learning, your efforts will surely be rewarded. You will create a child who is not afraid to question, to try, to take a risk, and to think for himself. These are qualities that will last him a lifetime. After all, as Malcom S. Forbes said, "Education's purpose is to replace an empty mind with an open one."

#20
"Hidden Treasure"

An accomplishment sticks to a person.
~Japenese proverb

Learn how to play Hidden Treasure! In a never-ending effort to make learning fun, we have created this game to be used with just about any area of the curriculum to help kids learn reading words, spelling words, definitions, and more. We haven't met a kid yet who didn't like to play (and beat us at) it! Basic play consists of these few steps:

1. Gather some note cards, a box, and two different kinds of counters (pennies and dimes work great!).

2. Write all words to be learned on index cards. Also create a few that say "Treasure!"

3. Place all cards in a box, mixed up, upside down. Take turns drawing a card and reading/spelling/defining it. (Hint: If spelling is the focus, either pass the card you pick to the other person quickly, so you don't see the word too long, or take turns picking words for each other to spell.)

4. If the person gets it right, she earns a counter worth 1. If not, no counter is earned. Once a player earns 10 single counters, she can trade them for a counter worth 10. (If a "Treasure" card is drawn, the player can trade in her single coins for one worth 10 regardless of how many she has.)

   To even it out if you are playing with your child, you can also let her read/ spell/ define your words, too; this lets her have the chance to earn more points! (On her turn she can spell/read/define the word she picks out and then, also, the one you had just picked, too.)

5. Play continues until all cards have been drawn. The winner is the one who has the most points.

Here are some different things you could put into the Hidden Treasure Box:

- reading words;

- sentences containing those reading words;

- vocabulary words with definitions on the back;

- spelling words;

- words from a story she is learning to read;

- challenge words (to read or spell);

- definitions for content words she is learning about in school (science, social studies, etc.);

- dates in history and their importance;

- basic math facts (addition, subtraction, multiplication, division); and

- math facts in other areas.

The workbook available for purchase at www.365teachersecrets.com has more detailed instructions for the game.

#21
Finding Success Every Day!

The sweetest of all sounds is praise.
~Xenophon

Praise at least one success a day. Even on a bad day, your child exhibits strengths. Look for them. Say them out loud. Remind him of his strengths when he is struggling, and encourage him to press on. Look back at the goals he set and focus on when those (or even parts of those) are reached.

Make sure, however, that it counts. Make a conscious effort not to overpraise. Parents, teachers, coaches, and many adults often think they will "give" children self-esteem if they praise every little thing they do. "Way to take out your crayons!" "Great job on drawing that line!" "You put that crayon back in the box so well!" Of course, these are exaggerations but sometimes not by much. Kids can't be *given* self-esteem. They have to *earn* it. They know the difference deep down. So, save the praise for when he really deserves it, and he really *will* feel proud.

Chances are, when you make a conscious effort to praise your child (at least once) every day, you may be rewarded when you hear him doing the same for others!

#22
Chores

He did each single thing as if he did nothing else.
~Charles Dickens

Studies show that having your child help with basic household chores does more than just get the house clean. By taking charge of a chore, a child learns about responsibility, consequences, planning ahead, establishing a goal, and planning how to reach it. (Not to mention the satisfaction that comes from a job well done!)

Giving your child too many chores may become overwhelming, though. Experiment to find an arrangement that works well for everyone involved.

The workbook on the 365teachersecrests.com website contains a sample chore chart.

#23

Kids Are Teachers, Too

> *By learning you will teach, by teaching you will learn.*
> *~Latin proverb*

From their youngest days, children like to do things independently. When they do so, they feel like adults. You can give them that chance. When your child has learned something, let him be a teacher to his peers, siblings, grandparents, and you. Look for ways to let your child teach something to someone else.

Research shows that children learn:

- 20% of what they *read*
- 30% of what they *hear*
- 40% of what they *see*
- 50% of what they *say*
- 60% of what they *do* and
- 90% of what they *teach* someone else.

See Idea #357 for more information about letting your child be the teacher.

#24

Displaying Work

> *If children live with recognition, they learn to have a goal.*
> *~Dorothy L. Nolte*

Your child will feel a great sense of pride when you hang up something she's made. Displaying her work shows that you are proud of her and what she's done. This will look different as your child gets older: from the first finger paintings to the cute little poem to the detailed reports she will write.

If your refrigerator gets full, try displaying things on the bedroom doors or even taking something to work with you to hang by your desk. Could Aunt Debbie hang something at her house? Think about the picture or writing and find the perfect place or person for it. You could save "extras" in a special basket for times when your child writes a letter to someone (like a thank you note, for instance). She could search through the basket to find the perfect item to send along with the note.

There are also websites where you can actually create a book of your child's work and then share it with family members. A popular one that many people use is www.Picaboo.com. You can take pictures of your child's work, upload them to the website and make them into a book. It's cool! It's one more way to show your child that she is very special.

#25
Unplug Yourself!

Technology is just a tool.
In terms of getting the kids working together and motivating them,
the teacher is the most important.
~Bill Gates

Just as you are developing a policy for homework, you may also feel the need to create one for the TV and other technology. Many parents underestimate the power that television and video games have over children. We will not discuss the nature of TV shows and video games these days or the physical and emotional effects they often have on children. What is important here is that certain things should take precedence over all the technology.

Only you can be sure what these things are, of course, but some may include homework, family discussion or "together" time, play, reading time, going outside, etc. For some families, setting a limit of one hour or one show a day works best. For others, it's best simply to have a list of requirements that must be met before the TV can be turned on. (For example, chores and homework.)

Can all members of your family completely "unplug" themselves for one hour a night and do other stuff? How about one whole evening a week? Or maybe just Saturday afternoons? Make it a big deal, a special time, and see how much fun you can all have (either together or separately) with no technology at all!

#26
The Value of the Library

Reading is to the mind what exercise is to the body.
~Sir Richard Steele

Have you been to the library lately? The library has a wealth of information and resources that can help you and your child with projects, reports, and so much more. All for free!

Talk with your family and choose library days each month. Make a goal to go at least twice a month. While you're there, apply for library cards for everyone.

You don't have to have a library card to enjoy the library's computers. Go to the children's or youth section and ask what programs are available that will interest or help your child. If you do not have access to a computer and the Internet at home, you can show your child how she can come to the library to do research. You may be surprised at the expanding multitude of resources that are available to help her.

#27

I Just Forgot!

If the person you are talking to doesn't appear to be listening, be patient.
It may simply be that he has a small piece of fluff in his ear.
~Winnie the Pooh

Do you find that when you ask your child to do more than one thing at a time, the task may only get partially done or not done at all? Perhaps it is less an attitude problem than you might be tempted to think. Children need practice building their memory and multi-tasking skills.

One way to improve your child's memory is by asking him to do a series of tasks. Use the words "first," "then," "next," and "finally" or number them 1, 2, 3, 4. Give him directions such as "First, go get your book bag. Second, put on your shoes and, third, wait by the door for me." It may be helpful to have a younger child repeat the directions first, before attempting to follow them. Ask him to visualize where these things are as you say them so he has a "picture" of where to go, too.

Another helpful aid is to find a song your child knows and likes. Borrow its tune and replace the words with the things he has to remember. For instance, use the melody from "Head, Shoulders, Knees and Toes" to remember to bring home all of his winter clothes from school: "Hat, snow pants, boots, and gloves." He can practice singing it every time he packs up to come home.

Find other ways in everyday life to help him increase his memorization capability. Give him 3, 4, or 5 things to remember when you take him shopping. Ask him, "What were the three things I asked you to remember for me?" With practice, his ability to remember things will increase.

Helping him at home should also increase his ability to remember multiple directions a teacher may give him at school. As the directions get harder and he accomplishes them, he will feel a sense of pride as well as improve his memory.

See the workbook available for purchase at www.365teachersecrets.com for a sample of a memory game.

#28

Learning is Child's Play

Play is children's work.
~Maria Montessori

We often transfer our hurried lives onto our children. We think they should always be busy with something and it had better be productive. Often, we do not allow them just to *be*. Just to *play*.

You remember that children learn best by *doing*. They are active learners. Young children learn more by their experiences than through words alone. That is why it is especially important for parents to provide a variety of experiences for their children. In this book, you will read about many ways to *work* with your child, but, please, do not forget about the importance of *play*!

Through play, cognitive, social, and emotional growth is accomplished. Through play and using their imagination, children learn about their world in ways no grown-up could have taught them. Through play, children can be in charge and be successful for they are making the rules. Through play, children can be children!

Here is what you can do:

- Understand the value of play.

- Encourage positive and age-appropriate play. (Just go by what you feel is right.)

- Provide a variety of appropriate materials.

- Get involved! Play with them! Get dirty together! Then get clean together!

- Don't forget to give them time to play alone, though, too.

#29

Get Ready... Get Set...

Blessed be the hand that prepares a pleasure for a child,
For there is no saying when and where it may bloom forth.
~Jerrold

Some of the activities that you will be introduced to in this book will require a little preparation. Maybe things will need to be gathered or cut out. Maybe you've decided to have your child help you cook a meal. Sound like more work for you? Not really if you think about the process of setting up for an activity as part of the fun to have *with* your child. He can learn a lot about planning, preparing, gathering, sorting, and organizing from just helping to *get ready* for an activity. Divide up tasks, or do all of the steps together.

Cleaning up will also go faster, too, if you ask your child to help you, and, again, many of those same skills come into play. At first, you may do a lot of "thinking out loud" to model how to do this: "Let's put away all of the refrigerated items first so they won't spoil" or "If you put away the rest of the ingredients, I will load all of the dirty dishes into the dishwasher."

These are life skills that your child will eventually need to know how to do. So, start now. It'll benefit both of you!

...GO!

#30
Some Habits Are Hard to *Make*

Habit is a cable; we weave a thread of it every day,
and at last we cannot break it.
~Horace Mann

Have you heard the theory that it takes 20 days to create a habit? If this is true, then some of the ideas you've read about (intended to last not only throughout the year but perhaps a lifetime) are probably not already a part of your family's routine. That's OK!

As Part 1 winds to a close, take a few minutes to review all the ideas and decide which ones you believe are beneficial to your child and your family. Which ones have you been doing? Which have worked? Which have you modified to fit your family exactly? Which ones do not appeal to you?

Now that you have identified which ideas are the most important ones, stick with them! Even if it's not always easy, remember that soon they will become a habit. Soon, they will be a part of the new routine that your family has created. This new routine is focused on making the most out of every day, and finding ways to work smarter, not harder. It's the routine that makes learning together a priority instead of just getting by year after year.

Abandon (or modify) an idea that continues to be *un*-fun. On the other hand, keep the ones you believe will help create positive, lasting qualities in your child.

#31
Creating a Learning Environment at Home

What is required is sight and insight—
then you may add one more: excite.
~Robert Frost

Part of helping your child succeed in school is creating a learning environment in your home. After all, you are your child's first teacher. You can create an atmosphere in which learning is valued by doing the things mentioned in Part 1. Here is a checklist of the main points:

- Have you found a good time for D.E.A.R.?

- Are the TV and video games turned off and your child turned on to another activity?

- Are you making it a point to be a good role model?

- Has your child set a goal for himself?

- Have you begun to set up ways (and spaces) to be better organized?

- Have you made a family trip to the library?

- Do you create opportunities to let your kids learn from everyday experiences and encourage them to teach you a thing or two, also?

- Have you played Hidden Treasure!? Have you won yet? (We didn't think so...)

- Is your family making attempts to work together on things?

- Are you praising when it's earned and playing?

Part 2
School Year Success

Part 2 helps give your child (and your whole family) ways to get the school year off to a good start and keep it running smoothly all year long.

"Back to school" means different things to different kids and their families. For many, it is exciting to meet new teachers, gather new hopes, and create new expectations. For some, it may be met with a few fears. As teachers, we have encountered many of these. We have dealt with them year after year. We hope that by sharing them here with you, we can relieve some anxiety, answer some of your questions, and give you some insight into ensuring a successful year for your child.

In this Part you will read about 30 of the most common areas about which parents usually have questions. You will learn ways to deal with potential or existing problems and issues. You will gain great ideas for becoming partners with your child's teacher and learn how to get the year off to a good start. Helping your child learn to love school now can set the stage for creating a lifelong learner.

#32
Develop a Plan

If you are planning for a year, sow rice;
if you are planning for a decade, plant a tree;
if you are planning for a lifetime, educate people.
~Richard Fenyman

Becoming a lifelong learner certainly requires persistence, but it also requires a plan. In Part 1 (Idea #4) you learned about setting goals by helping your child write down what he aspired to accomplish. Once the school year has begun, perhaps it is a good time to take a good look at those goals.

Now that he has embarked on a journey into a new grade, your child's goals and expectations may be changing. He may realize that the goal he had originally set for himself is a bit too ambitious or not quite challenging enough. Take time today to review his original goals or to write new ones entirely. Choose two or three from whichever areas he believes he could use the most improvement. Although some will undoubtedly be academic (*become a more fluent reader*), remember, they need not all be. *Become a more attentive listener* or *Learn to work cooperatively* are important life skills as well and certainly merit some conscious effort on your child's part. If he has trouble deciding what to pick, look back at his final report card from the last school year. What did his teacher mark as areas for improvement? You could also find out from his new teacher a few of the "big things" that he will be learning this year.

Remember these hints:

- Review your child's goals with him once a month or so. Talk about progress made and steps toward achievement.

- Choose an appropriate reward for your child when the goal is reached. ("Reward" does not have to mean money or presents.) Celebrate as a family!

- Create a new goal as each previous goal is met and applauded.

- Support his efforts in any way your family is able. (Do you need to listen to him read for 15 minutes each night, plan family projects that require cooperative efforts, find him a private tutor?)

- Don't hesitate to ask his teacher for ideas. His teacher has his best interests at heart, too!

- Display his goals so he can see them daily as a reminder to keep on track. (Try the message center, his study area, or his bedroom wall.)

- Don't forget that if everyone in the family does this, your child will see that learning is a lifelong process and that *everyone* has goals they have to strive to achieve. (He is not the only one who needs to work on something!) With the whole family working together and supporting one another's efforts, it is entirely likely that your child may even find a way to help you accomplish *your* goals as well!

#33
Review that Homework Policy

It isn't that they can't see the solution.
It's that they can't see the problem.
~G.K. Chesterton

Homework often becomes the dreaded "H" word around homes with school-aged children. Perhaps you know the feeling. You struggle with your child to get her to sit down and complete it, become frustrated trying to help her when she says, "That's not how my teacher said to do it!," or become stressed because your child can't even remember what she's supposed to do and you have no idea, either! So begins another year of frustration for your whole family.

Or does it? The goals of homework should be to practice skills learned at school, help develop study habits, foster a positive attitude toward school, learn time management, and show that learning takes place at home, as well. Studies show that completing homework can boost children's attitudes toward school, build self-discipline, and improve study habits. So, begin today to stop the unnecessary (yes, unnecessary!) frustrations that are bound to arise.

Try these tips:

- Review Idea #17's Homework Policy tips and the ideas for creating a space conducive to learning in Idea #18. If you and your child come up with an agreed upon time and place and method for homework (and write it down), it also makes things easier on you. It allows you simply to refer to it if your child tries to get out of doing homework. Instead of having to say, "I said you have to do it now," you get to say, "The Homework Policy says you've agreed to do it now."

- With your child's new fall schedule, do you need to modify her scheduled homework time? You may even have to find a different time each day to accommodate all of her activities. That's OK, as long as there *is* a specific time allotted each day.

- Ask your child's teacher to attach simple directions to each homework assignment if remembering the directions becomes a problem. Ask your child to explain the directions to you before she begins in order to avoid having to redo the assignment later. Some teachers require planners to be filled out each day. Others are now posting homework and other important messages online. Check into both of these options to see if they are available.

- Check in occasionally while your child is working to see if she needs help. Glance over what she's done, and let her know if she is off track but try to avoid providing answers. If you see she is making a mistake throughout, then certainly sit with her and show her how to correct her mistakes and move on. Guide, don't solve.

- Encourage breaks. A 5-minute break every 20 or 30 minutes works well for older elementary students. Younger children may need to stop more often.

- Discuss with her the reason for this homework. If she repeatedly does not know, you may want to talk with the teacher. Children are much more motivated to do any work if they know the reason for the assignment and how it relates to them. It is part of the teacher's job to explain this to the students. It is also helpful for you to know whether the assignment is an *introduction* to a new subject, a *review* or *practice* of one already begun, or work to be finished because it wasn't *finished* in class.

The types and amount of homework given will undoubtedly vary widely from teacher to teacher. Begin now to determine the homework policy of your child's new teacher. Know that when the right types of assignments are given, homework is an effective way to reinforce skills that your child is learning in school. It should be meaningful, appropriate according to the length of time given to complete it, and able to be completed with knowledge your child has been taught in class and with materials commonly found in the home.

If your child's assignments continually exceed these expectations, talk with her teacher to determine whether the problem lies with the student or the assignment. Ask for ways in which you can help make her homework experience successful. Ask about the role the teacher expects parents to play. Don't wait. Do it now. It will make for a much more peaceful year.

#34
Meet the Teacher

Teachers open the door, but you must enter by yourself.
~Chinese Proverb

Have you met your child's new teacher yet? If not, call or email him. Schedule a time when you both have a few minutes to chat. If he has sent home a lot of information, you may already have a pretty good feel for his philosophy, the schedule of the class, and his expectations for the year. You may just want to stop in to introduce yourself before or after school.

If you are full of questions, it is usually best to call or write to schedule a time that is convenient for the both of you to meet. Keep in mind that before school teachers are usually busy preparing the classroom and materials for the day's lessons. A lengthy discussion may be inconvenient then.

Even a quick "hello" one morning as you drop off your child can be helpful now. You could leave the teacher a summary of the times or ways you may be available to help out in the classroom. Writing the days and times down is helpful so the teacher doesn't have to try to remember what you said. Remember that this teacher has about 30 new children to get to know and twice that number of parents. Seeing your friendly face now and knowing that you want to be involved can be quite welcome to him.

A quick trip into your child's room before class begins for the day can ease your curiosity about how the room is set up, where your child sits, and the kinds of materials available for your child to use. You may even be able to answer some questions on your own. You can talk to your child later about what you saw and ask him specific questions about his new class. Meeting your child's teacher is just another way to help get the school year off to a good start.

#35
Keep Up Good Communication

We all need each other.
~Leo Buscaglia

The beginning of a new school year means many changes for your child. This time of year can be overwhelming and frustrating to some children. Your child may feel anxious about all the changes—a new grade level, a new classroom, different people in her class, a new teacher, possibly even a new building. That is a lot of changes for anyone!

As your child starts this new school year, remember that good communication between her and the family will be essential in making the transition smooth. Communicating regularly with her about her day and her upcoming assignments can help to avoid last minute panic about projects due the next day, misplaced homework, lost paperwork for field trips, picture day forms, and other such things.

Keep up consistent communication:

- Check her backpack with her after school every day. Have her pull out information and notices for you to look over or fill out. Create a routine out of this.

- Ask her specific questions about her day, the activities she's involved in, and the subjects she is currently studying. If you ask a generic question like "How was school today?" you will likely be met with an equally generic, "Fine." Opt for something more specific like "What did you cover in math today?" or "How many did you get right on your spelling test?"

- Consider hanging a corkboard on her wall above her homework area. Tack up any information sheets or projects that are forthcoming.

- Use the calendar at the message center to record important due dates for assignments or upcoming events or tests so the whole family is aware of her schedule and can help remind her of important information.

- Look over her completed homework with her. Ask her questions about the work. If she has doubts or can't explain the work she is doing, help her create a list of questions to ask her teacher.

- Check the family calendar in the message center together daily. Help her prepare for the next day. Try to avoid giving commands such as "Tomorrow is picture day. Get everything ready." Instead, *teach* her to plan for herself by preparing a mental (or written) checklist. "Tomorrow is picture day. What do you need?" See if she can come up with the necessary items such as clothes (are they clean and ready?), money, order envelope, etc.

Creating consistent communication habits with your child will help her enter into her new school year with excitement and confidence!

#36
Communicate with the Teacher, Too!

Make the most of yourself, for that is all there is of you.
~Ralph Waldo Emerson

Keeping up good communication with your child is essential, but chances are you will find that it may not be all that you need. Situations will surely arise that require talking to the teacher. Don't ever let this intimidate you! Your child's teacher wants what is best for her students and therefore wants and needs to know your questions and concerns.

If you have a few quick questions, perhaps jotting them down in a note or email would be the best approach. Chances are, conferences or a curriculum night are just around the corner and in-depth questions can be brought up and answered then. Teachers appreciate written communication because they have time to really think about the answers that they want to provide and can take time to respond when they are not rushed.

When it comes to communication, keep in mind these principles:

- If it's urgent, call. If you leave a message, let the teacher know what your call is regarding so she can prepare.

- If it is not urgent, it's probably best to send an email or a note with your child.

- Don't hesitate if you're unsure whether you should ask the teacher a question. She wants your child to be happy and to learn. It's true; no question is ever silly.

- If there *is* an upcoming curriculum night, some common questions may be answered there if they can wait. For instance, if you're wondering about the science curriculum for this new year, the teacher will probably answer this question then, as it is most likely on many parents' minds.

- Find out when conferences will be. Decide if your questions specifically about your child can wait until then. Don't forget, the teacher needs a few weeks to get to know your child's strengths, working habits, and areas for growth. He may not have the answers you need the first week of school. For more on conferences, see Idea #39.

Keeping up good communication with the teacher is good for everyone involved!

#37

Helping at Home

As you grow older, you will discover that you have two hands,
one for helping yourself, the other for helping others.
~Audrey Hepburn

Teachers have a tough job. They may have around 30 small children to get to know, for whom to determine the best methods for teaching, and for whom to create meaningful and exciting lessons. This often means preparing endlessly for many lessons each day. We have never met a teacher who didn't tote an enormous bag with her to and from school, full of "things to do" such as papers to grade, stories to read, shapes to cut out, folders to organize, projects to prepare, and book order forms to fill out.

We have also never met a teacher who wouldn't love a little help. It is not always possible for parents to come into the classroom and help with the students directly. You may have work, have young children at home, or have scheduling conflicts, but there may still be a way to help. You could offer to help out at *home*.

If you are unable to come into the classroom but are still eager to help, ask your child's teacher if there is anything you can do from home. Let her know if you are willing to type children's stories or spelling lists on your computer, check out books on an upcoming unit at the local library, fill out book order forms, cut out shapes for a bulletin board, organize classroom parties, or type a classroom newsletter. If you're not sure of the teacher's needs, simply tell her you'd like to help out from home and to let you know if something comes up.

Although most of a teacher's duties involve things personal to the students that she will have to do herself, there will undoubtedly be occasional activities for which she will be grateful for your help. How fun to have your child help you organize pieces for an upcoming project! She'll feel special to be able to tell the class she helped to prepare it!

#38
Volunteer

*Children of fathers with higher levels of involvement in their schools
were more likely to have positive school outcomes than those with low involvement.
(They were more likely to enjoy school, less likely to be expelled or suspended…)
~The Condition of Education, National Center for Education Statistics 1999*

You know that being involved in your child's education can greatly increase his chances for success. Unfortunately, many parents over the years have told us that they would like to help out in the class but don't really think they have anything to offer academically or aren't sure if they feel comfortable working directly with the students. Let us tell you that your help in any way, shape, or form will be greatly appreciated by your child's teacher. Don't let your fear of not being good at something stop you. You *do* have something very special to offer: your time!

There are so many ways to help out in an elementary classroom. Ask your child's teacher in which areas he could use the most help. From decorating a bulletin board to simply walking around during math time just helping those who need it, your help will be appreciated. Take a deep breath, and go in! Try it! If you like it, offer your services regularly so he can rely on you. (Whether it's every morning for a half-hour, every Wednesday from 2:00 to 3:00, or for two hours the last Friday of every month, commit yourself if you are able. The teacher will love to have you to rely on.) If you don't enjoy it, ask what else you can do. Here are some options to think about before you go in. You could help by:

- Listening to a book club (reading group). Perhaps you'd rather buddy-read one-on-one with a student who really needs extra practice.

- Monitoring a center at which children may need special guidance such as a scientific experiment, a cooking lesson, or a messy painting project.

- Cutting out pieces for a project.

- Organizing and hanging up murals in the hallway.

- Making copies at the office.

- Working with a small group on a remedial exercise. For example, helping children with the spelling words they're having trouble with, reviewing a math lesson, editing a story, and so forth.

- Recording assignments turned in.

- Driving and monitoring a small group on a field trip.

- Telling the class about a special skill you have by giving a demonstration.

As you can see, there are so many ways for you to help. Whether you enjoy working with groups of children, one-on-one with a child, or feel most comfortable helping around the room and school, there are so many ways that you can make a difference. You may even discover a particular love of something such as reading with children and decide to offer your services throughout the whole grade level (or school) as a partner for struggling readers or gifted readers who enjoy the extra support you can provide.

Whatever you choose to do, however often you are able to do it, never underestimate your potential for helping. Kids think it is fun for the class to have a Mom or Dad helping out in the room once in a while, especially if it is their own!

#39
Conferences

What we anticipate seldom occurs; what we least expected generally happens.
~Benjamin Disraeli

It begins before school even starts. You and your child are full of questions about the upcoming school year. By now, some of those questions have answered themselves as the days rolled by, but in their place, most likely, are *new* questions and concerns.

If you have a question that absolutely can't wait, of course it is best to call, write to, or visit your child's teacher. Many specific questions about your child can and should wait, though, until her teacher has had time to get to know her and she has time to discuss her with you in depth. For instance, you may want to know what your child's greatest strengths are, her areas for growth, and whether she is meeting the academic expectations of the class and attending to the variety of activities in the classroom. Conferences are set up just for that.

Being prepared for a parent-teacher conference is perhaps the most important thing you can do. Here are some ways you can do that:

- As soon as questions or comments begin to arise, write them down. Even though you *think* you will remember them, you may *not* once the discussion gets underway. This will also make you ask them. In the middle of a conference, there is the tendency to think, "Oh, never mind. That question is not really that important." Yes, it is. If you took the time to write it down, you must care to know the answer, so ask it! Add to this list as new situations arise, and delete questions that have been answered prior to your scheduled conference.

- Let the teacher begin if she wants to. Chances are she shares the same concerns you have and may answer your questions without you even asking them.

- Ask for suggestions for ways in which you can work with your child at home. If there is a particular area (or many) that need special attention, the teacher should be able to provide you with remediation techniques. If "everything is going great" she can offer you ways to extend and enrich your child's classroom learning.

- Take notes about what the teacher tells you. Again, even though you think you will remember everything, there is a good possibility you may not once you get home.

- Whenever possible, teachers usually prefer to talk with both of the child's parents. Talking with both Mom and Dad can offer her more insight and help you as well because you won't have to explain everything when you get home. In situations where the parents do not live together, teachers realize that it is often difficult to attend conferences together, but unfortunately, they may simply not have enough time allotted to them to schedule two separate conferences.

- Plan to show up on time (even early) to your conference. Be aware of how long your conference will last. (Usually around 15-20 minutes.) Try to adhere to the time limit. If you run out of time but still find you have much more to discuss, ask the teacher to schedule a separate time for you two to talk. Conferences are usually back-to-back and, just as you would not like to be kept waiting, neither will the family after you.

- Feel free to speak up. Don't let the formality of conferences interfere with their purpose- to discuss *your* child. The teacher is only a person just like you and may be just as apprehensive to talk with you as you are with her.

See our workbook available for purchase at www.365TeacherSecrets.com for some common conference questions.

#40
Report Cards

Behold the turtle. He only makes progress when he sticks his neck out.
~James Bryant Conant

Here's a riddle for you: what might you wait months to see and yet (sometimes) your child hates to show you? It's the *report card*! Even when children are doing well, they are often hesitant to show their report card to their parents simply because of the report card's implied seriousness. Many times, oddly enough, children fear the worst, believing that there must be some "bad stuff" written there by their teacher.

Here are some helpful Dos and Don'ts that may make report cards less scary for all of you:

- Do say something positive when your child brings his report card home to you like, "I can't wait to read the nice things your teacher wrote about you."

- Don't say something your child may interpret as threatening like, "I'll bet Mr. Croy has a thing or two to say about you."

- Don't sit right down with your child as soon as you get your hands on the report card. If you haven't had a chance to review it, you may say something you will regret later on.

- Do look the report card over yourself first, without your child around. This way you will have an opportunity to review it and plan what you are going to say to your child (and *how* you're going to say it) so that your discussion about it will be positive.

- Don't begin right away by asking your child about all the not-so-good areas.

- Do use the "sandwich method" to bring up any bad news. (First, compliment your child on something, such as progress made or a good mark in a subject. Then, discuss the bad-news area. End, again, with something positive.)

- Don't tell your child how he is going to have to do better and study more and improve or else.

- Do sit down and have a nice discussion. Offer to review the goals he set for himself. Does he need to add any? Can any be crossed out because they were met? Do the goals need to be more detailed? Does he need to create a plan for reaching the goals? Do you need to schedule a special conference with the teacher that your child can attend so that all parties involved can discuss the best things to do?

- Don't just focus on the areas for improvement, taking for granted the fact that there are many terrific marks as well.

- Do make sure your child knows how proud you are of every great grade he receives. Praise *improvements* and *effort* as well as good grades.

- Don't only focus on academics. After all, "working well with others" is a pretty important life skill!

- Do try to resist comparing his progress with that of any siblings. Each child is unique and has his own things he does well.

- Do remember: His report card should also give an accurate picture of how your child behaves, attends, gets along, and cooperates with others. All of these are important life skills and help to determine who he is and who he will become.

Many districts are now experimenting with a new type of report card. Educators have been discovering that "Sometimes," "Always," and "Never" are not always sufficient to describe your child's academic progress with the curriculum. Some new versions use keywords such as "Emerging," "Progressing," and "Achieving" and show a continuum to give a more accurate description of how children are doing.

No matter what type of report card your child brings home, take the opportunity to get to know and understand it. Identify areas for improvement, and celebrate the successes. Your attitude about report cards will undoubtedly influence your child's. Begin now to make report card time a truly pleasant experience for everyone. Remember: each report card is just a snapshot of your child's progress at one particular time, not an overall picture of who he is.

#41
R.E.F.R.E.S.H.

Breathe...Deep
~The Snuggle Fabric Softener Bear

Stress is not just something adults feel. Children can become stressed, too. Just think of what your child is expected to do every day. In one day, she learns new ideas and concepts in as much as six different subjects. When one subject is finished, it's put away, and the next subject is pulled out. She must switch gears within minutes, multiple times a day. In between the academics, there is the stress of getting along with classmates. On the playground, during lunch, or at recess, social interactions, both positive and negative, take place every day. How many times has your child come home and complained about what another student said or did that may have hurt her feelings? Teach your child at a young age to deal with her stress in a healthy, positive way. One nice way, is to think about the acronym REFRESH:

Renew - Every day is a chance at a fresh start. Tell your child that no matter what happened today, tomorrow is a chance to make it another great day or make it better.

Energize - What puts a spark in your child's eye? Encourage her to do the things she loves in her free time. Finding time to do the things she loves will increase her energy level, which will help her in every area of her life.

Food - You can never stress too much how important eating regularly and eating healthy is for children. Especially make sure you create time for breakfast before school. Healthy food provides energy she needs if she wants to perform at her optimum level at school.

Relax - Children must have a time to relax. Perhaps she needs a half hour after school to eat and relax before she even thinks about homework. Try setting up a place, free of electronics, where she can decompress from her day. A comfy bean bag next to a bookshelf is a great incentive to relax and de-stress.

Exercise - With so much technology around them, it's sometimes hard for children to resist the temptation to use it. It's easy to become sedentary and passive. Encourage your child to be active. Go outside and kick a ball around with her, take the dog for a walk, or find a jump rope and head outside. Exercising the body is just as important as exercising the mind.

Sleep - Experts state that school-aged children need 9-11 hours of sleep every night. Make every effort to start winding down your day about an hour before her bedtime. Avoid activities that will stimulate and energize her too close to bedtime. Before bed is a perfect time for her to write in her journal or read with you or alone. Quiet activities before bed will help her fall asleep faster so she can get the required sleep she needs.

Hydrate - Water is an important factor in your child's health and performance (in school and out). Many teachers recognize this and will let students have a water bottle on their desk during the school day. Check with your child's teacher about the classroom's policy. Whether she's allowed to drink in the classroom or not, make sure your child knows the importance of staying hydrated and the important role water plays in her health.

See our workbook available for purchase online for a reminder of this concept to display.

#42
Focus on Different Types of Success

Success is just a matter of attitude.
~Darcy E. Gibbons

As much as we love our children, it is often easier to pinpoint and observe their weaknesses rather than their strengths. Wouldn't it be a dream-come-true if all of our children excelled in all academic areas in school?

Some kids are strong in math but can't play a musical instrument. Some have the gift of art but have always struggled in reading. While academic subjects are important for your child, try not to focus only on the success, or lack thereof, in those areas. Is your child a kind and thoughtful person? Does he have an upbeat personality that reaches out and inspires people? Is he a positive role model for younger children? Does his attitude tell everyone that he does not give up and is determined to accomplish any task set before him? Praise him for it.

Not all children will be "A" students no matter how much we work with them. Does that mean that since your child has always struggled in math and may never be an "A" student in math you should give up? Certainly not! Our responsibility as parents and teachers is to provide our children with the best opportunities for optimal learning so that they have the best chance at success. (Remember, too, that many children just need more time than others to master certain skills such as reading. Perhaps all they need is some fun and authentic experiences with the subject and a little time.)

Remember the ultimate goal for teachers and parents is to prepare our children for their futures as independent, empathetic, contributing members of society. Even a child who does not always earn "A's" and "B's" in elementary school math can still become an engineer. If we do our jobs right, he *will* excel in some area and be a happy, well-adjusted, contributing citizen—certainly someone to be proud of! Success does not always have to be academic!

#43
Know the Rules

Be sure you put your feet in the right place, then stand firm.
~Abraham Lincoln

Do you know your child's classroom rules? Just like at home, every classroom has them. Teachers know it is very important for children to know and understand the rules and expectations, but children cannot follow rules or achieve the teacher's expectations if they are unaware of them. Many teachers have found that involving the children in making the rules helps the children feel invested in the classroom and more likely to remember and follow the rules. After rules have been established, good teachers know that the rules must be *practiced* and children must be *reminded* of the rules and expectations many times during the year.

In the beginning of the school year, you are likely to find your child's classroom rules posted somewhere in her classroom. Perhaps your child came home with a classroom contract that you and she had to read over and sign. If none of this sounds familiar to you, perhaps a talk with the teacher is in order so you can be aware of the expectations the teacher has for your child.

Understanding your child's classroom rules will help avoid conflict and confusion. By supporting the classroom rules and expectations, you and the school will be working together to create the best atmosphere for learning for your child.

#44

If Your Child is Having Trouble

If the student fails to learn, the teacher fails to teach.
~Anonymous

Even with the best intentions, you may find that your child is having trouble at school. You may be feeling frustrated, unsure of what to do. Be sure of one thing: His teacher is there to help you.

If you feel confident in helping your child with his problem, try that first. This book offers many ideas and activities that can be helpful and lead you to more activities that you create on your own. There are also many other helpful books out there that deal with specific problems. You might find some answers on the Internet. You might talk to other parents to see if they have ever dealt with similar problems. You can also talk to your child's teacher.

Your child's teacher will likely be the most helpful source you can turn to for support. He knows your child well and can probably give you specific things to work on at home. You might ask for specific curriculum goals and outcomes for your child's grade level so that you can judge for yourself how he is doing according to grade level standards. He will also know if your child should be referred to a specialist for testing. (If the assessment supports your concerns, he will receive special help at school.)

When a child isn't doing well in a particular subject (let's use reading as an example), he may begin to dislike it as well. As the frustration with not feeling like an adequate reader builds, he tends not to want to participate in reading activities at all. Of course, less participation will only exacerbate the problem. If this cycle continues without intervention from the adults in his life, the child may never become the reader he *is* capable of being. His teacher can probably offer you many ideas for ways you can make reading more fun and meaningful for your child at home. He is there to help.

Whatever the problem, it pays to search for solutions as soon as possible. Especially with reading, much of school success depends on skills learned early on. Falling behind in the elementary grades can have consequences in every subject in the future.

Also see Idea #50 for more about tutoring.

#45

If Your Child is Bored

A good teacher is one-fourth preparation and three-fourths theater.
~ Gail Godwin

A teacher is responsible for all of the children in her class. Just as she is responsible for providing remedial lessons and materials for students having trouble, she is also there to be sure every child is challenged if the material being covered has already been mastered.

If your child repeatedly talks about being bored in class, the first thing to do is to find out why. There are two very common reasons for this. The first is that your child is having a tough time paying attention or keeping up with the pace and academics of the class. It's easy to tune out something you continually don't understand and therefore become bored. If you feel this may be the case, try talking with your child's teacher. She will probably know exactly what you are talking about and have some suggestions for you. Also keep in mind what you read about in Idea #44.

The other main reason that your child may be bored is that she already knows the concepts being discussed in class in one or more subject areas. Most young children do not know how to occupy themselves constructively when they have finished work and need an adult to help direct them. If you suspect that this is the case with your child and find out that she is indeed doing very well with the classroom work, talk to her teacher. Perhaps the teacher could provide her with a slightly more challenging assignment or an extension or enrichment project to work on after she has completed (or instead of) the original assignment. Be sure that she is not simply given *more* work, though. Bright children do not need more work, they need *more challenging* work.

Some schools have Gifted/Talented programs or Talent Development Clubs for which your child might qualify. Teachers can also frequently work together to help encourage and challenge bright kids. For instance, some may let younger children read with a higher grade level's reading groups or join them for math lessons.

Try to determine the reason your child seems bored. Talk to her teacher. Try some of the ideas in this book according to the subject area(s) that she needs most. It's important to set the stage now for a lifetime of learning enjoyment. Behavior problems can sometimes arise when kids are bored, so it's best to catch this problem early, too. All children should be happy and challenged in school. Be sure yours is.

#46
Other Problems

Difficulties are meant to rouse, not discourage.
The human spirit is to grow strong by conflict.
~William Ellery Channing

There are various reasons why some children struggle in school, but not all of the reasons are related to academics.

Situations and problems at home can greatly affect your child's academic success. A sensitive child may not be able to focus or concentrate because of a change in family structure such as separation or divorce, a death of a loved one, or even feelings of guilt due to harsh words exchanged.

Your family's life is personal, as it should be. However, if there is a serious situation occurring at home that you feel is or could be affecting your child's academic achievement, it may be best to inform his teacher. Be assured that teachers are professional and the information you share in confidence will be kept in confidence. Teachers always have the child's best interest at heart and if there is any way that he can help smooth the rough road your child may be traveling, he will help in any way he can.

If your child's problems are related to conflicts with friends (i.e. playground troubles, bus problems), the teacher may not be the place to go. Teachers have very little control over what happens on the bus or playground. It may be best to see the playground supervisor, bus driver or principal for problems outside of the classroom. However, you may still want to make the teacher aware of the problem. He may be able to help by reinforcing simple rules such as kindness and cooperation.

#47
The Forgetful Child

Learning is not attained by chance,
it must be sought for with ardor and attended to with diligence.
~Abigail Adams, The Portable Life

Another common problem is falling behind on work. Does your child sometimes come home without books or her homework and then bring home a note about missing assignments?

As your child gets older, the volume and difficulty of the work she is expected to do will most likely increase. Very likely, if she misses an assignment or two, she will fall behind, which can result in a helpless, frustrated feeling. There are many reasons why children fall behind, but one of the most common reasons is that children simply *forget* to bring work home or forget what their assignments are.

If you find your child consistently forgets to bring her homework home or can't even remember or relate to you what she's learning in various subjects at school, a homework notebook and folder may help. (See Idea #13 for some ideas.) For the folder, go to the store and let your child pick out a folder she particularly likes. Maybe let her decorate it with stickers or drawings, too. If she has a folder she loves, she's even more apt to use it.

A homework notebook and folder can help in three ways. First, they can help your child remember which assignments she has finished and which she needs to take home to complete. Secondly, the homework notebook can help parents know what was covered in school that day. Third, all she needs to complete is in one place.

We have included a sample page from a homework notebook on our website. Look it over and adjust it to fit your child's schedule and needs. Remind your child to look over her homework notebook before she leaves school to help her gather the work she needs to take home. Have her put everything she needs to finish in that special folder. You may find at first that you will have to enlist the help of her teacher. A reminder from her teacher to write assignments down after each subject, and a few minutes given at the end of class to gather unfinished work, will help make the process smoother.

When your child gets home, make it a habit to find a time to sit down and go over her homework notebook together. As she finishes each assignment, encourage her to check it off as "done" and place it in her school bag right away to turn in the next day.

Using the homework notebook consistently can help your child feel more in control, be less overwhelmed, and teach her organizational skills that she will be able to use her whole life!

See our workbook available for purchase at www.365TeacherSecrets.com for a sample page from a homework notebook.

#48
Organization is the Key

Organize, don't agonize.
~ Nancy Pelosi

Many teachers agree: Organization is the key. To what? To everything!

If you are truly organized, you can achieve amazing things! The problem most people have is that organization itself takes time and energy. After a very busy and tiring evening of driving to and from practices or lessons and then dinner and homework, it is very easy to say, "Let's call it a night," and then relax. As enticing as this sounds, you may be paying for it the next day. As the bus pulls up, you may find yourself making futile, hurried attempts to get your child dressed, searching to find his backpack, or looking for a much needed field trip permission slip.

Taking the time and energy to organize yourself and your child in the evening can lead to a more pleasant, calm atmosphere in the morning. After all, who wouldn't like to start their day with a bit less chaos?

Try reserving a small portion of time right after school or at the end of the night to go over a checklist (written or mental) with your child. Statements such as, "Show me what you're going to wear tomorrow" or "Let's double check your school bag for completed homework and get it ready to go" can help teach your child important organization skills and lead him toward being responsible for himself. Consult your calendar at the message center to see if there is anything special to be aware of for the morning (such as gym day, a field trip, the due date for the final report, etc.) and get ready accordingly. The structure you provide by being organized will help keep your mornings calm and quiet.

Becoming organized and teaching your child to be organized may require a lot of effort and follow-through on your part at first. However, if you can reinforce organization now, the payoff will come later when organization becomes second nature to your child and he begins to take on responsibilities from laying out his clothes for the next day to keeping his study area clean and stocked and ready to use! After all, the morning sets the tone for the entire day, so get it off to a good start for your sake and your child's.

#49
Learning Styles

Learning is more effective when it is an active rather than a passive process.
~ Euripides

If you are like most parents, you have repeated yourself many, many times to your children. You may have even uttered the words, "How many times have I told you..." If this sounds familiar to you, perhaps you need to think about how your child learns and learn to work with that style.

How *does* your child learn? Consider the three types of learning styles: auditory, visual, and kinesthetic. Most children learn best through a combination of the three types of learning styles, but many children favor one over the others.

Auditory Learners: Hear

Auditory learners would rather listen to things being explained than read about them. These children can benefit from reciting information out loud or retelling it to someone after they have read/learned it.

Visual Learners: See

These children will often get distracted when the teacher (or parent) is talking. They may even *look* like they are listening, but if you ask them a question afterward, they have no idea and look confused. Visual learners need something to focus on. They benefit by looking at graphics, watching a demonstration, or reading.

Kinesthetic Learners: Touch

Kinesthetic learners learn best through a "hands-on" experience. You can't just demonstrate how to do a science experiment (or show them a video) and think they'll understand the concept. They need to actually do the activity to truly understand it. Even while studying, they must *do* something. They do not study best by reading a chapter in social studies; they learn best by writing things down which makes it easier for them to understand and remember.

Teachers know all about these learning styles. They try their best to incorporate all three in their lessons so they can reach all learners. When they are teaching subtraction, for instance, the students will hear (auditory) the teacher giving an example of subtraction by using a story problem. She might say, "Imagine you have 7 pennies but you give 2 away to friends. How many do you have left?" Then, the teacher may show the problem on the board and work through it (visual) while the students watch. Last, she may pass out manipulatives for the students to work with, such as real pennies, and have the students actually touch something and move them around to show how 7 - 2 = 5.

You may recognize your child in one, two, or all three of those learning styles, but chances are she will favor one over the others. Once you've discovered your child's style, try your best to incorporate it the activities you do at home. When studying spelling words, for example, consider your child's learning style. It may not be enough just to say the word and have your child spell it (auditory). You may want to have note cards with the words written on them (visual) so she can actually see the word, then turn it around and have her spell it. She can then look at it again to check for accuracy (and cement it in her mind). If she's a kinesthetic learner, you may want to have a small, lap size whiteboard where she can write the word after you say it, or use magnetic letters that she can move around to spell the words.

Using all three styles whenever possible will help your child develop all three types of learning styles. Just because she may have a dominant learning style doesn't mean the other types can't be improved. Help her understand her learning style so learning becomes easier and less stressful as she works toward reaching her potential.

#50
Tutoring

The mediocre teacher tells.
The good teacher explains.
The superior teacher demonstrates.
The great teacher inspires.
~ William Ward

It is not uncommon for many children to start falling behind in their work. If you are lucky, your child enjoys sitting down with you to work on material he doesn't understand. However, many parents find that their children work much better for other people, such as a tutor.

How do you know when your child needs a tutor? A learning disability, dropping grades, or concerns from your child's teacher that he is falling behind may indicate the need for a tutor. Some families choose to engage in the help of a tutor if they feel that their child could benefit from some one-on-one time with a professional for remedial help or even some enrichment if their child is inspired to go beyond classroom material and the parents are unsure of how to provide enrichment. Your child's teacher or principal can probably recommend a few tutors in the area for you.

The major benefit of a tutor is the one-on-one attention your child receives. A tutor is able to focus on a specific skill for a great length of time. For example, a child who doesn't understand fractions could work one-on-one with a tutor for an entire hour. The tutor can explain fractions in many different ways and can also use manipulatives to help him see the underlying concept. A classroom teacher also explains fractions and uses manipulatives but cannot possibly spend that much individual time with each student. A classroom teacher cannot possibly tailor each lesson to the exact needs of every single child on a minute-to-minute basis. It is simply impossible, but a private tutor can do that. She can judge how your child does every single thing and make decisions to either offer more practice or move on.

A tutor can also customize the lessons to your child's strengths and weaknesses. Therefore, before you decide on utilizing a tutor, you may want to meet with your child's teacher to make a list of areas the tutor can focus on and create concrete goals for your child to reach. Also, encourage the tutor to contact your child's teacher if possible. Together, they can create an individualized plan to best meet your child's needs.

How do you know if your tutor is top notch? Feel free to ask for references and credentials. Discuss each session, afterward, with your child to be sure he is learning and enjoying it. Most children love the individual attention and relaxed atmosphere tutoring provides. Although the learning may be challenging, it should be enjoyable. Remember that a good tutor will not just *tell* students how to improve or tell them when they're wrong. Instead, a good tutor asks questions when a child has difficulties such as, "Show me how you came up with that answer" or "Does your answer make sense?" Good tutors keep asking more specific, leading questions rather than telling your child the answer. You may also want to ask the tutor what you could be working on with your child at home to support his sessions.

Tutors can be expensive. Private tutors are generally less expensive than tutoring businesses. If tutoring is out of the question because of cost, try finding out what your child's school has to offer. Many schools have set up free peer-tutoring programs after school. If your school doesn't have a peer-tutoring program, perhaps now would be a good time to look into starting such a program in your child's school. You can also check with your local high school to see if any honor students offer free (or less expensive) tutoring. Sometimes high school kids need community service hours and love working with younger kids. Once you start spreading the word around, you may be surprised how well received your ideas are!

If you feel a tutor would benefit your child, don't delay. The earlier you can catch an academic problem, the better chance you have of doing something about it. Getting more help early on can help your child like school more and may also help him do better throughout the rest of his school years.

#51
The Multiple Intelligences

Do not let what you cannot do interfere with what you can do.
~John Wooden

The theory of Multiple Intelligences, created by Dr. Howard Gardner, is based on a belief that school systems focus on a very narrow range of intelligence. Dr. Gardner felt that the primary focus of the school system is concentrated essentially on verbal/linguistic and logical/mathematical skills. He acknowledges that these skills are vital but suggests that there are at least five other kinds of intelligence important to human development and that most people are able to develop all of these skills. Knowing what they are can help parents to understand that there are many different ways that kids can excel.

The seven intelligences, as described by Dr. Gardner, follow. We've also included some ways you can develop that intelligence further if you desire.

Verbal/Linguistic Intelligence: Involves reading, writing, speaking, and conversing. (This intelligence can be developed through reading books, playing word board games or card games, listening to recordings, using computer technology, and participating in conversations and discussions.)

Logical/Mathematical Intelligence: Involves number and computing skills, recognizing patterns and relationships, timelines and order, and the ability to solve different kinds of problems through logic. (This intelligence can be developed through classifying and sequencing activities, playing number and logic games, and solving various kinds of puzzles.)

Visual/Spatial Intelligence: Involves the visual perception of the environment, being able to create and manipulate mental images. (This intelligence can be developed by sharpening observation skills, solving mazes and other spatial tasks, and exercises in imagery and active imagination.)

Bodily/Kinesthetic Intelligence: Involves physical coordination and dexterity, using fine and gross motor skills and learning through physical activities. (Activities such as playing with blocks and construction materials, dancing, playing various active sports and games, participating in plays or make-believe, and using various kinds of manipulatives to solve problems can develop this intelligence.)

Musical Intelligence: Involves understanding and expressing yourself through music and rhythmic movements or dance, or composing, playing, or conducting music. (This intelligence can be developed by listening to a variety of music, playing rhythmic games and activities, and singing, dancing or playing various instruments.)

Interpersonal Intelligence: Involves understanding how to communicate with and comprehend other people as well as how to work cooperatively and collaboratively. (This intelligence can be developed through cooperative games, group projects and discussions, multicultural books and materials, and dramatic activities or role-playing.)

Intrapersonal Intelligence: Involves understanding your inner world of emotions and thoughts and growing in the ability to control them and work with them consciously. (This intelligence can be developed through participating in independent projects, reading illuminating books, journal writing, imaginative activities and games, and finding quiet places for reflection.)

Can you see a few above that fit your child? Try ranking them for her. Which is she strongest in? Weakest? Try it for everyone in the family. It's interesting to think about yourself in these ways. You and your child might decide that there is an area you or she wishes she were stronger in and can think of fun ways to develop it further.

Many teachers practice this theory and incorporate the different intelligences into their lesson plans. You can help at home as well by trying to incorporate them into the activities you do with your child. It's easy. Build some puzzles together, kick a ball around with your child, sing and dance together, and encourage her to reflect daily in her journal for starters. Many of the activities in this book also focus on a variety of them. You probably do an assortment of these activities often not even realizing how beneficial they really are!

#52

Internet Safety

Internet safety begins at home.
~ Mike Fitzpatrick

As your child progresses through elementary school, he will have many opportunities to use the Internet for school-related work. Students often use it for research when writing a report, playing educational games, or checking the classroom website that many teachers now have. It's important to talk about safe use of the Internet. It's not hard to imagine how a student researching Abraham Lincoln can suddenly be on a completely different website because he clicked an advertisement for a movie clip or a YouTube video, which may lead to inappropriate content. Help your child learn to use the Internet responsibly and safely by helping your kids understand they should:

- Never share their names, schools, ages, phone numbers, or addresses;

- Never send pictures to strangers;

- Keep passwords private (except to parents);

- Never open email from strangers; it may contain viruses that can harm a computer;

- Immediately tell an adult if something uncomfortable or mean happens;

- Only go on appropriate sites, and if they are not sure, ask.

Make sure your computer is set up in a public place in the house. Walk by often to check on your child's progress and to make sure he stays on task. Or better yet, show interest in what he's learning and looking at online. Visit the sites that are interesting to him and play some of the games he plays. You can also learn how to check the history of sites your child has visited. Your computer probably lets you set up limits on the websites your child is allowed to open which can stop a lot of problems before they come up. If you teach your child how to use technology responsibly now, your job will be easier when he starts to use the Internet more independently when he's older.

#53
Portfolios

A teacher affects eternity; he can never tell where his influence stops.
~ Henry Brooks Adams

There are many different ways teachers can evaluate their students' achievement. Some schools supplement the standard letter grades (or numbers) on report cards with portfolios. Portfolios are a system of tracking each student's improvement throughout the year. A portfolio consists of a large folder (one for each student) that is kept in a convenient place within the classroom. Both *student* and *teacher* can and should contribute to it.

Portfolios can be used for all subjects but let's use Language Arts as an example. Whenever a student writes a piece that she is proud of, she can place that piece in her portfolio. Portfolios are not meant to be collections of perfect work. A child may choose to add a piece because of the interesting plot, the particular attention she paid to spelling, the characters— anything she feels shows her growth as a writer. Teachers also add pieces they feel display the student's growth.

To get the most out of them, portfolios should be used during parent/teacher conferences or another time when parents, teachers and *the child* can view the portfolio together. As they all look through the portfolio, they can see firsthand how the child has developed in the subject area. It is easier to see her strengths and areas for growth when looking at a collection of work gathered throughout the semester or year.

Then, together, everyone (including the child) can discuss what she should be proud of, how much she's improved, and what area she can concentrate on improving next. This method allows students more control over the grades they receive. They are consistently aware of how they are performing, in which areas they are improving, and exactly what grades they will receive.

Portfolios are beneficial for parents, too. When their child comes home with a "C" in Language Arts it really means very little. The letter grade alone can't help them direct their child in ways to improve. Portfolios, on the other hand, can help parents "see" the reason(s) for the "C" as well as show them the areas of improvement that they can start looking for and working on with their child.

You can make a portfolio for home. It's tough to know what to do with all the work that comes home all year. Try saving favorite pieces and keeping them in a portfolio throughout the year. It can be a fun project when school gets out to sift through it and save what you both think best shows her progress. Years from now, she will love pulling out her portfolios from years past and seeing what she was like academically back then.

#54
Making the Grade

Have your child take responsibility for his grades.
Don't let him say, "The teacher gave me this grade."
Instead, have him say, "I earned this grade."

Has your child ever come home very upset because of a poor grade on a project or assignment? He might not understand why the grade was so poor and may even think the teacher was unfair in his grading.

Before you react, take a few minutes to sit down with your child and go over the assignment or project together. Can you see where he made his mistakes? Can he explain to you the goal of the assignment or project and then decide whether or not he achieved the goal? Together, you should be able to determine where he went wrong. If neither of you can find the errors that brought down his grade, make a list of questions for your child to ask his teacher about the project. If you have a young child, you may want to send a note with him to school asking the teacher to call you at a convenient time. On the note, tell his teacher which assignment you want to talk about so he can be prepared when he calls you.

Teachers don't enjoy writing poor grades in their grade book. A teacher's goal is to have every student master the material presented. A "D" on an assignment means the student has not mastered the objective. Like you, your child's teacher wants your child to learn the information, so here's a suggestion. Find out if his teacher will accept "extra credit." Talk with the teacher and your child to come up with a variety of projects he could choose from to complete and use as extra credit to bring up his grade (perhaps even just fixing up the assignment in question). Not only will the extra credit help improve his grade, but also he will be reaching the goal: learning the material he was supposed to master in the first assignment. Very few teachers would refuse to let an enthusiastic, willing child do extra work to improve his grade as long as the extra work being done will help the child learn the material.

If his teacher does not accept extra credit, still encourage your child to find and correct his mistakes. Even if the grade cannot be improved, doing the extra work will ensure your child has mastered this assignment's skills before moving on to new ones. If your child hesitates at doing extra work because he is not going to "get" something out of it, reassure him that he *will* be getting something very important: *knowledge!*

#55

This is Only a Test (Study Tips)

> *If we all did the things we are capable of doing,*
> *we would literally astound ourselves.*
> *~Thomas A. Edison*

Do you remember taking tests when you were in school? How did you prepare? Very often children are taught the subject matter but no one has ever taken time to show them how to take the information and use it to study for a test. Of course, the purpose of a test is to gauge how well a child knows the information being presented. Unfortunately, a child's lack of test-taking skills may be the cause of not-so-good grades.

Here are some suggestions for your child that may help her prepare for a test. Some of these will have to be taught to her. Others she may just have to be shown once and then she will understand. No matter what strategies your child uses, studying in a quiet place will help her concentrate. Studying in short chunks of time is usually more productive than one long chunk. Also, studying over a period of a few days is better than cramming the night before a test.

If the test she will take covers information taken from a textbook:

- Outline the chapter(s) being covered. (Idea #182)

- Make note cards with important information on them. Have a family member or friend "quiz" her on the information.

- Are there questions at the end of each section? If so, read them again and review the answers.

- Look over the headings and subheadings. The heading and subheadings tell the reader what is most important in that section.

- Reread the captions under the pictures. Pictures generally depict important people or events that may need to be remembered.

- Have her give her book to you or someone else and ask that other person to ask her questions. Often, when kids look over their textbooks on their own they think, "Oh yea, I know *that*. I remember those dates. I know all about that place." But to really know if she knows something, someone else should ask her questions and she has to recall that information out loud. Putting it into actual words may be the true "test" of whether or not she really knows the material. (Note: the person helping her study by asking the questions doesn't even have to know the material. Just look through the text for bold words, headings, or questions.)

If the test will cover information taken from a reading book or novel:

- Use the titles of each chapter to summarize (Idea #158) the chapters.

- Write the summaries on index cards and jot down any important events or characters from the chapter. Have a family member or friend use the index cards to ask her questions about each chapter.

- Have her try retelling the story to family or friends and have them ask questions when certain parts seem unclear.

- Record her retelling the story. Have her listen back. Are all the major events included? Does it make sense when listening to the recording?

You may find you will need to utilize many of these strategies to help your child prepare for a test. Or you may find that one or two particular strategies help her remember the information. She may even find her own way to study for a test. Whatever happens, start now by giving your child good study habits. Encourage her to study even if she feels she has the information down pat. Using good study habits now will help her through the rest of her education and beyond.

#56
Standardized Tests

I'm not young enough to know everything.
~James Barrie

Teachers learn about students' academic progress by using a variety of methods. They assess students by observing them in the classroom, evaluating their day-to-day work, grading their homework assignments, keeping close records of how they change or grow throughout the year (such as in portfolios), and administering tests.

One type of test many teachers administer is a Standardized Test. Standardized Tests are not created by the classroom teacher. Rather, Standardized Tests are objective tests that are usually created by commercial test publishers. Some names of standardized tests that you may be familiar with include the California Achievement Tests (the CAT), the Stanford Achievement Test (the SAT 10), the Iowa Test of Basic Skills (the ITBS), and the Stanford-Binet Intelligence Scale, to name a few.

Standardized tests are designed to give a common measure of students' performance. Since the same test is given to large numbers of students throughout the country or state, a "standard" of measure can be used to tell evaluators whether school programs are succeeding or to give them a picture of the skills and abilities of today's students.

Standardized tests can help teachers and administrators make decisions. They help schools measure how students in a given class, school, or school system perform in relation to other students who take the same test. Using the results from these tests, teachers and administrators can evaluate the school system, a school program, or a particular student. However, it is very important to understand that teachers *do not* use standardized tests to give report card grades. They are reported to parents separately.

It is important to remember that, while there are benefits to standardized tests, they also have some limitations. They are not the perfect measure of what individual students can or cannot do. Paper tests cannot measure everything that students learn. Also, your child's scores on a particular test can vary from day to day, and many factors can affect a particular score—whether your child guesses, receives clear direction, follows the directions carefully, is comfortable, has any test anxiety, and so on.

Because of the emphasis many schools place on the results of Standardized Tests, your child may be extremely nervous on the test taking day(s). Try not to let the seriousness of it upset your child. Help ease his anxieties by letting him know that this test will not affect his grade on his report card, but do encourage him to do his best. Let him know that the test will simply be used to help define his strengths and weaknesses in order to allow his teacher and parents to better meet his needs.

Your child's teacher will share with you the results of your child's test when they become available. Talk with the teacher about the results and discuss what they mean for your child. The percentages, statistics and graphs presented in the results can sometimes be confusing. Don't be afraid to ask any question that crosses your mind to help you better understand your child's performance. Together you and your child's teacher can come up with the best action plan for the success of your child.

See our website for test taking tips.

#57
Learning Differences

The greatest discovery of my generation is that human beings
can alter their lives by altering their attitudes of mind.
~William James

If your child continually struggles with school, you may have wondered if perhaps she has a learning disability. You may have heard one of the many acronyms for the various differences or disabilities, such as ADD (attention deficit disorder), EI (emotionally impaired), or LD (learning disabled).

Before you assume the worst, step back and consider not only how much your child is struggling but also what you have done to help her. Would a tutor after school help her? How about an older sibling, aunt, or uncle working with her on difficult assignments? Can the teacher find any assistance for her after school?

If you feel you've exhausted all your resources, a talk with the teacher would be your next step. Ask her if she has noticed your child struggling as you have. Ask for more suggestions to help her. If you truly feel your child has a learning disability, ask the teacher if your child can be tested by a specialist/resource teacher. Resource teachers have tests available to help determine if there is a discrepancy between your child's IQ and her achievement. Oftentimes, several different school personnel will get involved. You may even be asked to have a doctor evaluate her. Schedule a conference to talk in person with the resource teacher. Ask her about the procedures she uses and the process she follows to determine if your child has a learning disability. Then, discuss what happens if your child does have a learning disability.

If it is determined your child does have a learning difference, there are many things the classroom and resource teacher can adjust to help meet her needs. Modifying assignments to make them shorter, letting her use books on tape to support reading, even giving oral tests instead of written ones are all ways teachers can work with your child to provide the best opportunity for her to learn. She may even be able to provide you with an extra set of textbooks at home so that you can review the day's lesson or possibly *pre*view tomorrow's with your child.

Remember that a teacher's job is to provide all students with every resource possible to help them succeed. Many people are there to help.

#58
Be Open to New Ideas

It is best to learn as we go, not go as we have learned.
~Leslie Jeanne Sahler

Do you ever find yourself thinking or saying to your child, "When I was in school, we used to…"? Do you ever feel frustrated trying to keep up with new terms, philosophies, and methods? While it is true that many aspects of education have changed (some even drastically) over the past few decades, it does not necessarily mean they have gotten worse.

There aren't many occupations that remain static over the years because change usually means growth. In education, we are always striving for growth. The best thing you can do for yourself (your piece of mind) and for your child is to try to stay informed.

If your child brings home an assignment requiring a method that sounds like a foreign language to you, ask him to explain it to you! Remember that it will not only help you learn about this new way of doing things but also will help your child understand it even further by *explaining* it to you. If your child, unfortunately, does not know how to explain it to you, and you are unable to give him the help he needs, ask his teacher. He will be able to tell you everything you need to know.

So while there may be a new way to print letters, new terms for solving a two-digit subtraction problem, new ways to multiply, and new philosophies and methods for teaching science, be glad that the field of education is ever-changing. Think of it as continual growth and improvement. Ask questions, and try to stay involved. Don't fret. Of course, things aren't the same at school as they were 30 years ago. Would you really want them to be?

#59
Your Child is a Teacher, Too!

To teach is to learn twice.
~Joseph Joubert

As you may recall from Idea #23, having your child *teach* something she's learned to someone else is the best way to be sure she really understands the information and that she will remember it. So, don't miss an opportunity to allow your child to be a teacher, too.

There are many ways in which you can encourage this almost effortlessly. Try having your child explain what she's learning in science to your family at dinner. Can she retell a story to Grandma and Grandpa? Maybe a younger sibling would enjoy hearing her list the states and their capitals. She could impress an older sibling with her spelling of this week's tricky words. She could even explain the steps of long division to the family dog or her favorite stuffed animal if she's more comfortable with that at first. And wouldn't just about anyone love to hear her read?

Having your child teach things she's learned to others not only requires that she thoroughly understand the information she's discussing, but can also be a real source of self-esteem, too. She'll likely feel confident, important, and proud to be sharing her knowledge with others instead of always being the one to *receive* it.

#60
Your Role

You can preach a better sermon with your life than with your lips.
~Oliver Goldsmith

Your child is in school about 6 1/2 hours a day. His teacher is responsible for helping him learn during this time for about 180 days a year. There is the same number of days each year that your child does *not* have a schoolteacher to help him. However, he *does* have a teacher—YOU!

You are your child's first teacher, guiding him first to walk and talk and then later to read and write and more. Learning is continuous and does not end when your child walks out of his school building. In fact, it can be just getting started. There is so much you can do at home to supplement what your child learns in school.

This does not mean you have to provide formal lessons for your child every day. It just means that you can use everyday activities as learning opportunities to help enrich and extend your child's learning. You can also help by being a good role model for lifelong learning. (Idea #7.)

His teachers may be responsible for his formal education, but you have the pleasure of having all the fun. Use all of the tips you read about in this book (and hear about at conferences, curriculum information nights, and parent teacher organizations, etc.) to take an active role in the education of your child. Learning happens all the time, everywhere. You are there with him most of the time. Take advantage of it!

#61
Time Out!

There is more to life than increasing its speed.
~Gandhi

Many children participate in extra-curricular activities. Here are two very important things to keep in mind if it seems your child hardly ever slows down.

The first is to think about whether all of the extra things she is doing are taking away from her education. Many activities that children are involved in after school and on weekends (such as music, dance, and especially sports) are very time-consuming. Children too often are coming to school tired, saying they just couldn't finish their homework because their soccer game wasn't until after dinner and they didn't get home until late. Of course, if this happens once in a great while, it may be no big deal, but even a few times a month can begin to interfere with her school performance. If this happens, it's time to rethink your priorities. What kind of message are you sending when you let sports take precedence over school?

Another important thing is to make sure your child has time to just *be*. In Idea #28 we talked about the importance of play. Review it if you need to. Tell yourself that it is okay for your child to come home and play if she has no other pressing work to do. She needs time to be alone with herself and her thoughts and dreams. She needs time to make plans and decisions without the constant "busy-ness" so many of us fill our lives with, whether consciously or out of "necessity."

Allow her to slow down. Focus on quality over quantity. Take a step back and look at her life through new eyes. Is she living her childhood ideal or your own busy style? Discuss it tonight as a family after dinner. Does she need a time out from her hectic schedule? Do all of you? Make a plan today to begin to take life more slowly and make time to play.

Part 3
Narrative Reading:
Learning to Love Reading

INTRODUCTION: Part 3 is full of fun and motivational activities and ideas for ways to improve your child's comprehension and fluency and love of reading.

Reading is such a very important part of the elementary years. There are many ways to help children learn to read and become lovers of reading. Because of the overwhelming number of ideas we want to share with you on this extremely crucial subject, we have divided them up into two months. In Part 4, we will focus on reading *informational* text. Part 3, however, is dedicated to narrative, or story reading. It includes tips for encouraging your child to become an avid reader, ways to make reading fun, ideas for increasing comprehension, strategies for working with your child on various reading skills, as well as some common definitions that you may find helpful.

Try some of the ideas as you read them. You may want to save others for a time when they are more beneficial for your child. In the future, should your child ever need specific help, you can return to this month or next to find some help and ideas. It is never too soon to begin encouraging your child to become a proficient reader, and never too late to improve reading skills.

#62
Reading Together

The more a child reads the better reader he becomes.

Hopefully, by now, you have established a nice time of the day to curl up and read with your child. Previously, we discussed the benefits of doing this together (Idea #1). It is the single best way to make him a successful reader and foster a love of reading.

When you are reading aloud to your child, it is usually appropriate to choose a book that is at a slightly higher reading level (to check for reading levels, see #71) than one he would choose to read on his own. Children are often interested in reading higher-level books than they may actually be able to read alone. (They generally enjoy reading about characters a grade level or so above themselves.)

By reading aloud to your child, you are modeling how to read with expression and for meaning. Even older children and fluent readers benefit from hearing what good reading sounds like and experiencing longer books. It exposes them to more complex vocabulary and language structure, develops listening skills, and allows you to discuss meaning together while doing it. It also helps them fall in love with reading. In fact, one of the best ways to help your child understand the more difficult concepts and vocabulary he is encountering is to keep reading to him even after he has learned to read by himself. (An added bonus is cuddling-up together!)

For some variation, you can take turns reading (called buddy reading) if your child enjoys that. Remember that reading together should be comfortable, intimate, and warm. It should never feel like a test. Just relax, take cues from your child, and enjoy a good story together.

For some award-winning choices try the Newbery Award book list for "best children's book of the year": http://www.ala.org/alsc/awardsgrants/bookmedia/newberymedal/newberyhonors/newberymedal and the Caldecott Award book list for "best pictures in a children's book": http://www.ala.org/alsc/awardsgrants/bookmedia/caldecottmedal/caldecotthonors/caldecottmedal

See our workbook available for purchase online (and Idea #82) for a list to print out of every Newbery Award winning book.

#63
Be a Reading Role Model

A children's story that can only be enjoyed by children
is not a good children's story in the slightest.
~ C.S. Lewis

You've no doubt heard the familiar saying, "Actions speak louder than words." Telling your child about the importance of reading is good, but *showing* her is better. Without even speaking, you can communicate how important reading is as well as the joy of reading by letting her see *you* reading. You don't necessarily have to be reading a lengthy novel. Simply reading the newspaper, a magazine, or a short story will provide opportunity for your child to observe you practicing what you preach!

Try to have a special time set aside for everyone to read (even if it's only 15 minutes). However, just as important as the time spent reading is the time afterward *discussing* what you've read. Consider having informal "book talks" after reading. The book talks need not be long (even a few minutes would be beneficial). Discussing what you've read or having her talk about what she's read not only places value on reading but also is an excellent way to increase comprehension.

Now you have an "excuse" for reading the next chapter of that novel you've been stealing time to read at 11:00 at night or to browse through your new magazine. Right in front of the kids!

#64
Creating an Atmosphere for Reading

A general standard for reading has been that by the 3rd grade
a child is fluent in reading new text.

There are many different ways to help young children become good readers. You already know that reading to your child is perhaps one of the best. There are also other things you can do to create an environment at home that is conducive to reading:

- Labeling common objects in your house will create a print-rich environment for new readers. Simply use 3x5 note cards to clearly print the name of various objects and tape them on or very near the object. Read them to your child at first and then work toward having him read them to you.

- Have a variety of reading material available in your home—stories, informational sources, magazines, even comic books or joke books for reluctant readers. After all, reading is reading!

- Offer your child a collection of books to keep in his room. Let him choose the story for D.E.A.R. time most of the time. (You may want to make the choice occasionally in order to throw in a little something different here and there if he tends always to choose the same stories.)

- Remember to read together. It will seem more fun to him if you (and everyone in the house) are doing it, too!

#65
Not *That* Book Again!?!

If one cannot enjoy reading a book over and over again,
there is no use in reading it at all.
~ Oscar Wilde

Many children tend to have a favorite book. Right now you can probably name the book your child had you read to her over and over as she was becoming a reader herself. Perhaps now she has a book that you see or hear her reading time and time again to herself (and anyone else within earshot). You may be thinking that reading the same story again and again may be doing her no good and that she really ought to pick up something new and unfamiliar, but, actually, it does have its benefits.

Rereading a book over and over *is* beneficial to your child. It will help her increase her fluency as well as develop her self-confidence as a reader. She is probably feeling quite cozy with this book. She feels like a good reader because she knows all the words and understands the ideas in them. She feels like a good reader, like you.

Practice leads to proficiency, which eventually leads to pleasure. So don't fret. Eventually even she will tire of that story and naturally move on to find something more challenging. In the meantime, just smile and praise her for such a fine job!

#66
"I can't read like you…"

The best readers are those who love to read.
~Lucy Calkins, Ph.D.

Reading *to* your child is important, you've learned. It is also important for your child to read *aloud* once in a while. It helps him gain fluency, aids in his comprehension of the story, and can help him experiment with reading with feeling or expression.

Reading with expression (as the characters would really talk or a narrator would really read in order to maintain interest) is important because meaning can sometimes be lost without it. You can model expressive reading with a story at your child's reading level by having him *echo read* it with you.

All you need to do is choose a length of text that feels right for your child. Read it aloud to him using inflections and feeling. Have him echo you by trying to read it back like you did, perhaps adding in some of his own attitude. A beginning reader will do best with one sentence at a time. A fairly good reader can work with a few sentences, even a paragraph at a time to echo back to you. A fluent reader practicing expression can be challenged to hear how you read an entire page and then echo it back in his own style.

When your child reads expressively, (or "more like you"), he will most likely interact with the text more closely, comprehend better, and enjoy reading all the more! If your child wants to practice without anyone listening, tell him to read out loud in the privacy of his own room to a dog or even a stuffed animal!

See our workbook available for purchase online for a list of classic books for kids.

#67

Mind Monitoring

Reading without sharing is like watching a circus without saying anything—
like a commercial without a TV program—
like a frame without a picture.
~Nancy Whitelaw

One big step toward helping your child become a better reader is to make sure she is *actively* reading, which means paying attention to everything she reads and thinking about it as she reads. Good readers are always thinking as they read. (They make assumptions, predict, question, compare, and connect to their own lives.) You probably do this all the time as you read even though you don't realize it. Oftentimes in elementary school, kids are working so hard at *sounding* like a good reader on the outside that they are sacrificing actually *being* a good reader (comprehending) on the inside.

You can help, first, by thinking about what happens in your own mind while you read. Read something and see if you can be aware of how often you think of something you could say out loud about it. Now, sit down and do some buddy-reading with your child. When it is your turn to read, talk about what is going on in your mind. When it is her turn, ask her what is going on in hers. This is a great way for you to be a model; she can hear the things you say and learn to start thinking that way herself. In the beginning, and especially with newer readers, you might want to try stopping after every sentence and saying something. Later, or with more experienced readers, you can try after each paragraph. Soon, it will become a habit to be thinking while reading.

This may be tough for your child at first. If she is reluctant (or even just for fun), find a silly hat or a play crown and let her wear it on her head when it is her turn. Having something on her head may help her remember to be paying attention to what is going on underneath it! If she is stuck for ways to begin, jot down some sample things she might say to begin talking about what is going on in her mind. For example, try these:

- *I am picturing...*

- *I think the author said that because...*

- *That's sad (or funny or cool...)*

- *I have felt like that before when...*

- *I never knew that.*

- *I wonder if...*

- *I bet he/ she is doing that because...*

- *I don't think that is going to work out like they plan.*

- *I wonder why...*

- *That didn't make sense.*

- *I think _______ will happen next.*

- *I was confused by...*

- *If I were him I would...*

See our website for more ways to mind monitor.

#68
Reading Alone

Children who read for fun in their spare time
have higher reading achievement than those who do not.
Yet, about 30% of school-age children say they don't read for fun at all.
~Reading is Fundamental

It is perfectly normal for a child to resist reading aloud at first. (Even some adults do not like to read out loud!) If your child is resistant to the idea at first, encourage your child to read aloud to these:

- another family member, perhaps a younger sibling;

- the family pet;

- a tape recorder;

- a favorite stuffed animal;

- a grandparent.

These all provide a "safe" atmosphere in which to practice her reading-aloud skills, develop comprehension strategies, and increase her self-confidence as a reader.

Encouraging your child to read silently to herself is also important since that is the most common type of reading we do as we grow older. Casually asking her about what she read after a silent reading session can help you to see whether she is comprehending well. When children do not actually hear the words out loud, their minds may tend to drift at first.

This even happens with adults, occasionally, for that matter. Have you ever gotten to the end of a page and thought I *have no idea what I just read* because you were thinking about all of the things you have to do today instead? If this happens, you can try some Mind Monitoring together. Soon she, too, will be able to notice when her attention has been lost and go back to reread for comprehension on her own.

#69
Before, During and After

Before, During and After is a strategy to help *prepare* your child to read a book, keep her *engaged* while reading, and to check for *comprehension* after she's done with the book. Try these ideas and learn why they are helpful:

Before your child reads a book:

- Have her look at the cover, back cover, title and pictures within the book. Ask her to predict what might happen in the book. (While she is reading, she will be checking to see if her guesses were right and therefore checking her own comprehension.)

- Ask her to recall her prior knowledge (what she already knows). Does the book remind her of anything else she's read or knows about? (She will improve comprehension by making comparisons.)

- Ask her to think of a question that she thinks the book will answer. (She will be looking to see if she is right and, therefore, paying close attention.)

During the reading of the book:

- Stop several times and ask, "What do you think will happen next?" "What are you picturing" (to be sure she is comprehending). (See Mind Monitoring Idea #67.)

- Have her discuss why she made that particular prediction. Discuss her prediction, and ask, "Does it make sense?" (Again, to check for understanding.)

- Simply *discuss* the book with her, letting her lead the discussion. Try to evoke her reaction to the story.

After she is done reading the book:

- Ask questions about the main idea of the book.

- Check the predictions she made. Were they correct? How were they different?

- Discuss the author's intention. Did the author write to inform, persuade or entertain the reader? What did the author hope the readers would learn or feel as a result of reading the book? (Thinking about the author's purpose helps her understand different types of writing.)

- Ask how the book made her feel.

- Try having her retell the story using only main events and leaving out the secondary information.

- She may be interested in making a new ending to the story or placing the main character in a different situation and deciding what the character would say or how he or she would react.

See our website (and Idea #95) for a reminder of these ideas.

#70
The Library

Research has shown that a child's reading ability is positively linked with the amount of reading they do on their own, for fun.
~The Condition of Education, National Center for Education Statistics 1999

Hopefully, you have already set a goal to visit the library. Have you kept it? If you have, you've undoubtedly discovered all the wonderful tools the library has to offer you and your family.

One of the best attributes of the library is the *variety* of books it has to offer. If you've been to the library but haven't found your child reading and enjoying the books he's picked out, help him discover some different genres. Some children tend to look in one section of the library out of habit or familiarity. Your child may not even be aware of the different types of books available. Try choosing books from different genres every time he visits the library.

Here are just some of the different types of books to try:

- mystery;

- adventure;

- animal stories;

- how-to;

- poetry;

- realistic fiction;

- non-fiction; and

- historical fiction

Reading books from different genres can help him expand his knowledge about himself and the world. Information he reads in books can increase his background knowledge and enable him to relate information read in books to concepts he's learning about in school. He will be able to contribute more and may find it easier to write when asked.

If he finds a specific type of book he enjoys or a particular author he likes, encourage him to check out two or three books in the same genre or by the same author. Ask him to compare the books and discuss the similarities and differences.

#71
"The Rule of Thumb"

Educators are increasingly encouraging their students
to read and write on their own outside of school.
~The Condition of Education, National Center for Education Statistics 1999

When your child is looking at a new book and deciding whether to begin reading it (such as at the library or a bookstore), sometimes it may be difficult to tell if it is at the right reading level for her. A quick look at the cover (both front and back) of the book may tell you what grade level it is intended for. However, not all books carry that code and not all children are reading exactly at grade level.

A quick and easy way to judge whether a book will be too difficult for her to read can be called the "Rule of Thumb." Here's how to do it:

1. Simply have your child begin reading a page from anywhere in the book (not from the ending, though!).

2. Each time she comes to a word that she does not know, have her put one finger down starting with her pinky.

3. By the end of the page, if she has put her *thumb* down (indicating at least 5 difficult words), it probably means that the text will be too difficult for her and comprehension may be lost. Stopping to decode too many words breaks up the flow of reading and interferes with reading for meaning.

If she found too many difficult words but is still dying to read the book, perhaps it would be a good one to read aloud to her or buddy read together!

#72
"Hidden Treasure"

Each day of our lives we make deposits in the memory banks of our children.
~Charles Swindoll

Playing "Hidden Treasure" (Idea #20) is a perfectly fun way to practice reading words. Try making cards of:

- words in a story that your child is about to read for the first time so he can practice them before encountering them in the story;

- particularly difficult words in a story that your child is having trouble with;

- sentences with those tricky words in them so that he can practice the words in context; you may even try putting the word alone on one side of the card and a sentence containing that word on the other for reference if the word *alone* cannot be read;

- reading words his teacher has provided you;

- words similar in pattern (beginning letter[s], vowel sounds, rhyming chunks at the end) to words he is learning to encourage him to apply new word knowledge to other words; and

- challenge words for more experienced readers.

Many other subject areas, too, can be practiced with this fun game, such as spelling, math, and vocabulary words from other content areas like science and social studies.

#73
A Real Cliffhanger

I find it ironic that happy endings now are called fairytale endings because there's nothing happy about most fairytale endings.
~Joe Wright

Many of the long-running television shows accomplish their popularity by keeping the viewing public wanting more. They do this by ending each show with a question, problem, or situation that makes you want to watch it next time to see how it develops.

Books can do the same thing. Chapter books are often written so that each chapter ends in a cliffhanger, enticing the reader to continue and making it hard to put the book down. Picture books can also be read in a way to make your child want more. Try this with your child. After reading a chapter or a few pages in a picture book, stop. Ask your child to predict what will happen next. You will know by her answer if she is comprehending the book so far. If the answer is way off (and you know she is not just being silly!), you might consider rereading some of the text or important phrases or paragraphs to increase her understanding. In picture books, you can have her refer to the pictures to aid in comprehension.

By predicting the text, your child is now invested in the book. She wants to be right. She will pay particularly close attention to the story to determine if her guess is correct. If her prediction is not true, make sure she knows she is not *wrong*. Her prediction was probably a good one, but the author chose a different one. If she seems disappointed and thinks her prediction would have made a better story, challenge her to write the story *her* way. She can finish the story the way she thinks best and then compare it to the way the author chose to write it. (More experienced writers could be challenged to write their own ending in the *same style* as the author!)

To get a child interested in a chapter book, you might read the first chapter aloud to her during shared reading time. Tell her that's all *you're* going to read and that if she wants to know more (surely she will), she'll have to read it herself!

Two books we really like for this activity are *Abiyoyo* by Pete Seger for young readers, and *Tuck Everlasting* by Natalie Babbitt for upper elementary.

#74
Presidents' Day

Here is a great opportunity to visit the library with your child
to search for some age-appropriate books about any past presidents.

Presidents' Day is usually celebrated in February. However, no matter what time of year it is, it's always a good time to learn more about our past presidents. In honor of our past leaders, why not have some fun while reading about them? Try to find a book either at your child's reading level for him to read on his own or any interesting book to read *to* your child during shared reading time about any president they find interesting. You might even make a KWL chart of things that you've learned (Idea #94).

Once you've learned about them, challenge your child to make a birthday card for one of the former presidents. What kind of a personalized message or picture will he put on it especially for him, based on the information he has learned? Have him pretend to send it. Could you write back to him *as* the president himself and reply to his thoughtful message? Fun activities like this make reading all the more meaningful and fun.

#75
Every Day's a Holiday!

To show a child what once delighted you,
to find the child's delight added to your own,
this is happiness.
~J.B. Priestley

Holidays offer many ways to practice various reading skills in fun, motivating (and sometimes yummy!) ways. Try some of these ideas for some (or all!) holidays:

- Check out a book or two at the library about the holiday, then write out words associated with that holiday and play a special game of "Hidden Treasure!" with your child (Idea #20);

- Use those words to sort by features or put in alphabetical order;

- Write out the name of the holiday (or choose a large word associated with the holiday) and see how many smaller words your family can come up with using only the letters in that word;

- Cook a meal associated with the holiday, letting your child read the directions and measure the ingredients;

- Make personalized cards to send out;

- Leave her a special little love note in her lunch box.

Find ways to incorporate reading into specific holidays, such as doing any of the following activities:

- Read valentine heart candies to each other and then make up some sayings of your own. (Afterward, eat the candies, of course!)

- Make up an Easter Egg hunt with clues inside plastic eggs that lead your child to the next clue, with a special prize at the end.

- Write letters to the Easter Bunny, the Tooth Fairy, Santa Claus, etc.

- At Thanksgiving, take time for your whole family to actually write about things for which you are grateful.

- On the 4th of July, make a list of things we have/ do today that we did not have when America first became a country in 1776.

- Have your child write "old-fashioned" thank you notes to anyone who has given her a gift.

- Handwrite invitations to parties.

Expand on these ideas and use them for any holiday. Use a holiday as a special time not only for family and friends but also for having some fun with reading and writing!

#76
It's in the Bag

There is no friend as loyal as a book.
~Ernest Hemingway

After your child finishes a book, have him try this fun "book project in a bag" which uses visuals to aid in story comprehension.

Have him look around the house for objects that can represent the main characters and events of the story. If objects cannot be found in the house, encourage him to draw them or use clay, playing dough or any other odds-and-ends to create them. He can place each object in a bag or box and give a little presentation to family or friends. As he retells each main event, have him pull out the corresponding object for that event and place it on a table or floor in the correct order of occurrence.

For example, in the story of the *Three Little Pigs*, he may choose to put in his bag:

- a pig figurine, animal or drawing;

- a wolf animal or drawing;

- a piece of straw;

- a stick; and/or

- a brick (or playing dough brick).

If your child is having trouble deciding what constitutes a main event, you may want him to make a story map (Idea #81) first. If you find that his box or bag is overflowing with objects, he's probably put in objects that aren't related to the *main* events and should be encouraged to take out objects that represent minor details or events.

For extra fun, he can even decorate the bag like a puppet of the main character (here, a pig) and the puppet can retell the story from its point of view, sharing the items that were in the bag (and can then, later, be stored in it!)

Be a Perfect Person in Three Days by Stephen Manes is a fun book to use with this activity.

#77

A Friendly Debate

Deliberation and debate is the way you stir the soul of our democracy.
~Jesse Jackson

You already know that discussing a book after reading it can greatly increase your child's comprehension. If you want to liven up the discussion, try turning the discussion into a debate.

Choose two different books to debate. Take turns "arguing" whose character is more believable, which plot was most exciting, or which book had the funniest scene. Choose a different story element each time you debate. (Idea #84 has story element ideas.) Your child will quickly realize that arguing intelligently is not as easy as she thinks. She won't be able just to *say* her book's plot was the most exciting; she'll have to try to *prove* it with supporting details and information that will help validate her point. If she is able to argue with accurate details, you will know she has achieved comprehension of the story.

Make sure to set the rules for a proper debate. Remind her that no shouting is allowed and the person listening must wait until the person speaking is finished before responding. You might want to encourage her to have a notebook and pencil ready to jot down points she wants to argue after your turn is over. What a great way to practice all of the areas of language: reading, writing, listening, and speaking!

#78

The Tools in Your Toolbox

One of the greatest and simplest tools for learning more
and growing is doing more.
~ Washington Irving

You may be aware of the current tug-of-war many professionals in education struggle with year after year. It is the debate whether phonics or whole language is the best way to teach kids how to read. Luckily, as a parent, you do not have to commit to one or the other. You can simply commit to helping your child become the best reader he can be.

Simply put, *phonics* is the dissecting of a word into chunks* (or parts—letter sounds and symbols) and putting them together to form a recognizable word. However, the hard reality of the English language is that not all words are phonetic. In fact, *many* cannot be "sounded out."

This has traditionally been the primary way teachers have used to teach children how to read. First by letter sounds, then by putting letters together, and finally by putting those chunks of words together to create whole words.

In the 80's came the *whole language* movement. Experts felt that if a child is immersed in good literature and sees words often enough, he can learn to recognize them without ever having to sound them out. The reality here is that, sadly, many classrooms and homes are not equipped to provide an infinite supply of quality literature and endless opportunities to be surrounded by print. Even if a child is lucky enough at school and home to have this, there is no guarantee he will pick up on it all and become a good reader without any direct instruction.

You have the opportunity to balance these two very different approaches to teaching reading. You can learn to think of each concept as a tool in your ever-expanding toolbox of good ideas for helping your child become a good reader. If looking phonetically at a difficult word helps your child, do it. If he is learning to read by being read to and some of the other ways you are beginning to try from this book, then stick with that. Use both methods whenever they seem appropriate. A balance of the two should be the perfect recipe for helping your child learn to read.

*A "chunk" is a common term in elementary school for a part of a word. It is like a syllable. It consists of a vowel and the letters that come after it. Here are some examples: the "ale" in sale, the "ope" in hope, the "est" in best...

Phonics They Use by Patricia Cunningham is a great resource book that cleverly combines the principles of phonics with the natural practices of whole language.

#79
Readers' Theatre

*Children can use a play to explore concepts of the real world
without any of the consequences.*

One quite exciting and highly motivational way to get your child to read aloud with an incredible amount of expression is to conduct a Readers' Theatre. It is simply the acting out of a story using very minimal props and movements. It is a great way to work on all of the areas of language: reading, writing, listening, and speaking.

You can purchase a wide variety of books containing plays scripted out into the different characters' parts. This may be the best way to begin because your focus will be on the actual reading instead of the set up. Eventually, though, it will be fun and even beneficial for your family to work together to take a beloved story and turn it into a reader's theatre on your own. (Funny books work extremely well!)

Regardless of how you do it, it is a wonderful way for your family to enjoy reading together. You can make it as simple (sitting around a table reading parts) or as complicated (creating props, planning movement) as you wish. Older children may enjoy the challenge of adapting a favorite book into a play consisting mainly of dialog. You would certainly know how well they understood the meaning of the story when they turn narrative text into a character's words.

Through the practicing and perfecting of their lines, children who participate in Readers' Theatre gain skills in oral reading, comprehension, fluency, expression, and passion for reading. They will most likely be working with friends or family on the project, which also emphasizes the benefits of cooperation.

Try this website for some good ideas: http://www.teachingheart.net/readerstheater.htm.

#80
Top Ten Lists

To get your family involved in creating personal lists try 1,400 Things To Be Happy About *by Ann Kipfer. Your child can write his own unique ideas right in the book!*

If you asked a room full of children the same age the title of their three favorite books, chances are there would be a variety of different books chosen as the "best." Ask adults the same question, and you would *definitely* construct a list of many different books.

Children often read one type of book, such as *Diary of a Wimpy Kid, Junie B. Jones* or *Harry Potter* and enjoy it so much they want to read the whole set. There is certainly nothing wrong with this! However, when your child sees a list of other books that people consider the best, it helps open his eyes to the many different books available and might encourage him to delve into those books.

Start by having your family make their own Top Ten Lists of their all-time favorite books. Have each family member read each other's list. Keep them posted somewhere, such as the message center (Idea #6). As family members read new books, they may want to change their Top Ten Lists accordingly.

If you want your child to read different books at his age level, encourage him to collect data from family and friends around his own age (from two years below to two years above). For instance, if you have a 12-year-old, have him ask friends and family who are 10-14 years old. Encourage him to tally the responses. If a particular book shows up several times or one has an interesting title, go to the library, look it over, and if it seems appropriate, check it out! He might be surprised at how much he enjoys these new books and may want to revise his Top Ten List as well!

#81
Story Maps

Either write something worth reading, or do something worth writing.
~Benjamin Franklin

Story maps are a way to break down a story into important parts to help increase comprehension. Story maps generally contain places to record the story elements you just read about, such as:

- setting (time, place);

- characters (main and others);

- statement of problem or goal;

- events; and

- resolution (solving the problem or reaching the goal).

Children tend to find the setting and characters easy but may have difficulty with the statement of the problem and putting events in the proper order. When starting story maps with your child, try using a simple, familiar book such as *The Three Little Pigs*. The statement of the problem may be, "Three little pigs have to get away from a wolf."

The events, then, would detail how the pigs tried to escape from the wolf. The resolution should answer the problem and could be something like, "The three pigs escaped from the wolf by building a strong house of bricks that the wolf couldn't blow down."

Story maps are particularly useful in lengthier, more difficult books. They help your child clarify the problem and find the main events that relate to the problem. Being able to find the main events and eliminate the unimportant events aids in comprehension of the story. Therefore, this is a useful tool for comprehension to work on either *while* your child reads the story, or afterward.

You can make one, too, of a book you have read to give an example to show your child. Story maps can also be used in blank form to brainstorm ideas for a story your child is *creating*!

See our workbook available for purchase at www.365TeacherSecrets.com for a sample story map.

#82
Award Winning Books

Be not afraid of greatness:
some are born great, some achieve greatness,
and some have greatness thrust upon them.
~William Shakespeare

If you are not familiar with the great array of children's books available and don't know where to begin looking for quality, appropriate books, here's a suggestion: every year there are two major awards given to quality children's literature as determined by the Association for Library Service to Children, a division of the American Library Association.

The first is the Caldecott Medal, dedicated to Randolph Caldecott. The Caldecott is awarded annually to the artist who created the most distinguished illustrations in a children's book. Some of the most recent Caldecott Medal winning books are:

- *A Ball for Daisy* by Chris Raschka

- *A Sick Day for Amos McGee,* illustrated by Erin E. Stead, written by Philip C. Stead

- *The Lion & the Mouse* by Jerry Pinkney

The second award is the Newbery Medal, dedicated to John Newbery. The Newbery Medal honors the year's most distinguished contribution to American literature for children written by an American. Some of the most recent books to receive the Newbery Medal are:

- *Dead End in Norvelt* by Jack Gantos

- *Moon over Manifest* by Clare Vanderpool

- *When You Reach Me* by Rebecca Stead

On your next visit to the library, your child might try checking out some of the award winners from recent times or from years gone by. Compare them to other books he enjoys. Does he agree with the award? Why does he think the book was chosen to win the award? Can he find other books published the same year? Would they have been worthy of the award, instead? Why?

See our online workbook available for purchase, for a complete list of Caldecott and Newbery Award winners.

#83
Making Sense of Reading Mistakes
(How to Figure out Unknown Words)

*Remember: The main purpose for reading
is to gain meaning from text, not just to say the words.*

When you are listening to your child read aloud, you may be a bit unsure of what to do if she reads a word incorrectly. You may think you need to correct her right away so you don't forget. Or maybe you hate to mention it for fear of hurting her feelings. If this issue has ever perplexed you before, here are some tips based on research to make reading together a rewarding experience for both of you.

Studies show that it is best to correct any miscues (reading a word incorrectly) gently sooner rather than later (such as the end of the paragraph or page and then listing them all.) However, it is extremely important to give ample wait time. This means to allow your child time to correct her own miscue by waiting, at least, until the end of the sentence. This way, if she is truly reading for meaning, she will probably notice her mistake herself and go back and attempt to correct it on her own. (Ultimately, the amount of time you give will depend on your child's age, reading ability, what she is reading, the purpose for reading it, and generally just what feels right.) If she doesn't stop on her own, though, you might simply ask, "Did that make sense?" and let her figure out where she missed a word.

If she does attempt to figure out a difficult word but is clearly having trouble, here are some strategies that you can teach her to determine an unknown word:

- Context. Use the context of the sentence to determine what word(s) would make sense there. You might show her how to say "blank" for the tough word and reread the entire sentence. This might be all it would take for her to figure it out.

- First letter. Of all words that might make sense, which start with that letter?

- Chunks. Are there any chunks—or word parts—inside the word with which she is familiar? For example, *caterpillar* can be broken into known chunks such as *cat* and *pill*.)

- Illustrations. If there are illustrations in the story, they are often very helpful.

If these attempts all fail, tell her the word. Do not feel the need to correct any miscues that do not make a difference in the meaning of the sentence. Many children reading for meaning may read "mom" for "mother" or say "he said" instead of "he suggested." After all, the purpose of reading isn't to say all the words correctly but to understand the message, so miscues that do not affect meaning should be ignored.

You might suggest that your child reread a sentence again after all words have been decoded. This will help not only with fluency but also with comprehension because she will be able to hear the entire sentence completely, now with no interruptions that may make her lose her train of thought. If an entire section has been particularly difficult, with many places she has had to pause to decode words, you might suggest she reread that whole part so that she can understand it better.

See our online workbook available for purchase, for steps to figuring out unknown words.

#84
The Story Elements

Try this: Find the who, what, why, when, and where in a newspaper article that interests your child.

If you want to ask questions about the story your child is reading to check for comprehension, try starting with questions about the important elements of the story. These are called the story elements. They include:

- Who? (…are the main characters)

- What? (…is the problem, goal, conflict, situation, plot)

- Where? (…does the story take place)

- When? (…does the story take place)

- Why? (…do the characters act as they do)

- How? (…do the characters accomplish their goal or solve their problem)

If your child can answer these questions with detail, you can assume he has a good understanding of the story. You can use the story map to practice summarizing as well (Idea #158).

See our workbook for a blank story elements page to fill in.

#85
Tracking Progress

Remember: Becoming a lifelong reader happens one story at a time.

Parents frequently use sticker charts or similar incentive ideas to encourage their young children to do something positive or beneficial. Unfortunately, many children may resist reading, and similar forms of providing incentive can work wonders. Now, we're not talking about rewarding your child with a sticker each time he reads for a half-hour and a new toy once he gets ten stickers. What you ultimately want to do is encourage (not bribe!) your child to become a reader.

One way to do this in a completely positive way, focusing on increasing motivation from within herself, is to create some kind visible display of her hard work. A clever idea to "track" her progress is to cut out various colors of train cars from construction paper. Each time your child reads for a specified amount of time she can hang up one train car (or anything!), perhaps on a wall in her bedroom. When the train reaches a specified length or destination (ten cars long, across the wall, around the room) she gets the reward. Ideally, the reward will also help promote a love of reading, such as a trip to the bookstore to pick out a new book of her choice, a trip to the library for both of you and lunch out to discuss expectations for your new book, etc.

Focusing on *time* read may be better than *books* read because, as children grow into chapter books, it will obviously take longer to read a book than it did with a picture book. (If the goal is *books* read, young children might actually be encouraged to read fast just to get the book done and receive no enjoyment from it.) You can increase your expectation little by little each time the goal is met, making the reward a little more challenging to reach. You will probably see her pride and self-confidence as a reader grow with each new train.

Hopefully, this visual display of her reading efforts will encourage her to read more and more. When she has felt successful enough on her own, you will most likely see the motivation begin to come from within. With all that reading, she is bound to discover the joy in it and will be choosing to read on her own for pleasure in no time.

See our workbook available for purchase online for an example of a reading log—another way to track reading progress.

#86
For the Beginning Reader

Dr. Seuss and Eric Carle are two authors who write many books for children in a patterned, rhyming, and predictable way that are especially good for young readers.

You've learned a few ways you can help your child learn to read and become a better reader. Surrounding children with print, reading to them, and giving them experiences with a variety of types of books can all provide a good foundation for emerging readers. Gradually and naturally they will grow into trying to read books on their own. Patterned, predictable, and rhyming text can prove to be especially helpful here.

Stories that have predictable plots and or phrases are fun and easy for children to learn to read because they make sense to young children and are written in the language they speak.

Patterns make reading sentences easier because children can memorize the pattern and read it well every time. Rhyming text makes reading easier when children are helped to figure out words based on their similar sounds (rhymes) with words just read.

So, if you have a beginning reader, or even just a reluctant one, give some of these types of books a try.

See our online workbook available for purchase, for a list of predictable books.

#87
Love Letters

To send a letter is a good way to go somewhere
without moving anything but your heart.
~Phyllis Theroux

Don't you still love getting mail? *Real* mail… in your mailbox, addressed just to you from someone you care about? We don't do that nearly often enough anymore. With texting, emailing and all the forms of social media we use, there are so many quicker ways to get your message to someone. But if you still like getting mail, so will your child! What better way to practice reading than by reading something sent to her by someone who cares?

See if anyone—family or friend—would be willing to write to your child. It doesn't have to be long or deep, just something to get your child reading. Chances are there is someone who wouldn't mind sitting down for a few minutes and writing to her. Give them a heads-up as to her reading level, and suggest keeping the words more simple for young readers. (Also, remind them to print and not use cursive because early readers certainly cannot read that yet!)

A good *writing* project would be to have her write back to whoever wrote the letter. (You can take dictation for a very young child.) Reading is more fun when it is done in a natural way, and reading a letter from a loved one couldn't be more natural!

#88
Fun Reading Activities

Just play. Have fun. Enjoy the game.
~Michael Jordan

When your child finishes a story (whether he read it himself or you read it to him), the fun doesn't have to stop there. There are so many activities he could do or that you could work on together that would extend the enjoyment of reading and aid in comprehension as well. Here are just a few ideas for him to try:

- Draw a 6-frame cartoon sketch showing the book's plot.

- Select one character and explain why he would like to know him or her.

- Draw a map or picture of the setting described in the book.

- Create an advertisement for the book (a picture ad he might see in a magazine or a poster he might see at a movie theater).

- Write a poem about the book or main character. (See Idea #132 for a variety of poetry types.)

- Brainstorm questions he might ask the main character or author of the story in an interview. Could he find the author's address at the library and actually send the questions to him? Some authors do respond!

- Make a mobile of the story elements such as characters or scenes hanging from a hanger.

- Create a diorama of an important or memorable event in the book in a shoebox.

- Practice reading his favorite part. Video record it. Share it with the family, or send it to someone far away.

- Write a play based on the book and present it.

- Draw a picture illustrating what the story is about.

- Make a collage of items from the story. Be creative! How could you best display them?

See our workbook for blank filmstrips to brainstorm on.

#89
Summarizing

*As your child writes in her personal journal,
encourage her to try writing a summary about her day.*

Have you ever heard your child retell a movie or book to someone and listen to her go on and on and on? It may even be difficult for the listener to follow if he isn't familiar with the plot.

Teaching your child how to summarize can help her capture the plot and feeling of the movie or story without getting lost in minor events, thus increasing her comprehension of the main idea of a story.

Start by showing your child examples of good summaries. Good summaries (also called a synopsis) are not hard to find. You can find summaries on the back or inside cover of books. In the newspaper, there are synopses of movies and books. On the Internet, you can look up a title of any book and most often there will be a short synopsis of the book. (It can be fun to read a book together, work on a short summary together, and then go look the book's summary up online. See how similar yours is to "theirs." What's different?)

Once your child reads a variety of summaries, she'll begin to understand what they should look and sound like. When learning how to summarize, it may help to practice summarizing one chapter, a short story, or a picture book before tackling longer, more involved stories. You can even practice after a TV show. (Hey, summarizing is summarizing! We just need to keep them interested.) If she is still having trouble, you may want her to start by making a story map (see #81) and use the events to help organize her thoughts.

See our workbook for the steps of summary writing to print out.

#90
The "Pros" of Poetry

Poetry is plucking at the heartstrings, and making music with them.
~Dennis Gabor

Using poetry or verse as reading material for a change can prove to be very motivational for reluctant readers and quite enjoyable for all readers. Poems are usually short, sweet, and highly entertaining. Finding poetry that fits your child's interests (such as humor, nature, realistic…) is easy to do. A librarian or bookstore employee can help you find anthologies to suit any child.

If your child especially seems to enjoy reading poetry, you might try to gently suggest ways to increase academics through the use of poems. Perhaps…:

- You can pause, while reading him a poem, and omit the rhyming words for him to fill in.

- He can practice reading poems aloud.

- You could borrow the form of a beloved poem and help your child plug in his own words to create a unique poem all his own.

- You might encourage him to memorize his favorite poem and recite it to anyone he feels comfortable with.

Part 4
Informational Reading

INTRODUCTION: While Part 3 focused on Narrative Reading, Part 4 focuses on a different kind of reading: informational, or expository, reading. Informational reading is often tougher for kids to understand because it is full of "facts" rather than "fun." Luckily, there are many things you can do to help your child understand this type of text.

In this Part, you will learn about things you both can do before reading, while reading, and after reading that will all work together to help your child's comprehension of informational text. We'll also share some fun activities you can do with information from a non-fiction book. Hopefully, whether your child already likes to read these kinds of books or not, her skills and enjoyment of it will all increase. Reading for information is a skill she will use every single year of her academic life and possibly even in her career. Grasping comprehension methods early on, in elementary school, will set the stage for many years to come.

#91
Variety is the Spice of Reading

You don't get harmony when everybody sings the same note.
~Doug Floyd

As a parent, you want to encourage your child to read. Most experts agree the best way to do that is to read, read, read. You may think you need a library full of books at home to make that possible, but that's not necessarily true. Don't get stuck thinking that to be reading, your child must have an actual book. There are many different sources of reading materials besides books, and encouraging your child to read them helps expose him to different genres. It also may help him learn to love reading more.

Become aware of the different opportunities in your house and in your child's life for reading. Perhaps your child would love a subscription to a nature or animal magazine. Kids love getting mail addressed to them and might be encouraged to read it cover to cover if it is just for them. If your child likes comics, let him check them out from the library. There are some kid-friendly "graphic novels" that many kids feel success with because they are high-interest without as many words as a chapter book. If your family gets the newspaper, look for an article that may also interest your child and read it to him if he is young, or encourage him to read it himself if he can. Be a role model yourself and let your child see you read different kinds of materials. Find a reason to ask your child for help using a thesaurus to find a better word for something you are writing or using a dictionary to look up a word that is in something you are reading.

The goal is twofold: have lots of different kinds of reading materials around the house and encourage him to try out many of them. Whatever encourages your child to read, let him read it so he will simply read more. If he reads more, he will become a better reader. When he becomes a better reader, he will naturally want to check out tougher books/ material. So, don't be too quick to take away a comic book he may be reading. Reading something he loves, like a comic book or a magazine, can help promote his reading habit. The more he reads the better his comprehension will be; his vocabulary will increase, and his reading rate will increase. Don't focus on him reading the "right" material; simply encourage him to read whatever he likes and eventually he will move on when he is ready.

#92
Help Wanted!

Practice doesn't make perfect.
Practice reduces the imperfection.
~Toba Beta

As with many of the ideas in this book, most of the ideas in this Part will require your help. Whether your child is a new reader or a fluent reader, many of these strategies and ideas will be new to him. Perhaps he will recognize some from school. Perhaps not. Regardless, many will require some preparatory work from you and, especially at first, some *guidance* from you as well.

In the classroom, teachers recognize the need for different types of teaching strategies at different times. Often, when a subject is new, a teacher will share a lesson or explain a new skill to the whole class. The next step is not to send all of the kids back to their seats to work on something similar completely on their own. They know that students will need a little "guided practice" where their presence—and help—is required. They walk around and see how kids are doing and offer help as soon as it's needed. Eventually, though, students have had enough practice with that skill and they can work on it more independently; this is called "independent practice."

At home, you are the teacher, and many of these activities will require a bit of guided practice before your child can work on them alone. You will need to sit with your child and show him how a strategy works. He will need you close by at first, reminding him how it is done, modeling, checking all along the way to be sure he is doing things correctly. The goal, however, is to have your child working independently soon. Only you will know when he is ready for that step. Showing them a strategy once is all some kids need. For others (or for tougher strategies), they may need much more guidance. Just keep in mind that during elementary school you will start out helping a lot and end up not helping much at all. How much time in between is up to you and your child!

#93
Functional Reading

Once you learn to read, you will be forever free.
~ Frederick Douglass

Just as inside your home there are so many opportunities for reading, out in the world there are, too. While you don't want to turn every outing into a reading lesson, there are many ways you can gently, naturally encourage reading while you and your child are out and about.

Many young children learn to recognize store and restaurant signs and have fun reading them. Play a game, and see how many she can recognize during a drive. Point out that she is reading! At the grocery store, she may recognize cereal names and more. Can she read some items on the menu at the restaurant? Very early readers are helped along by reading common things around the house that you have labeled with notecards: refrigerator, stove, closet, bedroom, fireplace, table, chair, book shelf. Once she learns those words in their places, collect the cards and challenge her to read them out of context. Put up new ones, too.

If she is already reading a bit on her own, offer her more opportunities to read things that "need to be read." When she brings a note home from school, ask her to read it to you while you cook dinner, or have her read you the recipe. If your child loves video games, have her read the instructions, reviews, or strategy books. Most children love music. Consider printing out the lyrics of one of her favorite songs and have her read it to you. Is she into nutrition? Have her read the nutrition labels on her favorite foods. Putting together a swing set, bike or toy? Have her read the instructions while you follow them. There are endless opportunities surrounding you and your child every day once you start looking for them!

#94
Begin at the Beginning: KWL

The things I want to know are in books.
My best friend is the man who'll get me a book I haven't read.
~Abraham Lincoln

Perhaps the first step in understanding informational text is to start even before you read. How can you do that, you might ask? The KWL Method is one commonly used in elementary classrooms. It is usually done for one particular subject that a child is going to read about. Use a piece of paper turned sideways with two lines dividing it into three vertical sections as follows:

K= KNOW: Your child writes down (or you can write for a younger child) what he already knows about the subject. Write down everything, whether or not it actually is correct.

W= WANT to know: In this column, your child records his questions about the subject. What does he want to know?

L= LEARN: While reading and/or after, in this column he jots down the things he's learned. After reading is done, he can also look back at his "K" column; was each "fact" he wrote correct? If not, cross it out or edit it.

If there were any unanswered questions, encourage him to find the answers to them even if they were not in the book. Perhaps you can sit down together and look on the Internet or take a trip to the library for another book.

The three parts in KWL help set the stage for comprehension by getting him thinking and predicting before he even begins to read. Now, when he actually does read, he will have a purpose for reading beyond just getting it done. He will become an *active* reader. He will be reading to see if his knowledge was accurate, if his questions will be answered, and for what he can jot down that he learned. Having these purposes for reading greatly increases comprehension and, as we've learned, if kids feel successful at something they tend to do better.

See our workbook available for purchase at www.365TeacherSecrets.com for a blank KWL worksheet.

#95
SQ3R: A Reading Comprehension Technique

There are many little ways to enlarge your child's world.
Love of books is the best of all.
~ Jacqueline Kennedy

If your child has ever read something and afterward can't answer many questions about it, you know her comprehension was insufficient. It is possible for a child to be able to read out loud fluently, even expressively, and yet not remember much (or anything) of what they read. It is important to keep in mind the true definition of reading which involves not just *saying* the words but also *understanding* the words and constructing meaning from those words. If your child is not doing that, is she really reading?

Since informational text can be more difficult to understand and, therefore, to read, it is important to offer children strategies to better comprehend early on. One very effective method for understanding informational text is called SQ3R. The letters in SQ3R stand for these stages of reading:

S= Survey

Q= Question

R= Read

R= Recite

R= Review

At first, doing these five steps may seem tedious to her. In general, children just want to start reading informational text so they can be done. You can help change the way she thinks. Help her realize the goal of reading is to understand what she has read, not just to get it done. Once she uses this method a few times, she will realize she can finish her assignments more quickly without looking back through the text again and again. Once she realizes she's working smarter, not harder, she will embrace this strategy and use it frequently.

Still, not every single step of SQ3R needs to be done for every single thing she will ever read. However, practicing the steps now will help her build good habits that will last a lifetime. She will learn to use whichever steps are most helpful to her, modify her approach for each different text, and become a better reader.

The next five activities will explain in more detail each part of the comprehension technique, SQ3R.

See our workbook available for purchase at www.365TeacherSecrets.com for more information on SQ3R.

#96
SQ3R: Survey

A journey of a thousand miles begins with a single step.
~Confucius

Imagine walking into a crowded room at a party. When you walk in, you may stop and take a look around the room and gather information about what and who you see. You might see some friends, a table with food, an empty chair, etc. You use that information to make a decision on what to do next. You are surveying the room. Surveying a book works in a similar way. SURVEY, the first part of SQ3R, means to have your child give a quick look through what he is about to read and gather information.

Imagine he has a chapter to read in Social Studies about the *Declaration of Independence*. Here are some things to Survey:

- Have him read the title and guess what it's about.

- Look through the section for pictures and read the captions underneath.

- Pay attention to bold words; they are bold for a reason; he may need to know their definitions.

- Use the bold headings to predict what he will be reading about.

These all set the stage for good comprehension because he is already thinking about what he'll read before he reads. *While* he reads, he will be looking to see if his predictions were right. Whether he notices that he is right or wrong, IF he notices, he will know he is comprehending!

Depending on the length of what he has to read, this step can take as little as a minute, but it is worth so much because it may be the difference in comprehending what he reads... or not!

#97
SQ3R: Question

The important thing is not to stop questioning.
Curiosity has its own reason for existing.
~ Albert Einstein

Your child is full of questions about non-academic topics every day. You have undoubtedly answered the "Why?" and the "Why not?" question several times every day. You can use her natural curiosity to help her better understand what she reads. QUESTION is the second part of SQ3R. It means to set a purpose for reading by 1) reading any questions she will have to answer later *before* she even reads the text and 2) creating questions that she will be able to answer once she reads the text.

Many informational texts have questions after each section or chapter to test the students' knowledge of that section. Do you remember having to find the answers to those questions? It probably involved a lot of re-looking at the whole section with a lot of page turning and frustration. To avoid this frustration, encourage her to take a look at the questions in the back of the section/chapter *first*. Read them. Now she knows what the questions are before she even begins to read. Now when she reads, she is reading with a purpose—to find those answers. It helps keep her focused on the content and less likely to wander in her mind. It's actually like knowing the test questions before the test. Why wouldn't she take this step to make her learning easier?

Remember those headings she quickly read in the Survey part of SQ3R? Now, have her take each heading and turn it into a question. Imagine that section in her social studies book on the *Declaration of Independence*. Perhaps the two headings she reads are "Signing the Declaration" and "Forming the Future of the United States." She would turn those headings into questions like *Who were the signers of the* Declaration of Independence? and *How did the* Declaration *help form the United States?* After she's done reading those two sections, she should be able to answer her own questions, which would show complete comprehension.

Having a purpose when reading will make her an active, not passive, reader. Her purpose will be to look for the answers to the questions. She will stay more focused looking for those answers.

This step, too, takes very little time but is very worthwhile.

#98
SQ3R: Read

To learn to read is to light a fire;
every syllable that is spelled out is a spark.
~ Victor Hugo, Les Miserables

READ is the first "R" in SQ3R. It, of course, means to read the text, but a nice addition to this step is to get into the habit of reading with a pencil in hand. If the text is something he can write on, he can learn to annotate (more on that in Idea #103.) If not, if it's a school textbook or library book, he can take notes on a separate piece of paper. He can even jot down page numbers where he finds answers.

Another good strategy to use while reading, is to let pictures develop in your head. You probably do it all the time when you read. Try it and see. This is something you can encourage your child to do, too. When he is reading, stop and ask him what he "sees" in his mind. (See more on this "Mind Monitoring" in Idea #67 & #101.) If he "sees" nothing, you can help him by having him draw a quick picture after every paragraph or section of what was happening. Read it together, and help him at first. If he knows he will have to do this, he may begin to read purposely looking for things he can draw, and this is what you want! Reading for a purpose! Read so you can find out information!

Good readers also have conversations with the text while they read. Again, try this yourself, and see what kinds of things you say to yourself as you read. You might agree or disagree with what you read. You might compare it to something you already know or think *I did not know that*! You can model this for your child as you read together and show him that he should be thinking about the meaning of the words also.

It is important to mention here that good readers reread when they need to. How many times have you ever been "reading" and turn a page and think *I have no idea what I was just reading!* Even good readers' minds wander at times. Kids need to know that. Not-so-good readers turn pages without realizing that they weren't even paying attention. Good readers don't feel bad when that happens; they just reread!

As you can see, there are a lot of things going on while you are reading. Children don't always realize that. After just a few reading sessions together, you can help him to see how trying them out will help him understand what he's reading so much better. When kids start to feel more successful at reading, they like it more, and they read more. The more they read, the better readers they become!

#99
SQ3R: Recite

Stay at home in your mind. Don't recite other people's opinions.
I hate quotations. Tell me what you know.
~ Ralph Waldo Emerson

RECITE is the second R in SQ3R. It means to look back at the text as soon as your child finishes it. This is when she can answer those questions she created out of the headings and/ or answer questions assigned to her. She can take just a minute or two to look back at the headings and ask herself if she can explain what they mean. Ask her to do this out loud; otherwise, she may look at them and *think* she knows, but saying them out loud ensures that she does.

Let her play the role of teacher and "teach" you about what she's learned. After all, children learn best when they can teach someone else what they know - that's true comprehension.

While everything is still fresh in her mind, she should go to the questions (if there are any) at the end of the chapter/section and answer them with what she knows from reading. She can also look over her annotations or notes. Have her look back at any bold words. Does she know what they mean now? Perhaps she will want to add them to her notes, if she hasn't already. *Now* that she's read the entire selection, she may want to go back and highlight important parts or add them to her notes. Remember that highlighting *as* she reads is not very helpful because she doesn't yet know what is most important. But now, *after* she has read the whole text, she does know what is most important- and those things can be highlighted.

Looking back through the text to check for understanding will not take very long, but it is one extra way to ensure good comprehension, and, therefore, good reading.

#100
SQ3R: Review

A book must be the ax for the frozen sea within us.
~ Franz Kafka, 1904

REVIEW, the last of the 3 Rs in SQ3R, is a longer process. While reciting happens directly after reading, reviewing happens later, to prepare for an evaluation like a test or quiz.

A few days before the test, your child should begin to study. Here are some things he can try:

- Reread the notes he took during and after reading and look over the text itself if he annotated right on it.

- Ask someone to help him study. You are a good choice; you can create questions for the important points he has highlighted, underlined, or noted. Write the most difficult questions on note cards (with answers on the back) so he can even study alone later. Handing over the text and asking someone else to quiz him is a much better study method than doing so alone. If your child looks things over on his own, he may have the tendency to say "Yep, I know that" when really he is not *recalling* the information but simply *recognizing* it. If someone else quizzes him, he will not have the option of simply recognizing a fact; he will have to recall it.

- Each day, he should take some time to do this reviewing. Studies show that smaller amounts of study time spread out over a few days is better than cramming the night before.

By now you have read about all the steps of SQ3R. They may seem awkward at first or time-consuming. When your child goes through them for the first time, though, see if he does better on the assignment or test. If so, point out that doing all the steps helped him get ready to read, read more purposefully and with more comprehension, and review more efficiently. Again, he may not use every single step the same way every time. Trying the steps out now, though, in elementary school, starts a pattern that will likely help him out with every reading assignment in his future—and there will be many!

#101
Mind Monitoring

You may have tangible wealth untold.
Caskets of jewels and coffers of gold.
Richer than I you can never be –
I had a mother who read to me.
— Strickland Gillilan

The last several ideas gave you information about the system for better comprehension called SQ3R. During reading, it is important for your child to be thinking about several different things. Teachers often call this "having a conversation with the text." Try this out yourself: pick up something and read it. Pay attention to what you are thinking while you are reading. Are you connecting the words to anything you already know? Agreeing? Questioning? Predicting what might be written next? Good readers do this, often without even realizing it. Kids are very focused, especially at first, on *sounding* like a good reader and are most often praised for that. However, it is entirely possible for a child to read fluently and even expressively and yet have no idea what she read!

One terrific way to help your child get into the habit of thinking while reading is to read with her, out loud, perhaps taking turns. For instance, if you are reading a short children's book, you might read one page and then let her read one page. Before the next person's turn, though, stop for a few seconds and do some Mind Monitoring. In other words, talk to each other about what is going on in your mind. It is good for you to do this, too. For one, it gives her some suggestions for what she can say herself. It also shows her that you are thinking while you are reading, too, and that she should as well.

Part 3 also discusses Mind Monitoring but with narrative text. Here are some suggestions to get you started talking about what you are thinking while reading informational text:

- *I am picturing...*

- *I think the author wrote that part first because...*

- *I never knew that.*

- *That is interesting...*

- *I think I've read about something like that before.*

- *I think this is the part where __________ is going to happen...*

- *I wonder if/why...*

- *I think this is where the author is summarizing everything.*

- *That word is in bold probably because it is important for me to know.*

- *I don't really understand that part. Let me read it again.*

- *I think _______ will happen next.*

- *That still didn't make sense. I am going to mark that so I remember to ask about it.*

- *I remember reading about this last year in class.*

- *That's cool! I want to mark that!*

- *That's the answer to one of the questions! I will write that down/ mark it.*

- *In my head I am picturing...*

- *What does this graph show? Can it help me?*

- *Oh, look at that picture. It is helping me understand what the author is talking about.*

Young kids, or kids who are having trouble with comprehension, should stop after every sentence and Mind Monitor. Older kids can stop after every paragraph and eventually move up to every page. Soon, with enough practice reading out loud, she will begin to do this all the time on her own, internally. To help her do this on her own, you could jot some of the previous examples of things to say (and therefore think) on a notecard that she can keep with her at school or keep wherever she typically reads.

See also Idea #67 for more on Mind Monitoring and our workbook for a page of thoughts/ suggestions to print out.

#102
What's in There?

There is more treasure in books than in all the pirate's loot on Treasure Island.
~ Walt Disney

In Idea #95, you read about SQ3R. The first step is to have your child Survey the text he is about to read. Not every reading assignment will have all of the following parts, but if and when they do, they could be important to helping your child better comprehend. The next time your child brings home his textbook or an informational text of any kind, browse it together. We often assume our kids know what all the different parts are, but many have never actually been shown. Here are some things to seek out and discuss their purpose:

Title: Is it a creative title only, or can we predict what the text will be about from it?

Headings and Subheadings (usually in bold): They usually do tell exactly what that section is about.

Table of Contents: Shows all the major sections in the book. Show your child how to look through this, for instance, when choosing books for reports. Will this book be full of the information he really wants?

Captions: Many kids want to skip over pictures and graphs because they feel this is "extra stuff," and they don't want more to do! However, these visual aids are often included to show, in a quick, easy-to-understand way, something discussed at length in words. Talk about and interpret graphs together. Let your child make up questions to "quiz" you. Show him that looking at these can often help him understand more quickly and better than the reading alone.

Bold Words: Words that the author knows may be new or difficult for children are often bolded. It's usually a good idea to pay extra attention to them.

Glossary: A quick reference place to look up vocabulary words from this book. It is much quicker to use this than a dictionary.

Index: A detailed list of words and concepts in the book and the location of the information can be found in the Index. It is helpful to show your child how this can be used to help him answer tough-to-find questions.

#103
Notes on Note Taking

Learning is like rowing upstream; not to advance is to drop back.
~ Chinese proverb

In Idea #95, you read about SQ3R. During reading, this method suggests that your child take notes in some way while she is reading. There are several good strategies for doing this so that she can later look back and easily see the most important parts of what she read. It is nice to show your child a wide variety of options and then let her choose what she prefers. We don't all take notes in the same way. We also do not take notes the same way each time we do it ourselves. However, if we have lots of options we know about, we can pull from them and decide which would work best for us in any given situation. Here are two very helpful strategies.

HIGHLIGHTING: One terrific way to mark important information is to highlight it. However, if we just hand a kid a highlighter, chances are most of the text will end up highlighted! They simply love to use them and often don't know how to tell important information from not-so-important information. We have to show children how to pick and choose only the most important info to highlight. A good way to do this is to read NOT with a highlighter in her hand, but just a pencil. This first time she reads through something, she doesn't yet know what is or is not very important. So, instead of highlighting the things she thinks *may* be important, have her underline them. (Too much pencil is not nearly as distracting as too much bright yellow!) Then, when she is all done reading and knows what the whole text was about, she will better know what the main ideas were. Now, she can choose a few things per page to highlight. In general, some good things to highlight are answers to questions, first sentences of paragraphs (which often contain main ideas) and parts of beginning and/or last paragraphs which also usually contain main ideas. Remember the goal of highlighting is to look back at a page later and see just a few, most important ideas. Highlighting makes the important information stand out from the rest of the text. Then, when it's time to review or study, she can simply read the highlighted text and remember the important points. If too much is highlighted on a page, she will have to reread the whole text, which will not save her time and doesn't help her quickly remember the main ideas.

NOTES- Taking notes on a separate piece of paper, or right there on the text if possible, is another good way to remember the important stuff. You can even show her short cuts to note-taking like codes. For instance, instead of writing next to a paragraph "this paragraph contains many important ideas" she can pick a code like a star and just draw that at the end of the lines that she finds important. A happy face can mark a part she really liked a lot quicker even than writing a note about it. She can chose codes that make sense to her. Perhaps she might draw an arrow pointing up next to information she needs to look up or research more thoroughly. Or she could use a question mark next to a paragraph she needs to ask a question about or she doesn't understand. If she is writing a report, you can show her that taking notes on index cards can be more helpful than one sheet of paper because she can later move the cards around and organize them easily.

#104
"Hidden Treasure"

Little strokes fell great oaks.
~Ben Franklin

Every little thing you do with your child to practice reading skills is a great help to her. Every time you make an effort to find *fun* ways to do this, it makes learning to read (or becomimg a better reader) much more meaningful and motivational. In Part 1, Idea #20 explains how to play a game we made up called "Hidden Treasure." If you have not yet played, take a few minutes to play this easy and motivational game and reinforce just about every area of the curriculum. Of course, this includes reading.

If your child is reading a tough informational book or studying from a textbook, you can help her learn to read either high-frequency words (the most common words) from the text or new, vocabulary words—anything she is having a tough time reading.

The first step is to sit down and listen to her read the text. Make note of any and all words that give her trouble. Later, write these words on note cards. Try to include some not-so-tough words, too, so not every word in the game is new and difficult. Use these word cards to play "Hidden Treasure." On your turns, when you pick out a word card, model how you figured it out and note spelling patterns etc. that will help your child remember it, too.

After you've played the game, have her read the book again. Playing this game should make her more fluent. Every chance you have to make learning fun helps!

#105
Stashing Books

Plant a seed...READ!

Even though informational books can be a little tougher for kids to comprehend, they are often highly interesting. Whether your child already loves reading about real/true things or not, you can encourage him to read more by stashing those kinds of books in some planned-out places.

Many kids watch movies or play videogames in cars, in restaurants, in waiting rooms etc. Instead, try stashing some books that will capture your child's interests in the car. Encourage him to "unplug" himself and read instead. Think about his interests (bugs? cars? space? volcanoes? ponies?) and begin collecting books. To save money, look for used books online and in used bookstores. Perhaps grab a special box or bag to keep the books in (or find a plain old one and let him decorate it!) and change the books when you can for a surprise.

If a car ride starts to get boring, have your child open the special bag and pull out a book. Going in to a doctor appointment and know there will be a wait? Grab a book that's already in your car. Need a way to keep your child busy waiting for dinner out to arrive? Bring in a book. To make it even more interesting, ask him to read something to himself and then quiz you on it. Kids sure do love stumping their parents and feeling smarter than them on anything!

#106
Different Structures

The most interesting information comes from children,
for they tell all they know and then stop.
~ Mark Twain

Informational (nonfiction) books are written to inform, report, or describe information to the reader. In general, they are structured in one of six ways. If your child can begin to determine the structure the author uses in the text, she will be able to find the main ideas more easily.

Cause and Effect: In this structure, one event causes another to happen. The cause is *why* it happens, the effect is *what* happens. One event can have many effects. For example, if your child reads a book about smoking, there are many possible effects from that one event (coughing, shortness of breath, lung disease, etc.). Look for key words like *since, because, if, then, due to, because of,* or *therefore.*

Compare and Contrast: Texts that use the compare and contrast structure are helping the reader to view two or more different people, events or things and find what is the same and different about them (e.g., a book comparing alligators and crocodiles, or a book about two different presidents). Look for key words like *similarly, the difference between, likewise, however, yet,* or *nevertheless.* A Venn diagram (see Idea #143) works best for this type of book structure:

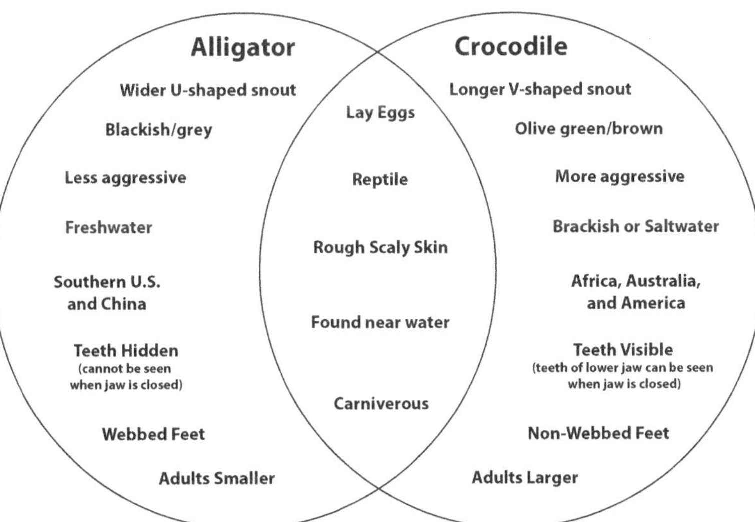

Problem/Solution: This structure is exactly as the title states. A problem is presented, and a solution follows (e.g., The problem is that the colonists didn't want to be ruled by a king; the solution is that they went to a new land).

Question/Answer: Your child may read many books that use this structure when he wants to find out something specific. How does a clock work? How does a caterpillar turn into a butterfly? Why does a volcano blow its top? Look for key words like *how, when, what, where, who,* or *how many.*

Sequence: A book that has an ordered list of events uses the sequence structure. Some key words to look for are *first, then, next, finally, after,* or *until.*

Description: A descriptive book will have an abundance of information about a subject (elephants, George Washington, or Alabama, for example). Using a mind map from Idea #157 is a great way to organize and remember all the information about the topic.

Understanding how an author presents information in a book can help your child find the important information more quickly. He will know what to look for and he can use a graphic organizer to help organize and remember what he learned. You may find that many books have more than one structure. Decide what the purpose of reading is first and you'll know which structure to focus on. If he's reading about the American Revolution, what is he trying to learn—the problem and solution or the events of the entire revolution (sequence)?

Regardless of which structure is used by the author, having a purpose for reading and using a graphic organizer will help your child stay focused and engaged as he practices being an active learner.

See our online workbook, available for purchase, and Idea #157 for an example of a mind map.

#107
Fun in Newspapers:

Wear the old coat and buy the new book.
~ Austin Phelps

Many people get their news electronically. Perhaps you still get an actual newspaper. Whichever way your family gets its current events or how your child might get his in the future, reading the news is one common form of informational reading that most people do. Nearly every job involves reading in some way, to some degree, but regardless of the type of career your child ends up choosing, he will still likely need or want to read the news. Therefore, it is not a bad idea to help him get familiarized with a newspaper now and make it fun while you are at it! Try these fun activities:

- Talk about the front page and what gets to go on it. Why?

- Read the titles of the front page articles and try to guess what the article is about. Read it. See if you were right.

- Find the want-ads. Take turns reading them to each other, leaving out the item itself. See if you can guess it.

- At the message center (Idea #6), start a family chain sentence. Let your child start by cutting out one word from the newspaper and gluing it to a piece of paper. It will be the first word of a sentence so have him remember that while choosing. Then, choose someone to go next, and choose a second word to go with the first to continue the sentence. Continue until a whole (often silly!) sentence is complete. Though you could all sit down together to do this, it can take place over time, too. How fun to watch the sentence grow day by day!

- Try the crossword puzzle together as a family. Let your child see how you use a dictionary or ask for help when you can't find an answer, too.

- Comic strips are like little plays. Assign each person a character in the comic strips and read aloud.

- A picture is worth a thousand words. Have him choose any picture from the newspaper and verbally create a story to match the picture he sees. Then, read the article and compare and contrast his made-up story with what really happened.

- After reading a few articles, create his own in a similar style. Have him write his own article about something that happened in the family. Maybe he can write about a recent soccer game his sister played, a description of his mom's cooking preparation or review of her dinner, or a review of his brother's piano recital—anything goes! Have him read his finished article to the family.

- Go "job hunting." Take turns picking a job want-ad and seeing what parts sound like fun—or not.

- You could even throw in a little math by reading the advertisements and making up math problems to go with them. Of course, let your child make up some for you to solve, too!

All of these activities are designed to bring a little fun to reading the news. It is a lifelong skill to be able to read and understand current events. Getting familiar with it now, while he is young, can have a lasting impact on your child.

#108
QAR: Question-Answer Relationship (Types of Questions)

You can tell whether a man is clever by his answers.
You can tell whether a man is wise by his questions.
~Naguib, Mahfouz

Earlier in this Part, you read that reading the questions your child will have to answer *before* she even reads the text is a terrific strategy. It sets a purpose for reading and helps her pay attention throughout. Reading *for* the answers is a much better strategy than going back and digging through the text for every answer.

Still, all questions are not created equal. The next time your child brings home an assignment with many (or any) wrong answers, take a look at the kinds of questions they were. How the questions were created is quite obvious: are they true/ false? Multiple choice? Fill in the blank? Short answer? Certainly, some children have an easier time with some of those more than others. But inside those questions there is something else to think about: what level are they?

Some questions are at a basic recall level, often referred to as "Right There" kinds of questions. These are literal questions. Often, the words used in the question are the same words found in the text. Your child usually does not even have to reread to find these kinds of answers. The answers are fairly obvious to a reader who has actually comprehended.

Then there are slightly deeper-level questions, sometimes referred to as "Think and Search" questions. These are sometimes obvious to kids, but more often the text needs to be skimmed back over to find the answers (if they weren't found as she read!). Sometimes, answers are gathered from several parts of the text. Still, whether they are easy to find or not, the answers *are* in the text.

Some questions require both knowledge of the text and knowledge from the reader. These types of questions are usually called "Author and You." For these questions, the answer will not be directly in the text, but she needs information the author has given and will combine it with what she already knows in order to respond to this type of question. For example, let's say she was reading about a certain bill that was trying to be passed. An "author and you" question might be *Do you think the law should be passed? Explain why or why not.* In order to answer this, she will need information about the law from the text and she will need to use her own knowledge of how that law might affect her and her community to respond to that question.

Often, the tougher questions to answer are at the next level, sometimes called "On my Own" questions. For these, the answers themselves are not actually in the text, either. Sometimes, these questions do not require the student to have read the text at all, but she must use her background knowledge to answer the question.

When you are looking over a test or an assignment, look beyond the number of questions she misses and see if you can find a pattern in the *kinds* of questions she misses. If they are usually the deeper-level, "on-your-own" kinds, go over the question with her and help her find a place in the text that she could have used to help her formulate an answer. This will help her the next time she encounters a question like that, as she certainly will! Of course, going over any incorrect answers also gives the added bonus of learning anything she may have missed!

#109
Reading Tests/Levels

> *The man who does not read good books*
> *is no better than the man who can't.*
> *~ Mark Twain*

If you have a child in elementary school, you have probably been told your child's reading level. Throughout the years, the tools used to measure and report these levels have changed. You may remember reading groups divided by levels when you were in school. There seems to be nearly continuous debate over whether kids should be grouped by ability or by interest instead. However your child's teacher does it, she probably also gives your child individual reading tests several times a year to show where he is reading at the beginning of the year and where he ends up at the end. These scores can be confusing if you are not familiar with them and can be worrisome if you feel your child isn't where you think he should be.

There are a few things to keep in mind when you get a reading score for your child. Probably the most important thing is to remember that it is a picture of your child's reading at one particular moment in time on one particular text. Though the texts are specially graded, there is still an interest factor; if *your* child is highly interested in the topic or is already very familiar with it, he may read it better than an unfamiliar text or one he finds boring. There is also the setting and formality to consider; sometimes a child may feel nervous about reading aloud for a reading test and may not do as well as he normally would. If you feel that, at home with you, your child reads much better than his score shows, those may be some reasons why.

More important than the actual number is to look for growth. Scores that don't change or change very little may indicate a problem. If your child is improving, though, talk with his teacher to see if that improvement is enough to be satisfied. Ask his teacher for a guide as to what the scores mean. Ask what you can do to help him at home if you feel he needs it. Try many of the activities in this book to not only help him learn to enjoy reading more, but to understand it better, too. While scores can be helpful tools for teachers and schools, keep in mind that they are just numbers. As his parent, you can use them however you want.

Just as kids do not always walk at the same time, or talk, or get their first tooth, they also do not always learn to read at the same rate, either. Resist the urge to compare your child to others. Most children (barring a few exceptions due to real learning disabilities) do learn to read in elementary school. So, don't fret if you hear another child's score is higher. You didn't spend months worrying that your child would never learn to walk or talk just because someone else's kid his age already was. You knew it would happen in his own time. Well, reading is the same. Expect improvement. Encourage practice. Read together. Read often. Talk about reading before, during, and after. Make it fun, and he will learn to read.

#110
Multiple Sources

The ability to read awoke inside me
some long dormant craving to be mentally alive.
~ Malcolm X

Remember writing reports when you were young? Did you even have a computer? If not, did you have to scour library aisles, search through an encyclopedia, or try to figure out how to find articles on microfilm? Years ago, we really had to hunt for our information. Today, kids are so lucky! With the Internet, information is literally right at their fingertips! However, that does not mean that the Internet is the only source of information. The next time your child has a report to do, offer her some other options as well. Give some of these ideas a try:

- Take a trip to the local library and search out some books on the topic. Show your child how to use the computer there for help and/or ask at the reference desk. Both are valuable tools she will eventually need, and it is great for her to see you asking for help, too.

- Can you find anything to help her in the newspaper?

- Can a magazine help? Perhaps the library has a copy of one your family does not get.

- People can be valuable sources of information. If your child is learning about the Great Depression, for instance, who better to ask than someone who may have lived through it?

As often as you can, let your child do the researching. Even if you are using the Internet, show her how to start off a good search and then narrow it down. Show her how to choose between good, helpful, informational websites, and how to spot a biased one set up mostly for advertising. The research tools you introduce her to now will help her throughout all of her many more years of schooling!

See our workbook available for purchase at www.365TeacherSecrets.com for sources for reports.

#111
Too Tough

> *One's mind, once stretched by a new idea,*
> *never regains its original dimensions.*
> *~ Oliver Wendell Holmes*

We've all picked up something to read at one time in our lives and have thought, "Whoa! What? This it too tough for me to read!" Possibly even as an adult, you have put something down because it was just too tough to understand. Of course, this happens to children much more often, especially very young readers. Idea #71 shared with you the "Rule of Thumb." The idea was that your child should begin to read any random page of a new book she is thinking of choosing. Every time she comes to a word that she does not know, she should put down a finger, beginning with her pinky. If she reaches her thumb (the 5th tough word) by the end of the page, chances are that it is just too tough of a book. Could she still *read* it? Probably, yes, but this may be a good indication that comprehension will be too tough.

Informational text is often full of new vocabulary words. A good writer will know that these are new words for kids and make a grand effort to define them in a way kids will not find interruptive. However, not all books are the same. If your child has to continually stop reading to look up definitions, her concentration will be broken and comprehension will suffer. The Rule of Thumb may help her to see, on her own, that that book just isn't a good choice.

What do you do, though, if your child comes home with an informational book that she *has* to read for some reason or is just really, really interested in? Here are a few choices:

- Preview the book with her, jotting down all words that stand out as tough. Look them up or otherwise define them together *now* before she even begins reading. That way, when she runs across them in her reading she may recall what they mean and not even break her reading stride. If not, she has a quick reference guide right next to her that she can glance at without stopping for too long.

- Buddy-read the book together. You can take turns reading sentences, or paragraphs, or pages, whichever seems to best suit your child. Discuss what you are reading along the way. Do some Mind Monitoring! (Idea #67 and #101.)

- You could even try echo-reading for very tough text or with very young kids. You would simply read a sentence first, and then your child echoes it back to you. Pointing to each word as you go (and asking your child to do the same) is important so she can begin to recognize those tougher words.

Having her choose and read a book that is way too difficult for her ends up being frustrating and can have a negative impact on her enjoyment of reading. When she is young, you want to do all you can to help her love reading, so encouraging her to put back a too-tough book is the right way to go. If she insists, or her teacher does, you can work together to get through it!

#112
Books as Gifts

Books make great gifts because they have whole worlds inside them,
and it's much cheaper to buy somebody a book than it is to buy them the whole world.
~Neil Gaiman

How many times has your child been invited to a birthday party and can't think of anything to buy his friend? When it is time for your child's birthday, is he stumped for ideas? The next time you are stuck trying to figure out what to buy as a gift for a child, think about a book!

Informational books about a specific interest a child has can be a great idea for a gift. Ask your child what his friends' interests are, and see if the two of you can find a book for a present. For your own child, do the same; think of some of his hobbies or things he is interested in right now. You might also ask a bookseller what is popular. If you would like your child to get more into reading informational books, you could request that his guests bring a book instead of a card that can sometimes cost just as much but will just be thrown away. You could do this as well when giving a gift; use a book instead of a card. Put a nice personalized message inside that the recipient will have for years.

Need more convincing? Here are several reasons why books are a great gift.

- They encourage connection—when you share a book with a child, you are creating a connection - especially if you share a book that was one of your favorites growing up.

- They are non-electronic—what better way to encourage your child to unplug than to offer a much-loved book.

- They are good for you—they help create a strong foundation for learning and reinforce that reading is important for their growth.

- It's like giving a vacation - reading a great book can take children places they've never been. It's a great and inexpensive way to escape and learn something new. You could give a book on a place he has already visited (perhaps a previous family vacation?) so he can revisit and remember a place where he's been before, or you can give a book about a place he would love to go so he can learn about it more before he may someday go there.

- They are inexpensive - Compared to the technology that so many children ask for and the price of expensive toys, book are quite a deal. They can hold the attention of the reader much longer than the newest fad toy or game.

- They are easy to give - Books can be purchased online and sent to children, or at big box stores, toy stores, gift shops, and even grocery stores!

- They have a wide appeal - Books appeal to everyone. Even children who believe they don't like reading can be excited about a book that appeals to their interest like a comic book or a book that is included with building a model plane.

Did you know February 14 is International Book Giving Day? What a great way to show your love for someone special!

#113
The Reading Response Journal

Look, then, into thine heart, and write!
~ Henry W. Longfellow

When your child has spent time reading about something and learned a little or a lot, then what? Of course, she does not always have to do something after she reads, but doing something after reading is a great way to Recite or Review (Idea #99 and #100), thus increasing comprehension. It is also a great way to share (or show off) what she's learned.

One way to do this on her own and for herself is to keep a Reading Response Journal. All she really needs is a notebook. (One she picks out herself may get used more often!) Whenever she reads a new book, you can encourage her to write in her journal what the book was called and what she learned. Young kids can start off with a picture and maybe a sentence. (Feel free to take dictation for a very young child.) Older kids could write a few sentences. Upper elementary kids can be challenged to write a paragraph, complete with a topic sentence and several details (Idea #161).

This journal can be just for her, to keep track of the books she's read (how fun to see the list grow!) or to be shared with you or anyone she wants. In Parts 5 and 6, you might also find other ways to write more creatively about what she's learned if summaries get boring. The idea is to do *something* with the information after she's read it. It helps with comprehension and gives her a sense of accomplishment as well.

See our workbook available for purchase at www.365TeacherSecrets.com for a sample of a reading response journal.

#114
After-Reading Fun

No matter how busy you may think you are, you must find time for reading,
or surrender yourself to self-chosen ignorance.
~Confucius

In Idea #113, The Reading Response Journal, you learned that writing in a journal is one way to increase comprehension of informational text. If your child is creative, you might sometimes encourage other ways as well to show what he's learned. If he has the project in mind before he begins to read, it can even make the reading more fun. It can be another way to foster good comprehension, too, because he will be reading for things he can use in his project. When planning a project about a book, think not only about the topic of the book but also about what your child likes to do. Does he like to build things? Paint? Draw or color? Write poems? Make up songs or games? Here are a few ideas to get you started.

- Use a simple paper bag to make a puppet. Decorate it like a person he learned about. Fill it with items from the book. Use them in a retelling done by the puppet. (*"Hi. I'm Abraham Lincoln. I was the 16th president of the United States. Here is the Emancipation Proclamation..."*)

- Use a poster board to make a game board and make up a game together, using information learned. (*"Recycle old newspapers. Move ahead 2 spaces."*)

- Fold some paper in half and staple it into a "book" in which your child can retell the story in words and/ or pictures.

- Make a video of your child telling what he learned. Have him gather appropriate props.

- Make a poster displaying the information learned. Get even more creative and have him pretend that book is coming out as a movie and make it a movie poster announcing the upcoming film.

- Have your child turn a person he has read about into a wax museum figure. Dress like him. Think about what he would say about himself and talk as if you were him.

- Build a model of what was read about. Make a spider out of craft items. Make an edible volcano. Use Legos or wood or clay—anything your child likes!

The idea is to have fun. Activities like the ones above can establish a purpose for reading and help your child review what was read. Both are terrific ways to aid comprehension and develop good readers who enjoy reading!

#115
Finding the Main Ideas

Those who bring sunshine to the lives of others cannot keep it from themselves.
~James Barrie

Earlier in this Part, we wrote about having your child highlight the main ideas in what she reads, but elementary kids often have a tough time knowing exactly what the main ideas are. You can help her by showing her some places where authors of textbooks and other informational texts put the main ideas. Here are a few places to point out:

> **Introduction:** Sometimes an author gives a separate introduction, usually before the regular part of the text or chapter begins. Sometimes, it is even called an overview or introduction. This contains information about the entire piece or chapter. It is often skipped over by kids because they just want to get to the "assigned" part, and it may look separate. However, reading this first helps your child know what the author considers the main ideas.

> **The first paragraph:** If there is no formal introduction, the author usually uses the first paragraph in any section to briefly state what that section is about.

> **Front pages of chapters:** Sometimes, an author will put key terms along the side of the first page or even all pages. Could those be some of the main ideas?

> **The first sentence in a paragraph:** This sentence is often the topic sentence, which generally contains the main idea. Authors of elementary textbooks find that putting them at the top of each paragraph is good for young readers. The first sentence tells the main idea and then the details follow.

Bold or italicized words: These words stand out for a reason. They are usually important words that help explain main ideas.

Conclusion: Just as an author sometimes begins with an overview of what the chapter will cover, so do they sometimes end with a concluding paragraph that sums up the main ideas of the chapter. Often, this is a stand-alone paragraph, sometimes called "Conclusion." Sometimes, it is just the last paragraph of the text. Either way, show your child that what is in it is valuable and should not be skipped over in a rush to be done.

Questions: If the chapter has questions at the end, they usually reflect the main ideas the author wants the reader to know.

Knowing some of these key places that contain main ideas can help your child spot the main ideas as she reads and afterward as well, when she is reciting or reviewing.

See our workbook for a printable reminder of where to find main ideas.

#116
Emphasize Quality over Quantity

I saw the angel in the marble and carved until I set him free.
~Michelangelo

Kids are notorious for "just wanting to be done" and rushing through certain tasks. Truthfully, though, we have been known to do that, too. As parents, we can feel so bogged down with evening tasks like driving kids to soccer and ballet, making dinner, and helping with homework, that it is tempting to cut corners.

Today, though, take a moment to think about quality over quantity, especially when it comes to your child's reading. In other words, don't focus on how *many* things you are doing with your child, think about how *well* you are doing them. Don't count up all of the things you haven't been doing. Think about the things you *are* doing. Now consider the things you think are the most helpful to your child. Is sitting with him and reading one of them? (Let me tell you it is even if you aren't aware of it!) So, make the times you do read together count. Most teachers would agree that there are a few Do's and Don'ts to focus on while reading with your child:

- Do read together as often as you comfortably can. Make sure you do some reading out loud to him even as he grows older. Even when he begins to read on his own, there may be books he is interested in that he can't yet read by himself. He also really benefits when he hears a good reader read. Plus, it's cozy!

- Don't focus on time, when you do sit together to read. Concentrate more on the quality of what you are doing. It is far better to spend 15 minutes with him going over steps to SQ3R (Idea #95) than it is to spend 30 minutes half-heartedly listening to him read aloud, missing words, stumbling over comprehension, while you mentally prepare your grocery list. Of course, you probably still do have to make that grocery list, but spend a few minutes only on that and the rest completely on him.

- Do know that even ten minutes away from video games or TV, reading with you, is infinitely better than taking no time for reading at all? Chances are, even if he complains, he will go to bed that night remembering more about you reading with him than those games, anyway.

- Don't rush through a book just to get done. If your child seems to be asking a million questions as he reads, or as you read to him, it is tempting to just skip over them and turn the page. *But you want the questions, the commentary, the connections!* So, resist the urge to plow through the book, and slow down. Let your child dictate the pace at which you go through the book. Know that every question or comment means that your child is comprehending!

- Do occasionally read above your child's level and challenge his mind.

Remember: when it comes to helping your child with tough reading, what you do together is often much more important than how long you spend doing it.

#117
3-2-1 Strategy

Organizing is what you do before you do something,
so that when you do it, it is not all mixed up.
~ A. A. Milne

The 3-2-1 strategy is another great way to help your child create the habit of thinking about what she is learning as she reads. Before your child reads an informational text, tell her when she's done she should be able to tell you three things she learned, two things she found interesting and one question she may have. You should consider modeling this first for her so she has a better understanding of what you want. You may find it helpful to set up a 3-2-1 sheet where she can write down her answers when she's done. Simply take a sheet of paper and draw two lines from the top of the paper to the bottom so you have three equal columns. In the first column, have her write the heading "3-What I Learned." In the middle column, she can write "2- What I Found Interesting." The third column could read "1-Question." When she's done reading, have her fill in the columns.

You should read the question she wrote in the "Question" column and encourage her to look for the answer to her question as she continues to read. If she doesn't find the answer in her continued reading, you can use this opportunity to research together, maybe on the Internet or at the library. It's a great way to encourage her curiosity and reinforce the importance of asking questions while reading.

This sheet may become very useful when it is time to study for a test. She will have many facts she needs to know right at her fingertips. She will spend less time looking back through the text and will be less frustrated.

See our workbook available for purchase at www.365TeacherSecrets.com for a blank 3-2-1 sheet.

#118
DRTA: Directed Reading-Thinking Activity

Oh, magic hour, when a child first knows she can read printed words!
~A Tree Grows in Brooklyn

Directed Reading Thinking Activity is a comprehension strategy that focuses on helping children ask questions about the text and make predictions before reading. This technique encourages children to be active readers and gives them a purpose for reading. It also helps them monitor their understanding of the text as they are reading. When your child has an informational reading assignment, you should preview the length and determine a few stopping points in the text where you will ask your child to stop reading. Before he begins to read, let him know where he should stop reading. Then, use the following outline to guide him:

> **Direct:** Ask him to make predictions about what he might learn in the text. Use the survey method in the SQ3R strategy for specific examples (Idea #96).

> **Read:** Have him read until the first pre-selected stopping point. Ask him about his predictions. Try to ask him specific questions about this section. Look for bold-faced words, and ask him the meaning. Look for pictures, and ask what they represent. Scan the page for names, and ask who they are and what they've done.

> **Think:** After reading, he should consider his predictions to find out if they were correct. Using what he's learned in the first pre-selected section, he may want to alter his predictions before reading the next section. Continue these steps for each reading section.

This comprehension method is helpful to many children who tend to wander while reading a longer text. For younger readers, you can create more stopping points. Have shorter sections where they will stop and have to think about their predictions and answer questions. In this way, they are more likely to stay focused.

You do not always have to be involved in this activity. For older children, you may need to guide your child through the stages at first, but eventually, he can learn to separate the reading selection into smaller chunks himself and learn to make predictions and check for accuracy or modify his predictions on his own. Whether he works on his own or works with a parent on this strategy, he will be strengthening his reading skills as well as his critical thinking skills.

#119
Until We Meet Again

Two roads diverged in a wood and I—
I took the road less traveled by
and that has made all the difference.
~Robert Frost

The two roads Robert Frost wrote about came together and offered him a choice. In the biographical books you read to your child or that she reads herself, rarely (if ever) do the paths of favorite people from different books come together. Wouldn't it be neat if they did? Could your child make that happen? Sure! Here's how:

1. Discuss with your child her favorite biographies and the people in them.

2. Have her choose her absolute two favorite people (from different biographies).

3. Help her make a list of the qualities, characteristics, likes, dislikes, etc. of these two people.

4. Now encourage her to think, draw, write—brainstorm in any way she finds helpful—what would happen if these two people met. What would they talk about? Where would they meet? (What setting would make sense?) What, realistically, would they do?

5. Now, she can write about it. Perhaps a paragraph would be a good goal at first. If she really enjoys the activity, you could try some of these variations. (You can take dictation for a younger child.)

Variations:

- Encourage her to write more, maybe even a short story about the encounter.

- *Give* her two people from biographies she has read about, and have her use those two for the project. (Or, if she hasn't read them, have her read them with this purpose in mind.)

- Write one at the same time she does, using the same two characters. Don't show each other until you are done. How alike or different are they?

#120
Writing Reinforces Reading

It is literally true that you can succeed best and quickest by helping others to succeed.
~Napoleon Hill

In this Part, you learned some ways to help your child conquer reading informational texts. There is one last way that deserves to be mentioned. Write! Yes, writing reinforces reading. It makes sense that the more a child reads, the better reader he becomes. The more he writes the better writer he becomes. Did you also know how much the two reinforce each other? The more a child writes the better reader he becomes, too. (And vice versa.)

So, in your quest to find new and better ways to help your child learn to enjoy reading an informational text more or understand it better, don't forget that encouraging him to write about real-life information is yet another way to do that. "Informational writing" could include writing about anything in his life that he is interested in, such as a special outing or trip, a movie or play review, a pet or animal around the yard, how to do something, etc. (See Part 6 for even more, specific ideas.)

— *124* —

Part 5
Creative Writing with Children

INTRODUCTION: This Part offers your family a variety of ways to help your child write creatively and to practice writing skills in fun, meaningful, and authentic ways.

Writing is a series of related ideas that communicate a message or tell a story. Writing is an important part of just about every area of your child's curriculum. It will most likely be a critical part of her job in the future as well.

In this Part, you'll find ideas for getting ready to write and creating finished masterpieces. Your child will discover ways to write for herself as well as for others. You'll get ideas for helping her with her writing skills and ways to motivate her to write on her own. Helping to foster a love of writing now can help your child become an enthusiastic writer for the rest of her life!

#121
Holidays

He who asks is a fool for five minutes,
but he who does not ask remains a fool forever.
~Chinese Proverb

So many children complain about not having anything to write about. The trick is to offer them real reasons to write, and then it will most likely be fun and easy for them to do. Holidays are perfect days to try this. From major holidays like Christmas and Hanukkah to fun ones like April Fool's Day, special days provide special opportunities for writing. Try the ideas below to get your child writing today for all the fun reasons!

- New Year's: Encourage everyone in your family to write down New Year's Resolutions and post them somewhere like the message center (Idea #6) where seeing them often will help encourage completing them.

- Valentine's Day: Write a love letter to your child. Ask him to write one to someone. If he's at an age where that does not particularly appeal to him, he can write one to the family pet or a favorite toy!

- St. Patrick's Day: Ask him to write about what he would do if suddenly he became magical like a Leprechaun just for one day.

- Easter: Write out clues to an Easter egg hunt. Hide clues in a plastic egg. Each egg found contains another clue that all lead to a special prize.

- Passover: Think about the meaning of Passover and write about what it means to your family.

- April Fool's Day: Write a joke book. Ask friends and family for help and ideas.

- President's Day: Write a letter to the President.

- Memorial Day: Write a letter to a Veteran. Writing to a Veteran can be an authentic learning experience for your child and allow him to connect with history.

- Mother's Day: Write a letter to Mom telling her all the things you love about her.

- Father's Day: Write a letter to Dad telling him all the things you love about him.

- Flag Day: Invent a flag for your family. What would it look like? Write a small paragraph to go with the picture to explain what each symbol or color represents. Is there something for everyone?

- 4th of July: Use the letters in AMERICA to create a poem or write a Haiku about the USA (Idea #132).

- Labor Day: Write a letter to his future self, describing the job he thinks he will have when he grows up. Save it for him and give it to him years from now. Was he right?

- Halloween: Write a scary story.

- Thanksgiving: Encourage the whole family to make a list of things for which you are all grateful. Can you collectively get to 100?

- Christmas: Write letters to Santa, send thank you notes, or create a poem or short story to give as a gift.

- Hanukkah: Write about a favorite holiday tradition.

If a holiday your family celebrates isn't on here, add it and brainstorm ways to write about it.

#122
Taking Dictation

Seek the wisdom of the ages,
but look at the world through the eyes of a child.
~Ron Wild

Many of the writing ideas in this book would be difficult, if not impossible, with children who are not yet able to write on their own. That's why we've included options for taking dictation whenever possible. But what does this really mean? How do you take dictation from a child whose ideas may be scattered or incomplete? Here are some things to keep in mind when recording your child's thoughts and observations.

Research shows that, while taking dictation, it is most important to write word for word what your child tells you without making grammatical changes. Always use your best judgment, though. The first few times you take dictation from a young child, be sure to accept and record her words as she offers them. This not only aids in her developing self-esteem and confidence as a writer but also provides her with text to read. Having a young child read her own words exactly as she spoke them is an extremely beneficial way to help her become a better reader. She knows what the words are so she can read them more easily than someone else's words in a storybook.

Once your child has dictated to you many times and you feel she is emotionally and intellectually ready, you may choose to offer some suggestions while recording for her. For instance, if she says, "Then I gotted more marbles than Justin," you might ask, "Do you think it would sound better to say, 'Then I *had* more marbles than Justin?'" Then, read it back to her to see if she finds your suggestion acceptable. Keep in mind that the goal is not perfection; it is to get her to read willingly and successfully.

Always be polite in the way you phrase your suggestions. Be careful not to say things like, "You shouldn't say 'gotted'; that's not even a word." Try not to suggest changes that are grammatically way above your child's level or to make changes without permission. Just write down what your child says.

Encourage her to make an illustration to go with the text. Display it. Show her she doesn't have to know how to write all by herself in order to write a story.

Variation for older kids:

You can even take dictation with older kids. Try writing a story together. When it comes time to write, sit next to each other and take turns writing sentences. It is not cheating; she is still writing half of the sentences. Even for older kids, it can be fun to tell Mom or Dad what to write. For one, it takes a little pressure off since they don't have to write *every* sentence. It also gives you an opportunity to do some modeling. When you are writing your sentence, you can say aloud things like:

- "Since our character is going to start talking here, I know I need to put a comma, quotation marks, and then a capital letter;"

- "Instead of saying 'he said,' I think I will write 'he cried' to make the sentence sound more interesting;" or :

- "*Space* needs a silent e at the end of it to make the "a" say its name."

And, of course, it is also a great opportunity to cuddle up together and create!

#123
A Writing Notebook

Man's mind stretched to a new idea never goes back to its original dimensions.
~Oliver Wendell Holmes

Chances are while reading this book throughout the year, you and your child will encounter many terrific ideas that he will want to remember. We've suggested earmarking the pages you find most interesting and useful, ones that you will want to go back to reference in the future. Another way to remember ideas you simply don't want to forget is to jot them down in a special notebook of ideas. That way, you have one place to go to find a bunch of your best ideas.

Your child can do this, too, for himself. If he finds a particularly helpful writing idea, for instance, he could write it in a writing notebook that you create together. (A spiral notebook works well.) This could have certain sections with titles at the tops of the pages. For example, he might choose to have a category for:

- *Million $$$ Words*: fabulously exciting words that he finds interesting enough to record for use in future writing pieces—see Idea #183;

- *Instead of* "Said:" other words that can be used. For example, *declared, informed, answered*;

- *Better than* "Good:" other words that can be used. For example, *fabulous, terrific, wonderful*;

- *Better than* "Bad:" other words that can be used. For example, *terrible, notorious, naughty*;

- *Super similes and metaphors* that he may want to include in his writing someday. For example, *The lake was a mirror reflecting the fall leaves.*

- *Spelling Strategies* he knows of or learns about in this book (see Part 10).

- *Frequently Misspelled Words* that he encounters in his writing.

- *Commonly Used Words* for spelling practice.

He could keep this writing notebook at his special study area or tote it with him for use at school each day. The idea is to have a quick reference available for him to use while participating in a writing activity. What children put into their writing notebooks will vary, but you can encourage your child to add anything he feels may be useful while writing.

See our workbook available for purchase at www.365TeacherSecrets.com for grade-level, high-frequency word lists for grades 1-5.

#124
Show vs. Tell

All I really need to know I learned in kindergarten.
~Robert Fulghum

Another way to encourage your child to write with greater detail and more creatively is to practice the idea of "Show vs. Tell." Most young writers tend to focus on the facts when they write. They are more concerned with getting done than they are with the quality of their writing. When you encourage your child to "show and not just tell," you can help her begin to see how she can spice up her writing quite easily.

To do this, find an area in one of her writings where she has simply told what a character did or felt. For instance, maybe she wrote, "Joey was so mad." Ask her to think of a way to *show* the readers Joey was mad without actually saying it. You can help her at first. Ask her what someone looks like when they are mad. What do they do? Act it out! Then, have her choose one or more ways and edit the story a little right there. She might change that sentence to "Joey's face grew red, and his hands were tightly clenched."

To practice this technique any time, even when she doesn't have a story to edit, you could make up some "Silly Sentences" (Idea #159). Make up a very basic story and have her liven things up a bit by revising those boring sentences that just *tell* into sentences that actually *show*.

#125
Snapshots

A good photograph is knowing where to stand.
~Ansel Adams

When we want to remember something important, we might decide to take a picture of it. That way, we can look back later and remember every detail. This concept can be used in writing, too.

When your child is writing a story, there has to be a balance of moving the story along and adding enough detail so the readers are intrigued and interested. One technique is to do an occasional "Snapshot" in writing.

To do a "Snapshot," first your child needs to find a place in his story that is particularly important. If he's a young writer, you can help him find these kinds of places. Perhaps this will be where the problem or goal is introduced. Maybe it's one of the main events. Often, it is at the resolution. Rather than focusing on moving the story along at these important places, he will slow it down instead by adding detail after detail. Not only should he tell what is happening but also what the character involved is thinking and feeling. Use the five senses. What does the main character see, hear, smell, feel, taste? Perhaps not all of these will apply, but the idea here is to add as many details as he can at a few crucial points in the story.

Using this technique will not only help his writing be more detailed, rich, and enjoyable for his readers, but it will also help him to recognize that there are a few, special places where these detailed "Snapshots" should occur. He will come to see that not every single event needs to be told in such detail and will realize that a story needs to contain both kinds of writing.

#126
Writing for Reading & Reading for Writing

Sometimes your joy is the source of your smile,
but sometimes your smile can be the source of your joy.
~Thich Nhat Hanh

Sometimes fabulous things are intertwined. When they are, you just can't lose. The same is true for many academic areas. So, if you've ever wondered how you can help your child to become a better reader or a better writer, here is a sure-fire strategy: Read and write!

When a child reads a variety of material (and often), she can become a better *writer* because she is gaining more command over the power and beauty of language. She discovers the multitude of ways in which words can affect people and evoke emotion, as well as the variety of ways and reasons to write.

When she writes often, for a variety of authentic and meaningful reasons, she becomes a better *reader.* She is learning to read her own words with feeling and expression, finding her own voice, and recognizing voices in other pieces she reads. She is also realizing that writing, just like reading, is done for the purpose of gathering meaning.

If your child needs practice with writing but loves to read even more, let her! If you know she needs to develop reading skills but resists reading every day, encourage her to write. These two skills reinforce one another beautifully and effortlessly. You can reinforce them, too.

#127
"Write" From the Heart

What a man thinks of himself…determines, or rather, indicates his fate.
~Henry David Thoreau

Is your child still writing in his journal? You might decide to reevaluate how often he does this. Does it feel like too often because he's hesitant each day? Do you think he's enjoying it and could really write in it more often than he has been? Talk with him today to see if he's feeling comfortable with the schedule. Remember, writing in his journal should help him to become a better writer by encouraging him to free write about anything and everything. It should be enjoyable. Try to find a schedule you can both live with.

You might also suggest that he try writing from the heart if he does not already. Children often tend to write about *events,* about what happened *that day.* You could encourage him to try writing now about his *feelings.* When children are able to do this, they can become better writers overall. Getting in touch with feelings and learning to write about them in safe environments (such as a private journal) can help your child learn to incorporate that type of descriptive writing in his other writing as well.

Here is an idea to try if your child's journal entries each day seem a bit short and event-oriented, without much feeling. Begin a trip down memory lane. Bring up a past event that evoked an emotional response from him at the time. Discuss the details with him and ask him if he's ever felt that way (or similarly) at another time. Then you could encourage him to write in his journal about it. Here are just a few ideas to get you started:

- His best day ever.

- The worst day he's ever had.

- The scariest thing that's ever happened to him.

- His saddest experience.

- The most exciting event that he's ever witnessed.

- A wish that came true.

If he "just can't think of anything," try taking turns *making up* stories about one of these topics. See who can be the most outrageous. Can he write about one of these escapades? Could you? You could both write your ideas first and then read them to each other.

After you've tried the silly stuff, try to get him to reflect seriously on his *own* life. Chances are, now he will be able to write about something that has happened to him and how it made him feel. If you encourage him to write about his feelings in his personal, private journal, it will not only be good for him emotionally, but also help to increase his writing skills and love of writing as well.

#128
Family Chain Story

Our imagination is the only limit to what we can hope to have in the future.
~Charles Kettering

Your family's imagination is the only limit to this activity. All it takes to begin is a piece of paper, a pencil and some creativity. You can begin (or let your child start) by writing a sentence on the paper. This will be the beginning sentence to a story so you might want to discuss a variety of ways to begin a story, perhaps by reading the first few sentences of a wide variety of books.

Now, post this paper somewhere for all to see such as the message center (Idea #6). Everyone else in the family has the challenge of adding one sentence at a time to the story. As long as everyone takes turns, the next person can add to it whenever it is convenient. Each new person has the opportunity (with her new sentence) to continue in the direction of the story so far or alter it as long as the new sentence fits into the context. The story may be serious, may get silly, may be true or made up. It doesn't matter. The idea is to have fun while practicing creative writing skills together.

This activity could also take place all at once with the whole family sitting around the table. The paper would just be passed around while each family member added his own idea right away.

Don't forget to read the whole story together when it is ended—if it ever ends! Everyone will delight to hear how their idea was perceived and added to by the others in the family. Chances are, it will create a few good laughs, too!

#129
Fun in the Funnies

The most wasted of all days is one without laughter.
~E. E. Cummings

Families who laugh together can also learn together at the same time! It's always more fun to learn (or practice) in fun and motivational ways. Here's an idea that will be fun for the whole family and will also help your child with his writing skills.

- Start by cutting out a comic strip from a newspaper or magazine. Choose one that your child enjoys but hasn't seen yet so he won't know what the characters are saying.

- Cut out the bubbles in which the characters' words are written.

- Tape or glue the cartoon strip with missing bubbles onto a clean sheet of paper.

- Have your child use the pictures to guess what could be happening in the strip.

- Once he has an idea what the cartoon may be about, he can fill in the bubbles using his own words and ideas to create a new, and perhaps even funnier, comic than the original!

The whole family may enjoy cutting out different cartoons strips and filling in the bubbles with humorous dialogue. It may also be interesting to show the whole family the same cartoon strip and have everyone fill in the dialogue separately. Then, you can all compare to see how differently everyone views the same pictures.

#130
Point of View

Teaching a child not to step on a caterpillar
is as valuable to the child as it is to the caterpillar.
~Bradley Miller

Your child is undoubtedly good at seeing the world through her own eyes in her own way, but how good is she at putting herself in someone (or some*thing*) else's shoes? Try this activity to help your child with some creative writing skills as well as practice critical thinking skills.

- Choose an object. This could be anything—a person, animal, character; for an example, let's use a caterpillar.

- Help your child make a list of things she knows and how she feels about the object (the caterpillar). Discuss with her and help her add many ideas. The more the better! For instance, she might list:

  - bug

  - lives in trees

  - eats leaves

  - creepy

  - lives with others

  - makes a chrysalis

  - changes into a butterfly

- Don't hesitate to do a little research if she picks a topic you are not too sure about!

- Now have her change her point of view and actually think about *being* that object. Have her write sentences for many of them as if she were the caterpillar, such as:

    - I am a bug.

    - I like to be in trees.

    - I eat leaves.

    - I crawl around with my many legs.

    - I live with so many brothers and sisters.

    - I know how to make a chrysalis and in it I change into a butterfly! (Has "she" decided she doesn't feel very creepy anymore?)

- Help her to turn the sentences into a paragraph.

- If she is interested in displaying or sharing her writing, help her to edit it and then encourage her to rewrite or type it. She could even illustrate it.

Variations:

- Could she send it to a relative and ask the relative to do the same by writing about something else in its point of view?

- You could even make this a game by writing them without telling what the object is and having the listeners or readers guess!

- She could even write a letter *to* an object or character. You could write back to her *as* that object. She would be applying her knowledge of the object and have so much fun reading your response! For instance, she writes to a tree and you respond by writing back to her *as* the tree.

- Try it the other way around. Write a letter yourself to an object, asking a lot of questions, and then challenge your child to answer you *as* that object. This time she will really have to change her point of view in order to give you a meaningful response.

Sometimes her opinion of things may change after this activity. She may treat things differently or develop more sympathy. Who knows, a few caterpillars may even be saved along the way!

#131
Poetry

Too many of us strive for new abilities
instead of striving to develop abilities
we already have lying dormant within us.
~Alfred A. Montapert

There is a poet inside all of us in one way or another. We tend to think of poetry in the traditional way of exquisite verse that rhymes perfectly. Many of us think *we* could never write like that, but poetry is so much more than that—and so much less. It is simply someone's view of the world put in such a way that may not have been done before; it's seeing something extraordinary in something someone else has not; it's the art of finding and interpreting ideas by way of the imagination; it's idealizing in thought and in expression; it's imaginative language or composition, whether expressed rhythmically or in prose; it's any communication (in blank verse or in rhyme) that evokes feelings and in which the language is highly imaginative or impassioned.

Yes, we *can* write like that, and so can children. We may just need to help them see that. Through poetry, children can see that words have the power to make something happen. Poetry helps others *see* what they *feel*. It helps kids:

- tap into what's important to them;

- see a new vision of their lives and the world;

- find their voice when their poetry is readily accepted and not criticized; and

- feel safe and free to write whatever's on their minds.

Perhaps the first step is to let kids know that poetry does not always have to rhyme or follow a specific meter. Sometimes, poetry is simply beautiful writing with no specific, metered form. You can encourage your child to write poetry like this by turning a simple sentence he writes such as *"I see a cat"* into poetry by adding a few beautiful, detailed words. You can show him how *"My eyes gazed at the cat's beauty"* sounds much more poetic. If he writes a paragraph and revises one sentence at a time in this way, he can begin to see how easy writing poetry can be.

At first, you may have to help him choose topics he feels strongly enough about. What does he love? Find beautiful? What moves him? Try suggesting that he use his five senses for this activity; he may find that helpful. Encourage him to experiment with using both long and single-word sentences for effect.

There are many forms of poetry to read and write. The greater the variety of poetry types your child is exposed to, the better he will become at *writing* poetry as well. Share your favorite poems with him, and explain why you like them. Read lots, and let your child discover poetry for himself.

Your child may also enjoy writing poems using specific frames to guide and support him. See the next idea (#132) for examples. He'll surely find out he's a poet and he didn't even know it!

#132
Specific Poetry Starters

Poetry is when an emotion has found its thought
and the thought has found words.
~ Robert Frost

Another fun and motivational way to get involved with poetry is to begin with a specific "frame" on which your child can fill in her own words. Here are some common—and fun—types of poetry kids love.

Couplets are fun, easy to write, and great for beginners. They are simply two sentences that end in a rhyme. An example would be:

I saw a green frog.

He was asleep on a log.

Now, try a *triplet* and make all *three* sentences end in rhymes!

I saw a green frog.

He was deep in a bog.

Asleep on a log.

Haiku (Hi-**Koo**) are 3-lined, Japanese poems, usually about nature, that try to capture a particularly profound moment in time. They are metered by the number of syllables in each line. Here is an example using the 5-7-5 word pattern:

The sweet raindrops danced.
Sunlight shone through dark gray clouds.
A rainbow was born.

Please keep in mind that it is the *beautifully written words* (the *feeling* being expressed) that should be the focus here, not the number of syllables the words contain. If your child is having difficulty with that part of it, forget it! Stop counting, and keep writing a haiku-*like* poem!

Limericks are 5-lined poems in which lines 1, 2, and 5 rhyme with each other. Lines 3 and 4 are shorter and rhyme with each other (a couplet!) but not with the others. They are usually humorous. For example:

There once was a monkey in a zoo.
But he didn't know quite what to do.
He wanted to be free
To run and climb trees.
So, he escaped and ran to Timbuktu!

Cinquains are also 5-lined poems, but are set up like this:

Line 1- one word title:	Dinosaurs
Line 2- two words that describe title:	Extinct reptiles
Line 3- three words that express action:	Roaming, eating, hunting
Line 4- four words that express feeling:	I think they're awesome!
Line 5- one word that renames title:	Giants

Use some of her favorite poems (from free verse to something structured) to make *Shape Poems*. Simply rewrite the poem in the shape of the object it is about. Sketch the shape lightly in pencil first so she'll have a guide.

Variations:

- Try some of these ideas, and then make up your own.

- Write a free verse poem with your child about the current season.

- Write couplets back and forth to each other. (Or you start one, she writes the other half and vice versa.)

- Give your child one of the frames and work with her to fill in her own special ideas. Soon, it will be a fabulous poem all her own!

- Go outside, smell some flowers, and write a haiku about them together.

- Display her favorite poem that she has written. Help her to memorize it.

- Write silly limericks about each member of the family.

- Memorize together one of her favorite poems written by someone else. You do the same!

- Read aloud silly poems, serious poems, long and short poems.

Try reading some fun poems by Jack Prelutsky or Shel Silverstein to get started. But don't forget to also read aloud poetry by such great poets as Walt Whitman, Robert Frost, Ogden Nash (and others that you may enjoy) to expose your child to other types of poetry as well.

See our workbook for 7 different poetry frames.

#133
Fun with Words

I like nonsense, it wakes up the brain cells.
Fantasy is a necessary ingredient in living.
~Dr. Seuss

Poetry is playing around with words in unique and wonderful ways. You can also do the same without creating a poem. Just make up some silly stuff! Try these:

Alliterations (sentences in which most of the words begin with the same sound):

- Have your child choose a beginning letter or sound. Let's use "m" as an example.

- Now have him brainstorm a wide variety of words that begin with that letter.

- He can now experiment with creating a sentence in which every word begins with the same letter: *Mary made many marvelous muffins.*

Tongue Twisters (alliteration used to create tricky-to-say sentences):

- Have your child choose a sound to start (such as "s", "ch", "dr").

- Then, have him make a list of all of the words that begin with that sound, have it in the middle, or have it near the end. He'll want to include various parts of speech such as nouns, verbs, adjectives and adverbs, if possible. (For instance, if he picks the "k" sound he might make a list such as: "Jack, lake, lucky, like, rake, snakes, take, skate, Jake, back, quickly, black.")

- Now, have him experiment with putting the words together to form some kind of a silly sentence. He should try to use as many of the words as possible and as few of any other words that do not follow the pattern as possible. Ideally, it should be a tad tricky to say as well. He might end up with a sentence such as: *Lucky Jake rakes black snakes quickly, and Jack takes snakes back to the lake.*

Acrostic Poems:

- Have your child write the letters in his name going down on a piece of paper.

- For each letter, your child should think of words that descibe him or the things he likes or likes doing, beginning with that letter. Older children could be challenged to think of a tongue twister or alliteration for each! It might look like this:

    Jelly

Octopus

Running

Drums

Ants

Neptune

Variations:

- He could rewrite his name poem neatly (or type it) and mount it on construction paper. Then, he could illustrate it with drawings of the things he wrote in his poem.

- He could surprise someone with one (the person's name) as a personal and touching gift.

- Could he make one for everyone in the house by interviewing each person quickly to find out what everyone likes? Hang them on each person's bedroom door!

- Try this with a word other than his name.

#134
Story Starters

When you have completed 95 percent of your journey,
you are only halfway there.
~Ancient Japanese proverb

Have you ever heard from your child, "I can't think of anything to write about!" If you have, you will probably recognize that this is a major hurdle. Of course, it will be tough to write about something if she can't even think of a topic to write about! The journey's *adventure* aside, she can't even figure out where to go!

When your child does not have a specific writing assignment, writing for fun can be enjoyable and can also help her increase her writing skills along the way. If choosing a topic is tricky, you can jump-start your child's imagination in a variety of ways.

Beginning with a picture can often spark her creativity and help with writing. If she can't even think of a picture to draw, here are some fun ways you can help her begin:

- Drop a blob of paint onto the open crease of a piece of paper. Refold the paper and gently press. Open up the paper and see the unique shape created. What could it be? Have her finish a drawing around it and write about it.

- Save cards your family receives in the mail. Let your child cut out interesting pictures to glue onto a piece of paper.

- Drop a string or piece of yarn onto a piece of paper. Glue it exactly as it lies. What is it?

- Draw a large number or letter on a piece of paper. Have your child turn it into something else.

- Cut or tear a hole in a piece of drawing paper. What could the hole be?

- Glue a cotton ball onto a piece of paper, or glue several. What are they now?

- Try it with a toothpick, coin, or something else that you find around the house.

Have your child determine what the picture will be and draw details all around it to complete the picture. Now, she has a detailed setting with which to begin creating a story. Chances are she will now be able to think of plenty to write about!

#135
Story Board

Obstacles are things a person sees when he takes his eyes off his goal.
~E. Joseph Cossman

When your child's goal is to write a story, it is often tempting to just dive right into it. Children are usually more eager to simply *finish* a project than they are motivated to do a good job at it. If you show your child an easy way to organize his ideas before beginning a creative writing project, he can create a much more detailed and complete story than he would have had he simply started writing. Here's a fun way to help him do that.

For young kids, not strong writers yet:

Draw a few rows of filmstrip-looking boxes on a piece of paper. (See our website for an example.) Tell your child he is going to be a moviemaker. He should try to think about the story he wants to write as if it were going to be a movie he is watching. What would be happening in the first scene? (He draws it with a moderate amount of detail in the first box.) What would happen next and then after that and so on until he has *drawn* the whole story?

Remember that this is a rough draft and does not need to be super neat and include incredible detail. Encourage him to add as much detail as he needs to remind himself of everything he wants to write about.

It may be helpful next to have him tell you the story based on the illustrations he has made on his story board. This will help him to see if he has left anything out that he wanted to say. It also gives you the opportunity to ask questions or make suggestions that might improve the meaning or flow of the story. If he finds that he'd like to add more detail than he can fit in the box, give him a new sheet, and have him draw in the new event. Then, he can number the boxes (including the ones on the new page) so that he will know not to skip the ones he's added.

By first illustrating the events sequentially and in detail, your child should find it rather easy to actually *write* the story.

Older kids and stronger writers can jot ideas down rather than illustrations. A "Story Map" is a great place to do that. They usually contain places for the major story elements.

(Characters, Setting, Beginning, Problem/ Goal, Middle, Resolution, Ending.) If your child jots down ideas for each of these, he has an entire plan for the story and knows all of the important things to include. Chances are he won't leave out anything important. Again, if he takes it one step further and explains the map to you first, you can encourage him to jot down any details he's left out. The result is almost always better than if he hadn't made a plan before writing.

See the workbook on our website for film strips (for younger kids) and a Story Map (for older kids).

#136
Be a Movie-Reviewer

> *You can have anything you want—if you want it badly enough.*
> *You can be anything you want to be, do anything you set out to accomplish*
> *if you hold to that desire with singleness of purpose.*
> *~Abraham Lincoln*

You've probably told your child that when she grows up she can be anything she wants to be. In activity #135, your child needed to pretend to be a moviemaker. Today, allow her to try to be a movie-*reviewer* in an activity that is sure to help increase writing skills in a motivational way.

Together, read some movie reviews in the newspaper. Discuss some of these:

- How the review was written;

- The intended audience;

- Length;

- The story elements covered (Idea #84);

- Beginning and ending paragraphs;

- Whether a synopsis helped (or would have);

- How and where opinions were included;

- References to other movies;

- Whether it had a rating (number of stars); or

- Whatever else you feel is important!

Now have her choose a favorite movie. Challenge her to write a review of it and give it an overall rating. She should support her rating with details. Should others see it? How can she tell her audience about it without giving too much away? If it is a recent movie, she could even send it into the local paper for possible publishing! If she does, don't forget to help her revise and edit it before sending.

Variations:

This activity could even be done with a favorite book, game, or magazine.

See our website for a blank movie review form.

#137
Until We Meet Again

If you don't know where you are going, every road will get you nowhere.
~Henry Kissinger

Chances are you have read a book (or several books) in which you have easily been able to identify with the characters. Perhaps a particular character reminded you of yourself or someone close to you. Your child has probably been able to relate to many of the characters he reads about also.

Today, talk with your child about his favorite characters in the books he has read. Encourage him to talk about two characters from different books. Discuss their similarities and differences, likes and dislikes. Then ask your child what he thinks the two characters might say to each other if they were to meet. For example, what would Nancy Drew think of Stacy in *The Babysitter's Club?* Would they get along? Perhaps they might work together to solve a mystery!

After verbally discussing the meeting of two characters from different books, ask your child to *write* a conversation between the two. Encourage him to use his prior knowledge (everything he knows about the characters) to make the conversation detailed and informative.

Could you think of two rather un-like characters (like Snow White and Peter Pan) and do the same? Try two "bad guys;" what would a meeting of Captain Hook and Cinderella's stepmother be like?

You could even try writing a letter to your child first as one character, and then ask him to write you back as the other.

If your child seems to enjoy creating this interesting dialogue, he may want to extend the experience into a whole new chapter or short story starring the two characters. He may even want to read his conversation or story to a friend who is familiar with the two characters. Together, his friend and he may come up with even more ideas to expand the story. Who knows where that may take them!

#138
Create a Sequel

When the soul of a person is on fire with imagination, impossibilities vanish.
~La Fontaine

Your child's imagination can sure soar here! Suggest this activity and let her imagination run wild.

Help your child choose her favorite book. Length does not matter. This could be a picture book or a chapter book. Discuss the plot with her. Remember, specifically, details about the ending. Now, let her be an author and create the *sequel* to the story. Have her continue with some or most of the main story elements (Idea #84). She could:

- keep the characters the same but change the setting and plot;

- use different characters in the same setting in a similar situation; and/or

- write about the same characters in the same setting facing a different problem.

If this is tricky at first, it may help to read a book and its sequel (or another in its series) to get a feel for it. Try *Rainbow Fish* and *Rainbow Fish to the Rescue* by Marcus Pfister for younger children and *The Indian in the Cupboard* series by Lynne Reid Banks for older readers. Upper elementary readers may enjoy *The Cay* and *Timothy of the Cay* by Theodore Taylor or the *Sarah, Plain and Tall* series by Patricia MacLaughlin.

This fun and motivational writing activity could be done also with a movie she watches or a play she has seen. The possibilities are endless.

#139
Alter the Story Elements

People do not lack strength, they lack will.
~Victor Hugo

Many children, when asked to write, are intimidated by the blank page set before them. It can be difficult to "pull" an idea out of thin air and begin to create a story. Another alternative to the story starting ideas you've read about is to take an existing story and add a little twist to it.

If he has already designed a story map from an existing story (Idea #81), have him look it over and choose one story element to change. For example, if he had a story map on *The Three Little Pigs*, simply changing the setting of the story (i.e. from the woods to the Arctic) will add an entirely new twist to the story. As he rewrites the story with the new setting in mind, the characters may change (pigs in the Arctic?), the characters' actions will change (a house of straw or ice?) and the resolution will be altered, thus creating an entirely new story.

Encourage him to share his altered story with family and friends. A discussion can take place afterward regarding how the story would have changed if the setting were in the desert or on a deserted island. Encourage his imagination. Even if some of his ideas are wild or unbelievable, go with it. Chances are Steven King's first stories were a bit out of the ordinary, too!

#140
Be the Character

Be absolutely determined to enjoy what you do.
~Gerry Sikorski

Think about what makes the books *you* read most interesting. Generally when people enjoy a story they express how fascinating the characters were or how much they could relate to them. Strong characters entice the reader to keep reading.

If your child truly comprehends a story she is reading, she will understand the characters and their actions. Try this discussion and writing activity that allows your child to *become* the character and write a diary entry from the character's point of view.

Have your child choose a main event from a story she is reading. Start a discussion about the main character and ask her to relate why she thinks the character acted as she did. Then, use her reading response journal (Idea #113) or plain paper to write a diary entry about the event as if she *were* the character. She would use first person ("I") and should write from the viewpoint of the character to describe how she feels after the main event takes place. If she needs a prompt, ask her:

- How do you think the character feels now?

- Why do you think she acted as she did?

- In hindsight, would she do anything differently?

Extension: Try having your child compose a diary entry *before* a main event takes place. Challenge her to put into words the feelings and thoughts going through the character's mind that help set the stage for the main event.

#141
Rewrite a Story

Energy and persistence conquer all things.
~Ben Franklin

Does your child have a favorite book that has to be read to him because it is too long or too difficult for his age? Here's an activity that allows your child to re-create that favorite book so that he can enjoy reading it over and over by himself or even to younger children.

Have your child choose one of his favorite longer stories and rewrite it as a picture book. This can seem to be an overwhelming task at first. If the book is particularly long, he may want to start by breaking this big project into a smaller, more manageable one by first:

- creating a story map (Idea #81);

- making a 6-frame sketch (Idea #88); or

- summarizing the story (Idea #158).

Using one of the above strategies will help him focus on the main events and eliminate the minor details to create a shorter, easy-to-read picture book. Remind him of his target audience (younger children) and suggest that he use simple, understandable words. After the story is complete, his younger siblings, cousins and neighbors will love to have him read it to them. He will feel a great sense of pride as he finishes reading the story to them and they chant, "Again, again!"

Extension: If your child enjoys recreating longer books, he may enjoy developing movies or plays into picture books to share with younger children as well.

#142
The Play is the Thing

Becoming a star may not be your destiny,
but being the best you can be is a goal that you can set for yourself.
~Bryan Lindsay

Your child already has acting experience whether she's aware of it or not, from over emphasizing a cut for sympathy to feigning sleep so someone will carry her to bed! When your child performs in "real" plays (whether for your family or for others) it not only increases her self-confidence but can also be a great learning experience as well.

Plays that are already written are a great place for your child to begin her acting debut. Friends and family can get involved by auditioning for parts, memorizing lines, and collecting or creating props.

However, if you would like to use your child's love of acting to increase her writing skills, consider having her write her *own* play. Look through her favorite stories to find one that is suitable for developing into a play. She will not only be using her writing skills but also other skills such as organizing, sequencing, directing, memorizing and exhibiting her comprehension of the story as well.

Variation:

If your child is having difficulty in a subject, such as social studies or science, ask her to bring her book home and look for ways to convert the information she is learning in school into a play format. In addition to using the skills mentioned above, she would be reinforcing the material taught at school! She could create a play to:

- demonstrate an important event (Boston Tea Party, Declaration of Independence);

- help memorize a difficult process (the water cycle, photosynthesis, life cycle of an insect); and/or

- remember more about an important historical person.

Involve the whole family in the creation of the play. You may just enjoy yourself while providing your child a creative and fun way to demonstrate her understanding of what she is learning at school!

#143
Compare and Contrast

Nothing is a waste of time if you use the experience wisely.
~Rodin

It is becoming increasingly popular to select a much-loved children's book and transform it into a movie. Given a choice (*seeing* the movie or *reading* the book), most children would choose to see the movie. As a parent, you have an opportunity to encourage your child to get the most out of the movie while also increasing writing skills in an authentic way. Take a trip to the library or bookstore with your child and find the book on which a movie was based. Encourage him to read the book either before or after viewing the movie.

After reading the book and viewing the movie, hold a family discussion about the similarities and differences. Which was "better?" Help him compare and contrast the book and movie by assisting him in creating a Venn diagram. (See our website for an example, or make your own by drawing two overlapping circles.) One circle would represent the book and the other the movie. The area in which the two circles overlap in the middle represents the similarities between book and movie where he would write what the book and movie had in common. Outside of the overlapping part, he should write the differences between the two.

If he chose to see the movie first this time, encourage him to read the *book* first the next time a book is made into a movie. He may find he gets more out of the movie because he has prior knowledge from reading the book. He probably won't even notice that he is using his comparing and contrasting skills while watching the movie when he has thoughts such as "What happened to..." and "Wait. Where's the....

See our workbook for a blank Venn diagram.

#144
Steal the Beat

The brighter you are, the more you have to learn.
~Don Herold

From a very young age, parents and teachers use song and rhyme to teach children information. From teaching the different sounds animals make in "Old McDonald" to learning the letters of the alphabet in the "Alphabet Song," children grasp concepts and information easier when it's presented in rhyme or song or both!

Keep that in mind when you see your child struggling with a difficult task or concept. Try brainstorming with your child a rhyme that might help her spell a certain word or remember a definition. It is usually easiest to utilize a song that everyone is familiar with. Songs such as "Mary had a Little Lamb," "Row Your Boat" and so forth are so well known that your child need only concentrate on the new lyrics and not the beat of the song. For example, many teachers like to reinforce the stages of the water cycle by singing this song to the tune of "She'll be Coming Around the Mountain:"

Water travels in a cycle; yes it does.

Water travels in a cycle; yes, it does.

It goes up as evaporation,

Forms clouds as condensation,

Then falls down as precipitation.

Yes, it does!

Encourage your child to write the words of the song she creates. This will be especially helpful when using a song to help her remember something long such as a summary of a book. She can add to the song as she remembers more information or change a verse or two around so the information in the song is in the proper sequence.

Your child will enjoy sharing her finished song with family and friends. Let her teach it to your family, and sing it together! You will be increasing her self-esteem as well as helping her remember the important information in the lyrics.

#145
Predict the Past

Continuous effort—not strength or intelligence—
is the key to unlocking our potential.
~Liane Cardes

This activity will provide your child with an opportunity to write creatively as well as learn about history: ask your child to choose one of his favorite books and pick an event he finds interesting or exciting. Ask him to draw an illustration of the scene including as many details as he can. Can he imagine how different the scene would be if it had taken place in a different time period or during a specific past event (100 years ago, the 1950s, when George Washington was President, during WWI)? You may want to ask him questions such as:

- What transportation would be available during that time period?
- What kind of communication did people rely upon?
- How were everyday tasks carried out?
- What did children do and play in that time?
- What parts of the scene would be impossible and why?
- What else would be there instead?

Together, discuss the above questions (and others the two of you may have). Suggest that your child rewrite the scene as if the characters were in the time period he has chosen. Most likely, your child will not know many of the answers to the questions about his time period, but he can find out.

Suggest that he start by creating a K-W-L chart (Idea #94). In the chart, he can write what he knows about the period and the questions he must find out. Finding the answers to his questions may require a trip to the library or a search on the Internet. Encourage him to take notes when he is reading. He may even learn more than just the answers to his questions. If he finds something particularly interesting, he can add it to the scene, thus making it more authentic.

Make sure he shares his finished scene with family and friends. Not only will they enjoy the rewritten scene, but they will be learning about a different time in history as well!

Tip: If researching is a tool that frustrates your child, he can still benefit from this activity. How about suggesting he use his imagination and describe the scene as if it were taking place in the future? This will not require any research, just an active imagination!

#146
Stay Tuned

Your work is a portrait of yourself.
~Unknown

Try watching the news with your child today. Ask her to focus on all the words and phrases the newscasters use to get the audience's attention or to emphasize an important news bulletin. Jot them down. Take notice of all the different segments within the broadcast (local news, world news, weather, sports). Record these as well. Have her pay attention to the way the newscasters speak and articulate their stories. Where they look, how they hold their arms, head—all these little elements come together to make the newscast professional and interesting.

Now, ask your child if she'd like to create her own newscast. Her newscast will be different in that it will not be broadcasting regular news but will focus on the information and characters from a book she's read. She can use the catchy opening and closing statements made by television newscasters and create her own newscast by writing her own articles, stories, and headlines.

For example, if she is focusing the news on the information and characters from *The Boy Who Cried Wolf* fairytale, her newscast can be complete with story headlines she writes such as:

- "Escaped Wolf on the Hunt for Food" (local news)

- "Local Boy Learns the Value of Truth" (moral, inspiring story)

- "Townspeople Get in Shape" (sports)

- "Perfect Weather for Outside Wolf-watching"(weather)

- "Sheep Herders all over the World learn a Valuable Lesson (world news)

Encourage her to write down the details of each headline story so the newscaster presenting it can deliver accurate facts. The more detailed her book, the more interesting and detailed her writing should be. The more characters she includes, the more angles she can explore.

The whole family can be involved in presenting the newscast. Everyone can help her by presenting a segment, directing, creating and holding cue cards. Add even more enjoyment to the activity by videotaping the newscast. Everyone will enjoy sitting down afterward and watching their "creation." Perhaps she'll think of more segments to add or different headlines. She may want to focus on different characters or different main events from the same book or even do another newscast from a different book.

Whatever she decides, she will enjoy utilizing her writing skills to design interesting headlines and detail the stories. She will also love applying teamwork to create a newscast, performing with her family and, most important, she will be exhibiting her comprehension of the story.

Consider sharing the recording with others. Chances are, they will see or hear all the fun and want to join your child in her next broadcast!

Variation:

Try this activity with a concept being taught in school. Having her (and a few classmates?) create a broadcast about it will definitely aid in comprehension and may even lead to further interest in the subject.

#147
Write a Test

Even if we study to old age we shall not finish learning.
~Chinese Proverb

Have you ever wanted to switch places with someone and do their job for the day? Your child has probably experienced similar feelings. He may wish to be a parent for a day and have fun making and enforcing the rules. He may even dream of being the teacher and making decisions such as a "no homework ever" policy!

You can give your child the feeling of being in charge by assigning him this important "teacher task." After he has finished reading a book, give him the opportunity to design his own test for the book. No doubt, he will try to be silly and create a question such as "What is the name of the book?" If this happens, help him to design more in-depth questions by challenging him to write questions even his teacher would have to think about! Tell him you will take his test, and so he should try to stump you.

Encourage him to include many different kinds of questions in his test such as:

- true and false;

- multiple choice;

- open-ended; and/or

- essay.

He should create an answer sheet to go along with his test, thereby requiring that he really comprehend the information. He can then use his test to help him study for an upcoming real test, share with his friends (who have read the same book) to help them study, or present it to his teacher. Who knows, his teacher may even use a question or two on the real test!

#148
Invent a Game

The only difference between ordinary and extraordinary is a little extra.
~Unknown

Parents and teachers alike know that anytime they can make learning seem like a game, children become active, interested learners! Help your child make learning a game by helping her create her *own* board game.

She can make a board game for any academic subject. She could create a game based on a book read for school, science information, social studies facts etc. Anything goes! Encourage her to look through all her board games at home to get ideas about how the game could look, how many players should play, and the objective and rules of the game.

There are many different surfaces to use as the actual board for the game, but poster board is probably the easiest. Encourage your child to make a small scale rough draft of her game to eliminate the frustration of erasing on the poster board. She may even want to play a game or two on the rough draft to avoid any inconsistencies or mistakes she may have missed and change them before creating the final game on the poster board.

How detailed the game gets is only limited to your child's enthusiasm. If she is a game lover, she just might surprise you with the details she includes in the rules of the game. You probably won't need to give many opinions or advice. Just sit back, and watch her go! If she's at all reluctant, however, get in there, and help her out!

Once the game has been tested at home, encourage her to take it to school (if the game is based on an academic subject). The whole class can benefit from your child's work. She should consider writing the directions out in detail and donate the game and directions to her teacher for next year's class to learn from and enjoy!

Variation:

She could also create a card game (using only index cards and her knowledge of a subject) to make a matching game. (For example, a "Lansing" card matches a "Michigan" card for state capital practice.)

#149
Move Over, Dear Abby

He that never changes his opinions, never corrects his mistakes,
will never be wiser on the morrow than he is today.
~Tyron Edwards

Many times your child has probably come to you with a problem or question in which he needs your opinion or advice. Today, try asking your child for *his* opinion on something. Depending on his age, choose a real situation in your life that you could ask his opinion about. It could be very simple or more complex such as, "I was really bothered by the way the repair man talked to me today in the shop. I'm thinking of calling his superior. What do you think?"

Giving advice and having adults and peers listen to them seriously increases children's self-esteem and confidence level.

Give your child an opportunity to practice giving advice by creating and writing his own advice column. It does not have to be a real column for the school newspaper (although that would be great!) but one that he can write in his own journal. He can consider a problem a character has in a book he's reading and write a column suggesting an action to take to help solve the character's problem. If he enjoys giving advice, he can also attempt to solve the problems of characters from movies or television shows that you deem appropriate. You could participate with him and begin by writing to him as the character. Here is an example:

"Dear Mr. Advice,
My name is Momma Bear. Lately, I think someone has been breaking into our house. The person is not causing any big trouble but is doing little things like eating our porridge. Once, the person broke my son's chair. I think the intruder might be a little girl. Once, I caught a glimpse of her long, golden hair. What should I do? I would appreciate your advice."

Have him look over the advice columns in newspapers or magazines. (You may want to preview the selection first!) Suggest that he pay particular attention to the way the person giving advice "speaks" to the person asking for advice. Encourage him to treat the character from the book or movie with respect and take the problem seriously, just as he would want someone to listen to him and take his problems seriously. You and your child (or whole family) could even take turns writing problems and advice back and forth to each other. (Have a drop-off spot at your message center.)

Being aware of other people's problems and assisting in solving them can help your child understand and use empathy with his family and friends, thus making him a more compassionate, caring human being—of which the world can never have too many!

#150
Spice Up Your Writing

Do not take life too seriously. You will never get out of it alive.
~Elbert Hubbard

Similes, metaphors, hyperbole—your child has probably used these figures of speech whether she was aware of it or not! Using this kind of language can really spice up your child's writing. Below is a list of some common figures of speech and their definitions. Read them over with your child. Encourage her to look for them in the books she reads and challenge her to use them in her own writing.

Simile: points out a likeness between two different objects or ideas by using a connective word (usually *like* or *as*); example: The water swept the sand like a giant broom.

Metaphor: suggests a comparison without using the connective words *like* or *as*; example: He's a sly fox.

Hyperbole: a huge exaggeration for special effect; example: I have a million chores to do every day!

Onomatopoeia: a word which is also a sound; example: Listen to the whoosh of the powerful machine.

Alliteration: occurs when the same sound begins most of the words in the same sentence; example: The playful puppy pounced on the prickly porcupine.

Personification: treating an object that is not human as a human being; example: The tree spreads her leafy arms to shade the tired boy.

It may help her to create a "Figurative Language" section in her writing notebook. She can record the figure of speech, give the definition, write an example, and perhaps even draw a picture to help her remember how and when to use it. When she comes across more figurative language ideas while reading, she can add them to her notebook as well.

#151
Using a Thesaurus

I do the very best I know how, the very best I can.
~Abraham Lincoln

To help your child be the best writer he can be, acquaint him with a variety of tools. A thesaurus is one valuable tool that helps add spice to anyone's writing. Children especially can benefit from the thesaurus because their vocabulary is generally not as diverse as an adult's.

Help your child create stories with interesting vocabulary by familiarizing him with the thesaurus. Try sitting down with him and reading a story he has previously written. Concentrate on looking for words that are overused (such as *said* or *really*) or mundane words such as *big* or *okay*. Write the chosen words on a separate piece of paper, and lightly circle them with pencil within the story. (Does he already have a page in his writing notebook (Idea #123) for some of these? If not, he could make one and have a perfect place in which to complete this activity.)

Now, choose a word and demonstrate to your child how to look it up in the thesaurus. After the word appears in the thesaurus, there will be a list of alternative words to use instead which mean the same thing (synonyms). Read them with your child, and have him choose a word that he feels is more interesting or creative and still makes sense in the original sentence. If possible, erase the original word from the story and rewrite the new word in its place. Have your child continue to replace words with "better" ones and write them into his story.

You could even incorporate this yourself into some "Silly Sentences" (Idea #159). Among other things you want him to edit, throw in some boring words and ask him to see if he can liven up the sentences with some "better" words.

When he is finished, have him reread the story with the words from the thesaurus in place. Even he will be surprised at how different, intelligent and interesting his story sounds with the new words! Soon, he will be using the thesaurus *on his own* to create entertaining stories with fascinating vocabulary!

#152
Probable Passages

If we do not change our direction, we are likely to end up where we are headed.
~Ancient Chinese Proverb

Probable Passages is an activity that works well for children who have difficulty deciding *what* to write about. Here's how it works:

The first part of probable passages will need to be done by you; the rest is for your child to complete. First, choose any age appropriate story; although this activity works best if you choose a story your child has never read before. Your part is simple: just leaf through the book and choose words, phrases or pieces of narrative from the book that sound interesting to you. Note: When you are choosing the fragments for this activity you should make an effort to pick words and phrases from a variety of story elements (Idea #84). Here are some examples of probable passages:

rain was pounding
stranger in town
steep bluffs
water is rising
cold
Aunt Betty
scruffy dog
boat is missing
lost
"Help is coming," she cried.
simple cottage
"Don't give up!" he pleaded.

Show these fragments to your child. Give her a blank story map (Idea #81) or a sheet of paper with headings labeled "Setting," "Character," "Problem," "Events," and "Resolution" written across the top. Ask her to write each fragment under the heading where she believes it fits best. Stress that there are no right or wrong answers. For example, she may choose to place "rain was pounding" under the heading "Setting" or "Problem"- either one would be fine. She should choose to put the fragments wherever they make sense to her.

Once she has all the fragments written under the different headings, she is ready to take the fragments and create a story of her own. Her story should include *all* of the words, phrases and narrative you provided her, but it's up to her to decide what events take place and how the problems get solved. Make sure you have chosen some words and phrases to guide her and give her many various directions in which to head. Remind her that all good stories have a beginning, middle and an end and therefore she will have to add many more words and phrases to complete her story. The object is not to write all the passages in the shortest possible paragraph! Rather, the object is to take the passages and use them to write a short but complete story with interesting characters, plot, and dialogue.

After her story is complete, show your child the story from which the words came. Read the story together. Compare and contrast the stories. Was her story similar or very different from the original author's story? You will both enjoy discovering how the author used the *same* words and phrases (along with many others) to create a story *different* from hers.

Variation:

You could even encourage *her* to set up this activity for *you* (or someone else willing to participate). Have her choose a favorite story and select words and phrases from it to give to you. *You* can try to decide what story elements they describe and write the story you think they create together. Read it to her. Now let her read the real story to you. Together, you can compare and contrast your version to the original. Not only will this get her writing and reading, but also *thinking critically* when she is carefully choosing fragments from all the story elements to provide for you.

Note: Younger children can enjoy this activity by dictating the story to you as you write down the words.

Part 6
Making Informational Writing Fun

INTRODUCTION: In this Part you will find a variety of ways to make writing for a purpose more fun and meaningful for your child as well as strategies for tackling grammar issues.

When we talk about writing, many things may come to mind. There's writing, and then there's *writing*. This month you will read about ways to encourage your child to write more *functionally*. Where creative writing comes from the imagination and the heart, functional writing comes more out of necessity with the purpose of informing, describing, and listing, but that doesn't mean you can't make it fun and have a good time doing it.

You will discover in this Part a variety of ways to make real-world, informational writing and grammar interesting and meaningful for your child. When children see a task as something important to them, they are much more likely to learn from it and enjoy it than they would be if it is simply seen as an assignment unrelated to their lives.

As always, read these ideas with your family, give them a try, and have fun!

#153
Functional Writing

Everybody walks past a thousand story ideas every day.
The good writers are the ones who see five or six of them. Most people don't see any.
~*Orson Scott Card*

In Part 5, you read about many ways to increase your child's interest in and love of writing for pleasure, but let's face it, out there in the real world most of the writing we do (and most of the writing your child will do outside of school) will most likely be for purely functional reasons.

At home, we may write letters to people, send thank you notes, or make lists. At work, we may have reports, memos, and summaries to write. This functional writing tells, explains, and helps us communicate information we need to convey. It is the most common type of writing most of us do in our daily lives. Therefore, it is important to help your child learn how to write effectively in this way and for a variety of purposes.

You can help almost effortlessly by just watching for opportunities for your child to write for real (functional) reasons. Try having him:

- Write (and organize according to category) the grocery list.

- Write thank you notes after receiving gifts.

- Write letters to relatives and friends far away.

- Write a "to do" list for you before setting off on multiple errands.

- Write a "to do" list for himself describing the chores or responsibilities he is expected to do.

- Write down goals he's set for himself (Idea #4).

By encouraging your child to write in these ways, you are helping to prepare him for the functional writing he will no doubt do for the rest of his life, both professional and personal. Besides, the more he writes, the better writer he is becoming!

#154
The Language Experience Approach

There is no greater agony than bearing an untold story inside you.
~ Maya Angelou

Teachers of young students often use the Language Experience Approach (LEA) to teach kids early reading and writing skills. This approach to teaching reading and writing uses words and stories from the student's own language and her own experience. The theory behind this approach is that when kids write about what is familiar to them, it is easier and more natural for them to read it back. The beauty of this method is that it can be done easily at home as well. All you need is a pencil, paper, and a little bit of *fun!*

1. Provide your child an exciting or interesting experience. (It can be a grand experience like a trip to a museum, a vacation, or party, or it can be simple such as baking cookies, going on a hike, or building a model.)

2. As soon as you finish, sit down with your child and write about the experience you had. If your child is young, you should take dictation, writing everything she says. If she is older, allow her to write it on her own. You may even choose to alternate writing one sentence (that she dictates) and then asking her to write one. Remember, it's not just making it a little easier on her (and therefore a little less of a "chore") when you write, too. It is also a terrific way for you to model good spelling and grammar. Talk out loud as you capitalize certain things and say why. Mention aloud where you place a period or comma.

3. Model reading the sentences back to her as you go. Encourage her to read them as well. If she is writing and reading on her own, this will help her to hear if her sentences are making sense along the way.

4. When she is finished telling or writing about her experience, there are many things you can do with the piece, depending on the age of your child.

For younger children:

- Read and reread it often to practice reading skills. Point to individual words as you say them.

- Type it or rewrite the words neatly (edited) to send to relatives. (You can read about editing in Idea #160.)

- You can write the individual sentences on strips. Mix them up, and have her rearrange them back into the correct order. (Of course, these can also be printed from the computer in a large font and still cut into strips.)

- Cover a word, and have her try to figure out the word using a variety of strategies. (See Idea #83 for various strategies.)

- Have her recopy the sentences in her neatest writing, even in cursive if she's learned it.

For older children:

- She can edit her own writing.

- Have *her* type it or rewrite it neatly to send to relatives.

- Make a brochure of the information. (Idea #163 for ideas.)

- Have her read it to siblings or other family members.

Don't forget to display her writing somewhere (at the message center?) for all to see. Writing about what your child knows (and has just experienced) should make the writing fun and meaningful. It will also help her to read it more easily because they are her own words.

#155
The Writing Process

We write to taste life twice, in the moment and in retrospect.
~ Anaïs Nin

Writing is not always easy. In fact, it rarely is. We often focus too much on the finished product rather than concentrating on how it came to be. This is especially true when children write. They just want to be done. Unfortunately, the content often suffers when this is the case.

Of course, there are many times when you (and your child for that matter) will write something just to do it and the content is *not* that important. For times when it *is* (stories, reports) a process must be followed to ensure the best final product your child can produce. While there are many good variations to the writing process, here is one that usually works well for reports elementary children write. (See our website for a Writing Process Check-Off List, or you may choose to write these steps on an index card for your child to keep handy in his study area.)

- Step #1: **Brainstorm:** While this step is often omitted or done quickly to save time, it is actually the most important. Here, your child decides exactly what to include. Without it, reports are often unfocused, scattered, and lacking in the depth your child is truly capable of. (See Idea #157 for super brainstorming ideas.)

- Step #2: **Write the Rough Draft:** In this step, the most important thing to do is to simply get the ideas down. Your child shouldn't worry about handwriting, spelling, grammar or finding the perfect word. That will all come later.

- Step #3: **Revising:** Now that the draft has been written, have him read through it once or twice slowly. Listen to the words and the flow of the report. Don't worry about the spelling; just make changes that will help improve the meaning and overall sound of the story. Turn boring words into exciting ones (Idea #183). Change overused dialogue into prose or vise-versa. Add sentences that will add to the meaning or detail, which will *show* the readers what he's saying. For younger kids, try reading the sentences to him one at a time and helping him record any changes he wants. It is fun to use a colored pen for revising and editing. It not only makes changes easier to see, but also kids like to use them and it can actually *encourage* them to make some changes!

- Step #4: **Editing:** When he has the report sounding exactly the way he wants, then it is time to fix it up. He should check for punctuation (capitals, periods, commas) as well as spelling. If he has a hard time spelling, you could suggest that he circle words he feels might be misspelled, and then you two can fix them together afterward. (At first, just learning to recognize a misspelled word is good enough.) Older kids can find and fix them on their own. For younger kids, you might try going through the report row by row and tallying up the errors in each line. Put the tally marks off in the left margin. Then, he will get to each line, see the number of errors, and try to find (and fix!) them. This just lets him know they are there to be found!

- Step #5: **Rewrite:** In this stage, the final draft is written or typed. (Additions and deletions are easier to see here when in colored pen.)

- Step #6: **Share it:** Depending on what your child wrote, for what purpose and for whom, he should find an appropriate way in which to share it. Could it be typed and turned into a book? Sent to someone who would enjoy it?

Breaking down a large task (writing a report for example) makes a seemingly overwhelming task simpler and will most definitely produce a better finished product as well.

See our website for a writing process check-off list and sample brainstorming forms.

#156
The Basic Report Format

If you have other things in your life - family, friends, good productive day work—
then these can interact with your writing and the sum will be all the richer.
~ David Brin

In upper elementary, children are often asked to write a small report, sometimes called a 5-Paragraph Essay. Even if it is not called this exactly, if specific instructions are not given, this is a good place to start. In this essay or report, there is a beginning, three supporting paragraphs, and an ending. Here are the basics of a 5-Paragraph Essay:

Paragraph 1: Introduction: This usually contains a *hook* at the beginning (something catchy to grab the reader's attention), some *background information* about the topic, and then a *thesis* at the end. (A thesis is a sentence that tells the main idea of the report.)

Paragraph 2: One support for the thesis: It usually begins with a topic sentence that explains what this paragraph is about. The rest of the sentences are details to support it.

Paragraph 3: Another support for the thesis: It usually begins with a topic sentence that explains what this paragraph is about. The rest of the sentences are details to support it.

Paragraph 4: A third support for the thesis: It usually begins with a topic sentence that explains what this paragraph is about. The rest of the sentences are details to support it.

Paragraph 5: The Conclusion: Usually one begins the conclusion by restating the thesis. Next, she reminds the readers of important facts she wrote about. Last is a strong ending, something powerful or interesting.

Of course, most teachers give out detailed instructions when it comes to report writing. But if the details are ever less than ideal, this is a good format to use.

See our website for Report Organizers and more on Hooks, Thesis Statements, Topic Sentences, and Endings.

#157
Begin at the Beginning: Mind Maps

I'm writing a first draft and reminding myself that
I'm simply shoveling sand into a box so that later I can build castles.
~ Shannon Hale

If you were going to take a trip across the country, you would not just go get in your car the second you think about going and take off. You would make plans first. You would decide on a route, what to bring with you, where to stop along the way, etc. If you do not, you might get lost along the way, miss wonderful sights, and not have what you want when you get there.

Well, the same is true for writing a report: you must make a plan! Most kids like to just sit down and start typing. No planning! They just want to get it done. The problem with that is, like the trip, their reports wander, might not contain important information, and may miss the mark completely.

Brainstorming first is always a good idea. Of course, brainstorming is only one part of the writing process (as you read about in Idea #155), but it is arguably the most important. With interesting graphic organizers, kids can not only learn *how* to organize their thoughts and facts first, but also have fun doing it.

Making a Mind Map is a very visual and efficient way to organize ideas. To start, have your child make a circle in the center of a sheet of paper. In it, he writes a word or two telling the main idea of the whole report. Then, for let's say a 5 Paragraph Essay, he will draw five lines radiating out of the center circle. At the end of each, draw another shape such as a rectangle. In each rectangle, he writes the main idea of each paragraph: one is the introduction; one is the conclusion; and the middle three are the best three topics he wants to write about that subject. The last step is to look through any sources and jot down facts next to the correct rectangle. He can attach them to the rectangle with a small line.

The result is a visual picture of the whole essay. All on one page he can see everything he is going to write about. The thesis comes from the middle circle. Each paragraph's topic sentence comes from the ideas in the rectangles. All of the supporting details for the paragraph are the ideas sticking out of it.

Now, when he goes to begin the draft, he is not just wandering aimlessly hoping to include the right stuff. He simply looks at the mind map, begins at the beginning, and follows along. All the planning is done, and he is well on his way to an awesome report!

See our website for examples of Mind Maps.

#158
Summary Writing (How-to)

> *So the writer who breeds more words than he needs,*
> *is making a chore for the reader who reads.*
> *~ Dr. Seuss*

In elementary school, kids begin to learn how to write summaries, and they use this skill in many ways throughout their schooling. However, learning how to write a summary is often a mysterious task for a child. An easy way to start out is to think about the "5 W's": Who? What? Why? When? Where?

To try it out:

1. First choose a small piece of text. Try an article from one of her magazines or a short book.

2. After reading it, talk about it together. Tell her what you think was important to remember about it, and let her do the same. Try to steer her away from including any minor details and to focus on the major ones. Also try to keep opinions out.

3. Then, write the five question words on a piece of paper, and jot down the important parts for each. Young kids like to trace their hand and put one question word in each finger; this helps them to remember that there are five. Some pieces of writing may not lend themselves to all five, and that's okay. (You might say, for instance, "Is the 'when' important in this article or could it happen any time?")

4. Once you have this important information down, have her try using just those five things to retell the plot. Remember to keep any thoughts or opinions out of a summary. (An older child could write this part.) Do you both agree what it was mostly about?

For fun, you could give a really "silly summary." Leave out some important parts and add in some minor, silly details. Ask her to tell you what was wrong with your summary. When she corrects you, it is helping her learn what to include (and not include!) in a summary of her own.

If you do this a few times, your child will come to realize that those five question words are a good foundation for a summary. It will help her to include the important stuff and weed out the not-so-important stuff.

#159
Silly Sentences (Editing)

I've found the best way to revise your own work is to pretend that somebody else wrote it and then tear it to shreds.
~ Don Roff

A super fun way to practice editing and grammar is something we like to call "Silly Sentences." It is easy and a fun way to sit and work with your child.

To do this:

1. Figure out a skill your child needs to work on. (For a young child, this might be capitalizing and high-frequency spelling words. For an older child, it might be proper punctuation and tougher spelling patterns.)

2. Now, write a few sentences, making sure to make plenty of mistakes along the way, specifically in the areas you want your child to practice. (This may take a little planning on your part!) It can be serious, funny, any way you want. For young children just trying this out, aim for maybe 5-10 errors. Older kids like to be challenged to find up to 30!

3. Tally up the number of errors you made and record the number at the top.

4. Give these "Silly Sentences" to your child and tell him you wrote something in which you think you made a bunch of mistakes and you would like *him* to be the teacher and fix them. Kids *love* when grown-ups make mistakes! And so many, all in one place, they feel like they've hit the jackpot and suddenly love to edit!

5.   Sit with your child and read it to him the way it "should be." Chances are he will see several mistakes right away. Each time he fixes something, make a tally mark so he can see his progress and see how many more mistakes he still has to find. Let him use a special colored editing pen, too, for added "professionalism" in editing.

PS. Have fun with it! Don't forget the "silly" in "Silly Sentences"! Throw in some "What is wrong with spelling 'what' 'w-u-t-t'?" or "We don't *really* need any periods in this paragraph, do we?" Talking about the errors and how to fix them will help him to not make them himself in the future.

See also Part 10, which is full of specific spelling help.

See our website for an example of some "Silly Sentences."

#160
When To Edit

There Are two Typos Of People In This world:
those Who Can Edit And Those Who Can't.
~ Jarod Kintz

Editing is a very important skill for your child to learn. As she gets older, she will be expected to do so on her own. The most obvious and simple way to help her learn to edit is to edit her own writing. The trick, of course, is to know what to edit and when. In general, these Dos and Don'ts should apply:

DO EDIT:

- Pieces that will be published in some form or displayed.

- School projects that you feel should be. (Her teacher will most likely let you know of editing expectations of homework assignments, such as book reports.)

- Letters etc. going to someone who may not be able to decipher her sound spelling.

DON'T EDIT:

- Lists she writes if the job can be accomplished without perfect spelling. (If she's helping with the grocery list and spells "soup" "soop", no one will care, and the job will still be completed!)

- Her journal writing.

- Letters to family and friends that will understand the message without editing.

If she is writing only for herself, her family, or her friends, formal editing can be replaced by a quick rereading to check for glaring errors that will distract the reader from the meaning of the piece.

When a long project does require editing, using a colored pen can be fun. Your child can be challenged to find as many of her own mistakes and correct or circle them in red. As always, working with you on the final edits will help your child learn to edit better and help her learn to enjoy the process as well. When you are editing with your child, be sure to have her sit next to you and watch as you say aloud why you are editing something. For example, if she is writing about a trip to Florida and she doesn't capitalize the 'f', underline it and say, "Florida is the name of the state (or proper noun for older children), so it needs to have a capital." By watching you and listening to your reasons, she will be more likely to find her own mistakes in the future.

Giving kids an "Editing Reminder Card" can also be helpful and empower kids to edit on their own. It doesn't have to be fancy; just jot a few basics of editing on a note card and keep it wherever she does her writing. For most kids, these four things are good editing reminders to write on the card:

1. Read it out loud (Check for missing words and endings on words.)

2. Capitals (Add them where they *do* need to be and get rid of ones you *don't* need.)

3. Punctuation (Do you have periods, etc.?)

4. Spelling (Circle words you need to fix.)

See our website for an example of an Editing Reminder Card.

#161
Writing Topic Sentences

The illiterate of the 21st century will not be those who cannot read and write,
but those who cannot learn, unlearn, and relearn.
~Alvin Toffler

Let's say your child has a writing assignment on the inventions of Benjamin Franklin. He's created a mind map (Idea #157) with great ideas on what he wants to write about Ben Franklin, but now what? Soon he will be faced with creating his first body paragraph, and he's unsure of how to start it. That's where an understanding of topic sentences comes in handy.

Very simply, a topic sentence tells the reader what the paragraph will be about. Beginning writers will find it helpful to have the topic sentence as the first sentence in the paragraph. That way, they are more likely to stay focused and not switch topics while writing the paragraph.

For example, let's say he wants to write a paragraph about Franklin's invention of bifocal lenses. A possible topic sentence would be "Benjamin Franklin's poor eyesight led him to create the first pair of bifocal glasses." The rest of the sentences in this paragraph would be *only* about bifocals—the need for them, their uses, how Ben created them, etc. He would not write about any other invention Franklin made. A paragraph on electricity could follow the paragraph on the bifocal lens and it would have its own topic sentence.

Learning how to write topic sentences that support the main idea will help him set a purpose for writing and help his writing stay focused and on topic. You can help your child write topic sentences by asking him, "What is this paragraph mostly about?" His answer will become the topic sentence. Older children can experiment with putting the topic sentence in the middle of the paragraph or at the end. No matter where the topic sentence is located, your child will find that creating topic sentences is easy, helps his writing flow nicely, and makes him proud of what he created.

#162
Writing *for* Information

The more a man writes, the more he can write.
~William Hazlitt

A great way to practice writing skills, you've learned, is to have your child write about what she knows, what she has just done, or information she has learned. Have you thought, though, about encouraging her to write *for* information? You can help her to learn how to compose brief requests *for* information from a variety of sources. For instance, if your family is about to go on a trip, she could write the Chamber of Commerce in that city for tourist information. She could hand-write or write an e-mail to museums and other places she would like to visit and ask them to send her a brochure. She could even learn to properly address envelopes with this activity.

She will surely enjoy the responses she will receive in the mail (or in an e-mail) addressed to her. She can read through the information and maybe even organize it to save. Three-hole punch the information and put it into a binder or organize responses in folders on the computer according to category. Soon, she will have quite a collection!

#163
Kid's Brochure

Until further notice, celebrate everything.
~Tim Hansel

Have you ever been persuaded to take a trip or visit some place simply because of what you've read on a brochure? Brochures use words and pictures to create imagery in hopes of convincing the reader that this is someplace he just *must* visit!

Look through your home for brochures you may have collected or saved from past trips. If you don't have any brochures, consider writing a letter to a vacation spot you'd like to visit (Idea #162). You could also visit local museums, historical buildings, or interesting sites and collect their brochures. Look through the brochures, and notice how the writers use descriptive phrases and colorful pictures to keep your attention.

Some brochures are made to entice the reader to visit. They may be informative and full of facts. Still others are full of information to explain a specific place, person, animal or event.

Your child could highlight or circle any words or phrases that he feels got his attention and he would like to try, too. Have him start keeping a list of his favorite phrases and words. Ask him to create some of his own descriptive phrases.

Now your child is ready to create his own brochure. Have him fold a piece of paper into thirds. You now have a homemade brochure ready to fill with interesting information, facts, pictures and descriptive paragraphs. Your child can design a brochure for any number of things:

- a place he has recently visited (another state, museum, play, musical);

- a place he would like to visit (real or imaginary);

- a past event or one approaching (county fair, parade, festival);

- an animal he learned about at school or the zoo;

- a special event taking place in the family (reunion, wedding, shower);

- the town you live in;

- his school;

- a team sport he is on; and/or

- a brochure to detail material that he has learned (i.e. the effects of pollution, information about his state, an endangered species).

Your child can use crayons, markers, glitter, real photos, magazine picture clippings, clip art or anything else he can think of to help him create his own brochure. Older children who are comfortable with the computer can use Microsoft Word to create a brochure. There is a template on Word that is easy to fill in, save and print. Your child is still practicing writing but also using the computer as his tool for creating the brochure. Whether he does it by hand or on the computer, this should prove to be quite a motivational writing experience!

#164
Vacation Memoirs

Our greatest glory is not in never failing but in rising up every time we fail.
~Ralph Waldo Emerson

Here is an activity that is fun, easy, inexpensive, motivational, and rewarding for years to come. (It will help increase your child's love of writing and writing skills as well!)

Become a collector of postcards everywhere you go. Vacation spots are an obvious place to find them, but they can often be found in museums, shops (even rest stops!), and other places that people visit often.

Encourage your child to write briefly about her experiences and feelings, after visiting the place depicted, on the postcard. She may also want to include notes about things to bring or do the next time she visits. She might write about the best parts of the visit or a funny thing that happened while there. You may want to pick up a few postcards in certain very-fun places that you anticipate might warrant a lot of writing. It may help your child to discuss the trip with you and the family before she writes. Not only will it help her focus, but it will also teach her a little about summarizing!

If your child is young, take dictation and write on the postcard for her. If she is older, she can write it herself. You could save them and add them to a binder for safe keeping. A great collection can be made after a few years, and what a treasure to take with her and add to later when she begins traveling on her own. If she does all the writing each time, your child will be able to look back and see her growth throughout the years as her skills increase with each new card.

#165
Commas

You may be disappointed if you fail, but you are doomed if you don't try.
~Beverly Sills

Have you ever read a story written by your child (or anyone) where, within the entire first page, there is not a period or comma to be found? Correct use of punctuation, especially commas, is one element of writing that teachers try to impress upon their students. Improper use of commas can change the whole meaning of a sentence and sometimes of the story. Commas can even save a life! (Well, not really, but look at the following example). Imagine a child writing this:

Let's eat Grandpa.

What he really meant to write was *Let's eat, Grandpa.*

In lower elementary school, children are taught to use a comma when there is a pause in the sentence. The most common uses of commas are below.

- Use commas to separate three or more items in a series.

  - *She wanted a new bike, a jump rope, a book, and a puppy for her birthday.*

- Use commas to separate city and state, and dates and years.

  - *Atlanta, Georgia*

  - *May 1, 2015*

- Use a comma in dialogue to separate the speaker from the dialogue.

  - *Her mom shouted, "Be careful!"*

Older children can learn more complex comma rules:

- Use a comma after introductory phrases.

  - *If she studies for the test, she will do well.*

- Use commas before a coordinating conjunction joining two independent clauses.*

- *She wanted to go over to her friend's house, but her mom wouldn't let her.*

- Use commas to separate extra information (put the extra information between commas)

  - *Her best friend, Beth, is always late.*

(The fact that her friend's name is Beth is extra information.)

*Definitions:

Coordinating conjunctions: Think of "FANBOYS" as a way to remember the connecting words: *for, and, nor, but, or, yet, so.*

Independent clause: a group of words that can stand alone as a sentence.

The above comma rules are the most common rules used in elementary school.

Here are other basic punctuation marks you and your child should concentrate on when writing. (You may want to consult his teacher to be sure of the punctuation marks required for his grade.)

- **Period:** ends a complete sentence;

- **Quotation marks:** used when a character in the story is talking. Put the first set of quotation marks before the person speaks and the second set of quotes after the character has finished speaking and after the end punctuation mark. When a new character speaks, a new paragraph should be started.

Try to find ways to practice punctuation in a fun and interesting way. For example, your child could use his favorite cartoon strip from the newspaper to practice the correct use of punctuation. Cartoons are usually full of quotation marks, commas, periods, exclamation points and question marks. You can discuss how the author uses them and why. Your child could use crayons or highlighters to color-code punctuation, such as all commas are yellow (for pausing), all periods are red (for stopping), and all quotation marks are green. The funnies work well for this because they are not in a book that you would prefer your child not write or color in. They are also usually highly interesting and fun to work with. You could even use Idea #129 from Part 5 and have your child write a comic of his own (or rewrite one already drawn), using the correct punctuation.

See our online workbook, available for purchase, for more examples of correct commas usage and a list of Do's and Don'ts.

#166
Follow Your Heart

Learn to listen. Opportunity could be knocking at your door very softly.
~Frank Tyger

If your child is struggling with informational writing or the grammar involved in writing, try switching gears and do a little experimenting. You probably know the things your child is most interested in. Try tapping into her love of animals or art, sports or space, and involve her in writing activities about these subjects. Children are much more willing participants in projects that interest them.

So, if your child has to write a book report, help her to find and choose a book that really captures her interests. If she has a choice of people to write a biography about for school, go to the library together and browse through many books, discussing along the way. She will be so much more excited to delve into the life of a person she's truly interested in rather than someone she knows only from pulling some book off a shelf.

If you'd like to practice informational writing skills in general, try tailoring the ideas you read about in this part to your child's specific interests, too. If she's curious about endangered animals, find addresses (or e-mail addresses) for places to write about organizations, fund-raisers and more to help the cause. Many places she will write to will send free stickers, posters, books etc. along with the information requested.

Whether you have a reluctant writer or a willing one, ensuring that your child's writing experiences are meaningful and interesting to her will make a world of difference not only in her attitude but also most likely in the finished product as well.

#167
Be Ready for Writing

He who would leap high must take a long run.
~Danish proverb

You've already read about the importance of creating a study area for your child in your home (Idea #18). Certainly, that would be the most appropriate place for your child to write a report for school or even maybe a letter to Aunt Jamie, but think of all the fun that he could have writing in *other* places.

Have you ever considered stashing note pads or notebooks in various shapes and sizes in your car for those long rides or unexpected traffic jams? Stuff a bag with colored pencils, lots of paper, cute erasers, and a pocket dictionary and drive away. With a fun variety of tools to use, your child might be compelled to take on a writing challenge on the way to the zoo, such as finding and recording something that starts with each letter of the alphabet or listing animals he predicts he will see. On the way home, he could draw his favorite exhibit and write a short paragraph about what he learned while the ideas are still fresh in his mind. Not only is this an extremely motivational and fun way to get kids writing, it may also help to keep them from complaining, "Are we almost there yet?"

#168
Interviewing

Remember, we all stumble, every one of us.
That's why it's a comfort to go hand in hand.
~Emily Kimbrough

A terrific way to motivate kids to write, you know, is to have them choose a topic that interests them. For most children, their parents' and grandparents' lives seem vague and intriguing. How about offering to let your child interview you or setting up time for her to interview another family member?

There are so many skills involved with interviewing, and a great deal can be learned. Of course, if your child is young, you can help her with many of the steps and even take an abbreviated path. Here are some informational writing skills you could focus on along the way. For instance, if your child is going to interview Grandpa Larry, have her:

- Brainstorm what she already knows about Grandpa as well as questions that she has about him.

- Choose a focus for the interview based on some of the things she wants to find out, such as what life was like for him as a child.

- Make a final list of the questions she has decided to ask during the interview, having narrowed her focus and eliminated unnecessary questions.

- Arrange a meeting time and find a quiet place the two can be alone. She should bring the questions and a pencil or two.

- Take notes during the interview either right on the question sheet if she's left room for answers or on a separate piece of paper. (She may want to record the interview so that she can listen to it again if necessary.) (See Idea #103 for note taking strategies.)

- Write a rough draft using the information she learned during the interview keeping in mind her focus. (Of course, this will be later, after Grandpa goes home.) She may want to listen to parts of the tape again if she realizes she has missed something. Idea #173 has paragraph writing techniques.

- Revise and edit the paragraph(s). (Idea #160)

- Rewrite or type the final draft on the computer.

Think about what she would like to do with it. Could she send Grandpa a copy? How about other relatives that might be interested to find out the things she's learned. Be sure to send Grandpa a thank you note! This is a lengthy project but one that is extremely rewarding for your child, Grandpa, and everyone who will get the pleasure of reading her finished paper.

See our workbook on our website for a checklist for this activity.

#169
Writing About Reading

Opportunities multiply as they are seized.
~Sun Tzu

The more your child reads, the better reader he becomes. The more your child writes, the better *writer* he becomes. Since the two go hand in hand, the more he reads, the better writer he will become, too, and vise versa.

Another way to increase informational writing skills in a motivational way is to begin with your child's growing love of reading. If he is reading something informational, encourage him to write a short paragraph about it. (Idea #158 discusses summarizing hints). He could create a poster about it, illustrating various points, and then write captions for them. The ideas are endless.

If he is reading a fiction book or picture book, try something fun like challenging him to write a journal entry (sometimes called a reading response journal), pretending to be one of the characters in the story. What would that character write about tonight before going to bed? What would she be thinking, feeling, doing, or hoping? If the story is long, such as in a chapter book, try having him do this once after each chapter. See how the entries change after new events have occurred. If you are reading a book together during shared reading time, maybe you could take turns writing entries (buddy writing) so that you can model the thinking strategies as well as the writing.

#170
Pen Pals (Letter Writing)

The proper definition of a man is an animal that writes letters.
~Lewis Carroll

A terrific way to practice writing for real and meaningful reasons is to have a pen pal or someone with whom your child can write and receive letters or e-mails in return. Perhaps you know of a friend of hers that has moved away, a cousin in another state, a grandparent who may enjoy a correspondence. Anyone willing will do.

A person out of state works well because you can encourage your child to ask questions about the life and land where her pen pal is and she can compare and contrast to where she lives. Regardless, help her to think of a variety of questions to write each time so that the recipient will automatically have a lot to write by answering her questions. Help her learn to set up a letter (greeting, body, ending) and address the envelope properly if she's mailing it. Collect and send postcards back and forth as an exciting change once in a while or send pictures to each other. The possibilities are endless!

If you are having a hard time thinking of someone to write to, ask around at work, family gatherings, dance lessons, etc. Chances are someone will have the perfect candidate for your child to write to. Try asking your librarian for help. Your child's teacher may also have suggestions for finding the perfect pen pal. If you're still running into dead ends, try writing to her yourself! You can both still address envelopes (no need for stamps!) and stuff letters in your mailbox (or underneath each other's pillows) for each other.

Your child will love receiving letters in the mail from her new pen pal. And chances are, she will learn to love writing a little more, too.

See our website for an example of a proper letter.

#171
Persuasive Writing

Whatever you can do or dream you can, begin it.
Boldness has genius, magic and power in it. Begin it now.
~Goethe

Chances are your child has resorted to begging when he really wants you to give in on something. Now you can give your child *permission* to beg—in an articulate way. Challenge him to persuade you, verbally at first and then through writing, to see his point of view.

For example, imagine your child is trying to persuade you to believe that he absolutely *has* to have an expensive pair of jeans. Ask him to stop and collect his thoughts, reasons, and ideas about why he feels he needs them. Have him write his arguments down on paper and practice what he will say to you before he tries to persuade you. Suggest that he remember his target audience (parent) when giving his reasons. Right away he should know that "they're cool" will not suffice.

This not only allows him to put his reasoning into articulate sentences, it also gives him practice at a real life skill. Even as adults we try to persuade people to help with a task or grant us a much-deserved raise or more vacation time. Very often, children will have difficulty coming up with valid arguments and may stop begging or perhaps arrive at a better solution such as doing chores to earn the money.

Once your child has had practice persuading you on issues most important to him, encourage him to tackle more involved and thought-provoking issues such as persuading:

- people to vote;

- family and friends to donate blood;

- people to wear seatbelts or bike helmets; or

- smokers to quit.

He might enjoy taking on issues more closely related to his school or town such as the advantages or disadvantages of:

- a longer or shorter school day/year;

- after school programs;

- school dress codes; or

- curfews for adolescents.

When your child has had practice verbally persuading you or others, he will be ready to write down his arguments. A persuasive paper starts by identifying the argument and then detailing the pros or cons. His paper should be written so that anyone reading it will understand his position and begin to see things "his way." Remind him of his target audience. He will write a paper differently for adults than he would for his peers.

If his paper is well thought out and contains valid points, he may want to consider asking it to be published in the school newsletter or even the local paper! Who knows, simply writing a persuasive paper for fun could bring about a positive change for your family, town or school!

*Try the editorial section of any newspaper for examples of persuasive writing.

#172
"Write" Across the Curriculum

If you think you can, you can. And if you think you can't, you're right.
~Marykay Ash

In classrooms all across the country, informational writing in the *academic* areas is coming to the forefront. Writing across the entire curriculum has been shown to increase comprehension of the material as well as help children become proficient writers.

There are various ways to provide opportunities for your child to write across the curriculum. Start by making (or purchasing) a journal to write in. She could use the journal for any subject. Below are just a few suggestions:

- Math Journal: When your child conquers addition, have her use *words* to describe how to solve a simple addition problem. She can imagine herself explaining how to solve the addition problem step by step to someone else and write down the directions to solve it. She may choose to write in paragraph form (First…Then…Next) or by using steps with numbers (1. 2. 3…). (To determine if her directions are accurate, suggest that someone try to solve the problem by reading her words. This will help her find areas where she needs to be more specific or clear.)

- Science Journal: When completing a science experiment, she could explain in her journal the conclusion of the experiment and the reasons for the results. She may even wish to write down a few ideas for future experiments!

- Social Studies Journal: After learning about an event or person, she may choose to write her own thoughts and opinions about what she's discovered.

- Spelling Journal: In her journal she can describe the ways that help her remember how to spell her words (little clues, rhymes or patterns that help). (See Part 10 for many ideas!)

#173
Paragraph Writing

Act as if it were impossible to fail.
~Dorothea Broude

Does your child receive any magazine subscriptions? If you are considering subscribing to a magazine for your child, consider subscribing to one that contains factual, informative articles. Magazines such as *Ranger Rick* and *ZooBooks* have informational articles about animals, people and different places around the world. If you want to try out a magazine before committing to it, you may want to visit the library. The library has many different magazines to peruse that will help you decide if it is appropriate for your child.

Here's an activity your child can utilize after reading informational articles from a magazine or book. This activity will help with both her writing skills and increase her comprehension of expository texts.

While reading the articles, ask your child to look for three things: topic, main idea and supporting details. Here's a brief explanation:

Topic - what the article is about.

Main idea - the most important idea about the topic.

Supporting details - little bits of information that support the main idea.

Read this example below:

HORSES (topic)

There are many things you must do before saddling your horse (main idea). First, you must brush your horse's back where the saddle will be placed (one supporting detail). You should also check the saddle and blanket for anything that might hurt the horse (another supporting detail).

A good informational paragraph will have these three components. Look with your child through some of her magazine articles. Challenge her to identify and highlight the topic, main idea and supporting details of the article. By identifying these components, she will be increasing her comprehension of the article.

Once she becomes proficient at identifying the topic, main idea and supporting details, ask her to create her own article with these important components. Suggest that she write about something she is familiar with and cares for. Start with something simple such as an article about her pet, friend, family, or the importance of her room or privacy. Anything will do!

See our website for a paragraph worksheet.

#174
Step By Step

Yes, risk taking is inherently failure-prone.
Otherwise, it would be called sure-thing-taking.
~Tim McMahon

There are things we do every day without even thinking. We get dressed, make our beds (maybe!), cook meals, drive to the store and so much more. Yet, we rarely stop to think of all the steps involved in completing these tasks. If we did, we might go crazy. Well, here's your chance to drive your child crazy for once! This is a super fun writing activity that is sure to have the whole family in stitches. Here's how it works:

- Have your child choose something very common that people do every day. (For an example, we'll use making a peanut butter and jelly sandwich.)

- Ask him to write down all of the steps involved in the task (the making of the sandwich). Tell him he needs to be extremely specific. Skipping lines in between the steps will be helpful. Another good idea is to write each direction on a numbered note card. Both allow room for adding details later.

- Now, gather as a family where the task will be completed (the kitchen). Choose which family member will follow his directions. (Let's say Dad.)

- Have your child read the first step on his direction sheet aloud slowly and exactly as written.

- Dad should listen carefully to the direction read and do exactly as he heard, being careful to not do anything unless it was specifically stated. (For instance, if your child's first direction is to spread peanut butter on the bread, Dad could use his fingers, instead of a knife, if he wasn't specifically told to get out the knife!)

- If your child realizes he wasn't specific enough, allow him to quickly add in the missing directions and reread it to Dad. Now, will it work?

- Have him read through the rest of his directions, one at a time, while Dad follows them exactly as stated. (How funny when Dad decides to add the jelly into the peanut butter jar, instead of to the bread, because he was just told to "add the jelly"!)

- Try it again, this time having your child listen carefully to the directions written and given by Dad (preferably on a different task.) Encourage your son to listen for opportunities to be very specific and funny. (For instance, if Dad's telling him the steps for getting dressed and says to put his socks on, but forgets to say on his feet, whisper to your child to put the socks on his hands if he hasn't already picked up on the idea!)

Don't forget to have fun together. The idea here is, of course, to show how details in writing can be extremely important, not to frustrate your child. He'll probably also gain a new insight and respect for all of the completely complicated things he does all day so well. And you'll surely all want to enjoy peanut butter and jelly sandwiches together afterward, too!

#175
Rainy-Day Lists and More

> *Some men see things as they are and ask why.*
> *Others dream things that never were and ask why not.*
> *~George Bernard Shaw*

If your child is like most, you've undoubtedly heard the infamous words, "I'm bored. There's nothing to do." Be prepared for the next time you hear those words. Sit down with your child and create a rainy day list of all the *things she likes to do.* This list is not just for rainy days when she is unable to go outside, but for anytime when she is having difficulty finding something to do that interests her.

When the list is complete, brainstorm together for some other things she could do but has never tried or a list of things she would like to learn to do. She could even make a "Bliss List" of all the things she really and truly loves. This may lead to discovering interests she'd never even thought of before! Keep the lists available, and add to them when she (or anyone) has an interesting activity, game or other idea.

The next time she utters those words, pull out one of the lists and look at it together. Encourage her to choose something appropriate for the day. You may even find her referring to the list by herself for some interesting and different activities to try!

#176
Weekend Writing

> *Think for yourself and let others enjoy the privilege of doing so too.*
> *~Voltaire*

Have you ever had a tough day and immediately felt better after talking to someone about it? Simply verbalizing our frustrations can let us put everything back into perspective and lessens the stress.

If your child tends to keep everything to himself and doesn't like to share the events of his day with you, he may prefer to write about it. If he enjoys writing, he may want to write about his day in his journal. If he is a reluctant writer, suggest that he write on the weekend about the previous week. He could write about one particular day, the best or worst thing that happened, his friends and the activities they did together, or events that have transpired at home.

Many good things can come from this activity; your child will be practicing his writing skills, he will be strengthening his memory by recalling events from the previous day or week and he will be releasing his feelings and thoughts which will hopefully lessen any stress he may be feeling!

If your child is comfortable with sharing his journal with you, it will provide an excellent opportunity for discussion and also keep you informed of the events happening in his life. If he is hesitant about sharing his writing with you, try writing about your day or week at the same time and then share it with him. He may just be curious enough about your day to share his with you!

#177
Goofy Grammar

Nostalgia is like a grammar lesson:
you find the present tense, but the past perfect!
~Owens Lee Pomeroy

No doubt your child can write or tell you a sentence, even a story, that sounds quite wonderful, but when asked to identify the grammatical components of it, are you met with a blank stare? Could even *you* identify the all of the nouns, verbs, adjectives, etc.?

Knowledge of the parts of speech, for instance, can ultimately help your child to become a better writer. While rarely in her life outside of school will she be asked to specifically identify the passive verb in a stock report, she will most likely become a more competent and descriptive writer having been exposed to the basics of grammar.

A fun way to help your child understand the parts of speech (such as nouns, verbs and adjectives) is to use her own writing. Select a short story (or the equivalent) that she has written. It works well if she does not know the story you've chosen. Type or write it out leaving blanks for about 10 words or so. Choose to leave out some:

- Nouns (people, places and things such as *child, Disney Land, flower*; you could reinforce the concept of plurals here also.)

- Adjectives (words that describe nouns such as *beautiful, silly, red*)

- Verbs (action words such as *run, sing, play*; you could also use various forms of verbs such as present and past tense, too.)

- Adverbs (words that modify verbs such as *slowly, quickly, gently*)

Label the blanks according to the parts of speech they represent. Part of it may look like this:

"Once upon a time, there were two ______________ ______________ who lived down
                                   (adjective)   (plural noun)
by the ______________. Every day they would ______________ around looking for
       (noun)   (verb)

some _________________ to eat. They would _____________________ _______________
     (plural noun)   (adverb)   (verb)
through town."

Now, gather your family together and get ready for some fun. Look for your blanks, and read the part of speech to the players. (Do *not* read the story yet; just ask for words separately!) They can collaborate or take turns offering suggestions to fill in the blanks, having no idea what the story is about. Encourage your child to be creative, even funny with her responses. It will make for an entertaining story!

After all of the blanks have been filled in, read them the story they have created. Of course, it will not sound like the original. That's the point! It will be a new, silly version of the one she had written. It may sound like this:

> "Once upon a time there were two fluffy dinosaurs who lived down
> by the ice rink. Every day they would skip around looking for some
> TVs to eat. They would quietly dance through town."

If your child enjoys this, encourage her to write one of her own. She could use something she's already written, a story from a book, or make up her own specifically for this game. She can choose which words to omit and will need to identify the part of speech they represent in order to ask you for a new word that would fit. It will get her writing, planning, creating, and learning some grammar along the way. It is sure to get your whole family laughing, too!

The "School House Rock" educational video series is a catchy and entertaining way to teach math, grammar, history and science.

You can purchase "KID LIBS" that are already set up in the format of this activity for some ready-made stories.

#178
Brighten Up Someone's Day with Writing

Being considerate of others will take your children further in life than any college degree.
~Marian Wright Edelman

When children write for themselves, it can be very rewarding. However, many children feel a greater sense of enjoyment, pride, and self-esteem when they write to please someone else. Have you ever witnessed a sparkle in your child's eyes as she delivers to you a special birthday card or gift she has made herself?

Give your child an opportunity to brighten up the day of another person. How about looking into a local nursing home? Many residents would love to "adopt" your child and have her write a letter each week or every other week. Your child will enjoy receiving letters as well as writing them! Have her send a picture she drew, too.

Help your child to notice when other people have done something nice for her. Perhaps a librarian has helped her locate a special book or a sales person at the department store helped search high and low for her lost charm! Encourage your child to write to thank these special people. Her letter will surely bring a smile and may even be displayed inside the store for others to read!

#179
An Autobiography

Never look down on anybody unless you're helping him up.
~The Reverend Jesse Jackson

Children read and write stories and articles that they can relate to, understand and find most interesting. What could be more interesting, motivational and relevant to your child than a story about himself?

Suggest your child compose his own autobiography. It may help to first have him design a timeline of the most important events in his life. Interesting main events can be anything your child considers meaningful. Even if you don't agree, let him decide what's significant in his life. If his timeline looks sparse, help him recall events he might want to include. He can use the events in the timeline to guide his writing. The timeline will help him remember all the events he wishes to include and help him put them in chronological order as well.

Consider helping your child design a front and back cover for his autobiography and bind it together. Don't forget to add many extra pages in the back to record more important events as they unfold. Get creative, and enjoy time searching through old photographs to add, too.

This could be an activity for the entire family. Your life may not seem very interesting to you, but your child will enjoy reading about himself and other family members as well as learning about you when you were younger!

See our website for a timeline template.

#180
Biography

An expert at anything was once a beginner.
~Unknown

Activity #179 asked your child to compose her own autobiography. In addition, she may be interested in writing a biography of someone *else's* life. Suggest that she compose a biography of someone she knows and cares for such as a parent, grandparent, aunt, or uncle.

The first step would be to interview the chosen person (Idea #168). Using the information obtained from the interview, encourage her to create a timeline of the person's life before she starts. Creating a timeline helps to keep the events in order as well as guide her writing.

The benefits of this activity are numerous. Your child will be increasing her writing, interviewing, and organizational skills all while learning about someone she cares for. Be sure to share the finished product with the whole family. Consider making copies to share or email it to far away family members.

#181
Family Newsletter

Many candles can be kindled from one candle without diminishing it.
~The Midrash

Whether you have a large or small family, here is an activity that can emphasize the importance of family while giving your child another opportunity to sharpen his writing skills.

Gather the members of your family together, and discuss the possibility of creating a family newsletter. Consider the different sections your newsletter could contain. (Letters from the editor, sports section, school happenings, favorite recipes or activities, a riddle or brainteaser section, even the classifieds! All ideas can be considered!) Brainstorm snappy titles for each section such as "Spectacular Sports," and don't forget to give your newsletter a title.

Everyone in the family can participate. Each member can be responsible for a specific section, or the whole family can write it together. How often your family creates a newsletter is up to you. You may start by planning to create just one to send out in holiday cards. If you realize there is very much going on, you could make one per season. Grandparents, aunts and uncles are perfect recipients of family newsletters.

You may have a computer program that provides a newsletter format to utilize. If you do not have a computer, you may choose to simply write the newsletter. Writing with pencil or pen gives your newsletter character. It also allows you to be more creative with the space you have available. You might even want to add a photograph or stickers to help decorate it. In addition, if you write your newsletter (as opposed to typing it) your child will be practicing penmanship as well as spelling and grammar.

Consider sending your newsletter to family members that you don't see very often. Even if you choose not to send out your newsletter, you have spent valuable time with your family and worked together to create something to be proud of. Place the newsletter on your refrigerator, message center, or another visible place as a reminder of the wonderful things happening in your life and the value of a close family. Wouldn't it be great if others responded by creating their own family newsletters to send out for all to enjoy?

#182
Outlining

It's a funny thing about life;
if you refuse to accept anything but the best,
you very often get it.
~W. Somerset Maugham

Has your child ever been asked to create an outline from information she's read in a school textbook? Outlining is usually very frustrating because children haven't had practice at identifying a text's topic, main idea, and supporting details (Ideas #161 and #173).

Once your child has mastered identifying the topic, main idea and supporting details, outlining an article or story will be much easier. Consider this example once again:

HORSES (topic)

There are many things you must do before saddling your horse (topic sentence). First, you must brush your horse's back where the saddle will be placed (one supporting detail). You should also check the saddle and blanket for anything that might hurt the horse (another supporting detail).

Horses require a lot of care (topic sentence). They like to be on a schedule and they must be fed two times a day, usually at the same time each day (one supporting detail). Their feet must also be taken care of. If the horse will be ridden, its feet must be trimmed regularly. It must have shoes and the shoes must be cleaned before and after each time it is ridden (another supporting detail).

Once you've identified the components, outlining is easy:

Horses (topic)

    I. There are many things you must do before saddling your horse. (main idea/topic sentence)

          a. Brush your horse's back (one supporting detail)

          b. Check saddle and blanket for harmful objects (another supporting detail)

          c. (More supporting details here)

    II. Horses require a lot of care. (main idea/topic sentence)

          a. They must be fed two times every day (supporting detail)

          b. Their feet must be trimmed and have horseshoes (supporting detail)

          c. (More supporting details here)

Your child can practice outlining stories, articles, or chapters from her school textbooks. Outlining her text books will help her identify the important information in the book, increase her comprehension, and, when it's time to study for a test, she'll be ready with her outline of important information to study!

#183
"Million Dollar" Words

Many of life's failures are people who did not realize
how close they were to success when they gave up.
~Thomas Edison

Here's an activity that can help increase your child's vocabulary and encourage him to experiment with unfamiliar words. Work with your child to create a "Million Dollar" Words book. Simply fold several 8 1/2 by 11-inch sheets of paper in half and staple them together. Let your child create a cover for the book and inscribe his name as the author.

While your child is reading, encourage him to be on the lookout for new, unfamiliar or interesting words. When he finds one, have him add it to his "Million Dollar" Words book. For young kids, dedicate one word per page. Have him put the new word on top of the page and write his own sentence using the word near the bottom of the page. In the middle, encourage him to draw a picture to represent the word. (The picture will also help him to remember the meaning of the word). Older kids can put several words on a page and may not want or need the illustrations.

Now, introduce the thesaurus to your child if he hasn't used it already. A thesaurus is a book that contains a multitude of words used often and gives other, "better" words to use instead (synonyms). Words in the thesaurus can help liven up sentences, create more descriptive writing, and eliminate repetition.

Take a look at this sentence:

"That house is big!" she said.

By locating the words *big* and *said* in the thesaurus, your child can create a more descriptive sentence such as:

"That house is immense!" she exclaimed.

When your child looks up a word from his "Million Dollar" Words book in the thesaurus, have him write down three more interesting words on the bottom of the page. He may choose to write another sentence using one of the synonyms found in the thesaurus.

If you notice that your child tends to use a particular word repeatedly (such as *said* or *good*), encourage him to look up the word in the thesaurus. Use one of the pages in his book and dedicate it to all the other words he can use instead of *said* or *good*. Challenge him to find other words he tends to overuse and fill up a page with synonyms found in the thesaurus.

Look for opportunities to use the words from his book in everyday writing and speaking. The whole family can get involved by sharing words they may have come across during their day and posting them on the message center for your child to use.

Part 7
Math Made Easy

INTRODUCTION: Part 7 is dedicated to improving your child's math skills.

The beginning of this Part contains ideas and activities to use with your child in specific areas of math such as estimating, measuring, and graphing. Some activities can be done with children of any age. But if necessary, we've given suggestions to *extend* the activity for older children or *simplify* it for the younger elementary student. Some activities might not work for you and your child and that's OK. Some will work so well you'll want to build onto the activity according to the interest level of your child.

The second part of this Part is filled with exciting, child-appealing games to help build basic math skills in addition, subtraction, multiplication and division. These games are meant to be played over and over again, and most can include family and friends. They are designed to reinforce basic facts without the boredom of traditional pencil and paper math. The more the games are played, the more your child's math skills will improve and facts will become memorized.

We will specify which operation(s) the game reinforces and the materials you will need to play. Find those that work best for you and your family. If a game doesn't seem to be right for you at first, mark it and come back to it at a later time. You may find it will work perfectly with what your child is learning down the road.

#184
Making Math Meaningful

*I have come to believe that a great teacher
is a great artist and that there are as few as
there are any other great artists.
Teaching might even be the greatest of the arts
since the medium is the human mind and spirit.*
~John Steinbeck

For so many children math seems like something completely unrelated to their lives, just a subject taught for 30 minutes during the school day that gives them a lot of homework. Of course, a good teacher will show how every area of math relates to the children's world. Since you are a part of that real world, you can, too.

If you are aware of the specific math subject being taught in school you can find opportunities in your daily life to point out how you or someone else in your family is using that very concept. (If you are not, just ask! Teachers love having concepts reinforced at home!) Point out that math is everywhere. For instance, a trip to the store offers endless opportunities to demonstrate how you use math all the time in real life:

- estimate discounts, tax, etc.

- round prices

- count money

- compare values

- find unit prices (if it costs $10 for 6, then how much is just one?)

- find the price for many (if 1 is $3, how much for a dozen?)

Also, don't forget to show your confidence in math. Studies show many children, especially girls, have a low self-perception of their math skills. Your attitude can do a lot to change that. Instead of balancing your checkbook saying, "Boy, I hate all this adding and subtracting," say, "I'm sure glad I know how to use a calculator to check my adding and subtracting." Or try enlisting your child's help and let him type the numbers in!

#185
Estimating

No great discovery was ever made without a bold guess.
~Sir Isaac Newton

You can help your child *estimate* in math by finding real life situations where estimating can be fun. Our ability to estimate well improves with experience so helping younger children learn this skill in interesting and exciting ways now can benefit them in many ways later.

For all children, estimating the answer to a problem before solving it allows them, afterward, to answer the question, "Does the answer make sense?" If their answer is way off the estimation, they know to go back and recheck the addition, subtraction, etc.

Here are some ways to work on estimation with her (and your whole family!) in your everyday life:

- How many bites do you think it will take to finish your bowl of cereal?

- How many seeds do you think are inside your apple?

- How many teaspoons of water will it take to fill up your cup?

- Fill that cup to the brim. Estimate how many pennies you will be able to add without the water spilling over. (You may be surprised at the answer, thanks to surface tension!)

- How many inches tall is Mom?

- How much does Dad weigh?

- How many days old are you?

- Let her "pay" for purchases or bills at a restaurant. Before paying, estimate the amount of change she should get back. When she gets change she'll know if the cashier has given her correct change if it is close to her estimate.

Encourage her to make up some estimating questions for you!

#186
Time Well Spent

If you don't have time to do it right, when will you have time to do it over?
~ John Wooden

The most obvious way to help your child learn to tell time is to look at an actual clock (Do you have a standard one available?) and practice with your child. Again, it is an important life skill and is a concept most meaningful if tied to everyday experiences.

Besides simply asking, "What time is it?" try these problem-solving questions:

- How many minutes until dinner?

- How many hours did you sleep?

- How many hours are you in school? (Or try minutes for older kids!)

- How long do you think it will take us to walk around the block? (Do it, and time it. How close were you to the actual time?) (Yea! More effortless estimating practice!)

- Older children can be challenged to try elapsed time word problems. The following is an example: *Sam spent 90 minutes working on a school project. If he started at 5:35 P.M., what time did he finish?* Create your own word problems that are specific to your child's daily activities. It will become more relevant and interesting to your child if you use information from his everyday life.

Having a clock to manipulate will be helpful to your child. Try making one by using and/ or recycling household items. (Paper plates, construction paper, for instance.) Make up games with your child. He can move the hands around to figure out the answers. This will all be so much more fun on a clock he has actually made himself.

For fun: Try reading *The Grouchy Ladybug* by Eric Carle. It has a clock on each page to note the time the events are taking place and can open up a discussion about telling time!

See our workbook available for purchase online for some blank clocks.

#187
Patterns

The outline of your future path already exists,
for you created its pattern by your past.
~ Sai Baba

Patterns are everywhere! Kids love them! Recognizing patterns in numbers, geometry, and measurement helps get elementary kids thinking in a complex way that will help with the more abstract mathematical concepts they will study in higher grades.

See how many patterns you and your child can find in your everyday lives. (Time, months, seasons, numbers, schedules, wallpaper prints, stories. . .) Start a family list at the message center of patterns everyone finds. Be on the lookout *every*where.

You can also create opportunities to develop your own patterns. Try a family challenge. Place a bucket of coins on the kitchen table. Challenge each family member to create a unique pattern using any variety of coins. Then, see who can figure out each pattern and even add on to it!

For more permanent patterns, color hollow noodles (see below) and string them to create patterned necklaces your whole family can wear and enjoy!

To make colored noodles:

1. Place a few cups of hollow, uncooked noodles in a plastic, zip-close bag.

2. Add a few drops of food coloring and a tablespoon of rubbing alcohol.

3. Close bag and mix with your hands until all noodles are colored.

4. Spread noodles out on a paper towel to dry.

5. Do the same for each color desired in a new bag. Have fun!

Older elementary students will enjoy finding missing numbers in a sequence. For example, provide them with the following numbers and ask them to find the pattern: 1, 1, 2, 3, 5, ___, ___. Ask what comes next. If your child doesn't get it in three or four guesses, tell her the next number is 8. Have her guess the next number (13) and the next (21). Ask her to figure out the rule that tells how to generate the next number in the sequence. (The rule is to add the previous two numbers.). Encourage your child to create a pattern for you or other family members to figure out. You may find that her patterns are more difficult than any you may create for her.

Brown Bear, Brown Bear What do you See? by Bill Martin is a pattern book that young children are sure to enjoy!

See our workbook available for purchase online for some pattern activities.

#188
Tally Charts

When things get too complicated, it sometimes makes sense to stop and wonder:
Have I asked the right question?
~ Enrico Bombieri

Learning to make and understand graphs is an important skill. Before you can make a graph, however, you need to have collected some information. One easy way to organize information is in a tally chart. (Under each category are bundles of five lines. The first four look like |||| and the fifth is placed diagonally through the first four.)

To help make this concept fun, you and your child could think of something you would be interested in collecting information about. Perhaps:

- Tally the favorite ice cream or favorite color of the family. Could you call, write, or e-mail others you know to make your data collection larger and tally the results as they come in?

- Predict five things you might see on a walk around the neighborhood or at the zoo and tally them each time you find them.

- Toss a coin 100 times, and tally the results after each flip.

- To make a boring driving trip more fun, tally the colors of cars you pass.

Save the results (the tally charts) for future graphing opportunities (Idea #189). Don't forget, tally charts and graphs can be made and used for a wide variety of subject areas!

By reading *Caps for Sale*, by Esphyr Slobodkina, you have a perfect opportunity to tally. Try tallying all the different caps!

#189
Different Kinds of Graphs

Doing mathematics should always mean finding patterns
and crafting beautiful and meaningful explanations.
~Paul Lockhart

Graphing is a tool used to help people see relationships between certain things. They are everywhere and are a helpful part of textbooks if you know how to read them. You can help your child by explaining that graphs are just pictures of this information. Children are usually introduced to three basic kinds of graphs in elementary school: pie, line and bar. Try finding examples of them together tonight by browsing through magazines or the newspaper.

Perhaps the most common and easiest graph to create and interpret is the bar graph. You may want to start your graphing endeavors with this type. Today, think of all the ways you and your child could create a graph. Could you make one on:

- The computer?

- Poster board by drawing or gluing on pictures?

- Graph paper?

- An old window shade that is easy to roll up and store?

Creating a graph can be simple or complex depending on your child's skill level, available items, the purpose of the graph, and the limits of your imagination! If you help your child to see the graph as a picture that represents the information you've collected, it may help her to determine the type of graph she'd like to use and the way she'd like to display it.

*Newspapers are a great source to find different types of graphs and see how they are used in the real world for a variety of reasons.

See our website for different types of blank graphs.

#190
What Should We Graph?

Organizing is what you do before you do something,
so that when you do it, it is not all mixed up.
~A. A. Milne

To make the most of graphing, have your child chose something that interests him to graph. If you've created a tally chart (Idea #188), you've already done that. Some graph information can be collected rather quickly, but you could also use other high-interest areas to begin gathering data:

- Plant a seed; measure its height every day or week after it sprouts.

- Record the temperature for a month.

- For a very long-term project, record the number of sunny days each month for a year.

Now, use that collected information to create your graph. Be resourceful. How about borrowing materials from a neighbor or bringing some home from work to use?

Often, the amount of time or effort spent on collecting the information will determine how your child will choose to graph it. The purpose for the graph is also important. If he has spent a long time collecting data or would like to display his final graph at the science fair, the type of graph and how he creates it will be different than one he will do quickly for his own use. That's okay. That's life.

Don't forget to share the results with everyone who helped participate in the data collecting. They'll be interested to see how their choice compares to the others. (When your child explains the graph to others, it will enhance his understanding of it!) If you display it, it will make him feel even more proud of his accomplishments.

#191
Calculators

Teaching kids to count is fine, but teaching them what counts is best.
~Bob Talbert

Although you may hesitate to let your child use a calculator, there *is* a time and a place for it. If the purpose of an assignment is to demonstrate your child's knowledge of the multiplication facts, for instance, then obviously you will want her to work through the problem on her own.

However, a calculator *can* be a wonderful tool for your child. Below are some appropriate situations where a calculator can be used without diminishing the effectiveness of the assignment:

- It can be used for checking answers to difficult problems such as long division.

- Calculators can be used after estimating to find the actual answer which can then be compared to the estimate for accuracy.

- Story problems often lend themselves to calculator use. Most story problems are set up to have your child sort out the important information and numbers, decide which operation to use, and formulate a reasonable answer. The actual *calculation* is secondary.

Give your child opportunities to use the calculator in real life situations:

- At the grocery store let her total the bill as items go into the cart.

- Let her compare prices and find the best buy. (Which is better - 32 oz. for $3.29 or 64 oz. for $6.75?)

- Play the dice game (#211).

- Find the price of an item on sale.

#192
Grocery Shopping

It's easy to stop making mistakes. Just stop having ideas.
~Anonymous

If you're like most parents, the thought of taking your child grocery shopping probably isn't on your list of things you just can't wait to do, but maybe it will be now. Grocery shopping is actually a wonderful opportunity for learning. Your child practices many skills like:

- neatly writing the grocery list;

- organizing the list by sorting items by section or food group;

- clipping and organizing coupons;

- carrying those coupons and searching for the items;

- comparing the cost of the item with its coupon and similar product prices to determine the best value;

- estimating the total of the grocery bill as items are going into the cart;

- using a calculator to calculate the correct total as the items go in.

Of course, you won't want to do all of these things every time you shop with your child. You'd never get your shopping done! Choose one or two that fit in with what he is doing in school or that he needs to practice. As an added bonus, you will probably hear a lot less of "Can I have this?" and "Can we get that?" because it will keep him busy!

#193
Money

*A little thought and a little kindness are
often worth more than a great deal of money.*
~John Ruskin

Money is an integral part of every family's life. You can help your child learn to count money by letting her handle money in real life situations whenever possible. Encourage her to pay the bill at stores or restaurants.

At home, work with your child to set up a store using real money. It can be a grocery store or a toy store where her toys are on sale. Take turns being both buyer and seller. When you are the seller, you can model how to count back change to your child. Before you give her back the change, ask her to practice her estimating skills and *estimate* how much money she should receive. When you are the buyer, don't always give exact change for your purchases and have her practice counting change back to you. Of course, depending on her familiarity with coins and their values, make the prices very simple to start (i.e. "An apple is 10¢, can you count out 10¢?") and more complex as she learns more (i.e. "Here is $10.00 for a ride to soccer practice that costs $3.42, so how much change will I get back?").

Involve the whole family in your store. Younger siblings can play, too. Exposing your child to money early may help her grasp the concept easier when her time comes to be responsible for it!

Alexander Who Used to be Rich Last Sunday by Judith Viorst and the poem "Smart" in *Where the Sidewalk Ends* by Shel Silverstein are great resources with the concept of money in them. Your child can actually work right along with them!

#194

Manipulatives

*Not everything that can be counted counts,
and not everything that counts can be counted.*
~Albert Einstein

You remember that children learn best by *doing*. If your child needs help learning a new concept, manipulatives may be the answer. Manipulatives are simply anything that the child can move around (manipulate), count, stack, sort, etc. In school, manipulatives are traditionally used when a new math concept is introduced so the children can experiment with the idea in a concrete way before doing it with pencil and paper.

Manipulatives can be anything your child is able to move around that help him *visualize* the process of a math problem. Manipulatives can help the abstract become tangible as your child uses pieces of cereal, candy, buttons, or raw macaroni to actually "see" the process of addition, subtraction, multiplication, or division.

Dominoes are wonderfully fun to play with and are actually a great teaching tool for younger children. They are dotted with the standard configuration of the numbers. When children have a lot of exposure to viewing them, it makes *visualizing* numbers easier, which, in turn, makes mental math easier. (For instance, when learning to add 14 + 5, children can visualize four dots in the corners and one in the middle and use that to count on five versus using his fingers.)

#195
Fractions

Life is hardly more than a fraction of a second.
Such a little time to prepare oneself for eternity!
~Paul Gauguin

The word *fractions* often instills fear in many children and adults as well! Perhaps this is because it is another subject that is just not often made to seem relevant to children. You can help your child see that fractions, too, are a part of everyday life.

Begin by explaining the concept of fractions as parts of a whole thing. The bottom number (denominator) tells how many equal pieces there are in all, and the top number (numerator) tells how many of those pieces are being used. (Many kids find a pizza or candy bar easy to visualize when discussing fractions.)

Here are some ways to make fractions more meaningful:

- Slice an apple into 8 equal slices. (Name one piece as one-eighth and count off all the eighths. Then group 4 together and show how it can be four-eighths *or* one half.)

- Make a pizza together, and put certain toppings only on one-fourth or three-fourths of the pizza.

- Cut a sandwich in half. Halve it again. Name the parts.

- Look for 1/2 off signs while shopping at the store. Estimate totals.

- Challenge your child to fold any piece of paper in half more than 8 times. Try it. (Then, speculate why this is not possible!)

- Play a game of Fraction War with a deck of cards. (Idea #208.)

Eating Fractions by Bruce McMillan is a perfect way to introduce fraction concepts to your child. Don't forget to try eating some of the ideas you read about! *The Toothpaste Millionaire* by Jean Merrill is another good fraction book to read with older children.

See our website for step-by-step instructions for adding and subtracting fractions and fraction strips.

See Ideas #208 and #216 for a fun way to practice comparing fractions.

#196
Shape Up!

You're in pretty good shape for the shape you are in.
~Dr. Seuss

Help your child get a jumpstart on geometry by being able to find and name many different shapes. Younger children can be on the lookout for these shapes:

- Circles
- Rectangles
- Squares
- Triangles
- Ovals

Older children can be challenged to look for the above geometric shapes as well as:

- Trapezoid
- Parallelogram
- Hexagon
- Decagon
- Octagon
- Rhombus

To encourage your child to be on the lookout for shapes, try declaring this week "Shape Week." Pick one shape a day (or over several days) and look everywhere for it in objects at home or around town. Keep a list and challenge your child to make it as long as possible.

If one shape a day isn't enough, try making a tally chart (Idea #188). Write all the geometric shapes he'll be looking for across the top of his chart and use tally marks underneath the shape to keep track. Feeling ambitious? How about making a graph of the results (Idea #189)? Share the results with family and friends. His teacher will surely love it, too!

Tangrams are another fun way to learn about shapes. The tangram (which literally means "seven boards of skill") is a dissection puzzle consisting of seven flat shapes, called *tans*, which are put together to form shapes. The objective of the puzzle is to form a specific shape (given only an outline or silhouette), using all seven pieces, which may not overlap. Younger children will enjoy trying to create the shapes and older children should be able to name the shapes of each tan as they solve more difficult tangram puzzles.

The Secret Birthday Message, by Eric Carle is a neat shape book for young children, or try *Grandfather Tang's Story* by Ann Tompert for a great story for older children.

See our website for the tangram shapes and a few pictures (easy and more difficult) to create from them.

#197
Practice Makes Perfect

A journey of a thousand miles begins with a single step.
~Chinese Proverb

In order to excel at anything—sports, music, art or academics—children must practice. Our challenge is to find different ways to practice the same things over and over again while still keeping them exciting. Utilizing different strategies can make practicing math interesting and fun.

Many times children are bored with the prospect of practicing math, using the standard pencil and paper. The interest level of children rises significantly when they are offered alternative ways to increase their skills. For instance, you may want to invest in a lap-size dry erase board and some colored markers for a unique medium on which to practice. It's a small price to pay for your child's willingness to practice. Here are some suggestions for ways to use them:

- Flash cards can be fun again when she is allowed to write the answer on the board instead of saying it verbally or writing it on paper with pencil. Pick ten flashcards and hold them up one at a time while she writes the answer on her new board. Put aside the flashcards she has difficulty with and add to the next pile of ten. Let her check her answers and give herself stars!

- Give your child the answer and have her come up with the equation(s). As an example, for addition, you might say "6." She would write "5+1" or "3+3."

- You can write the problems on the board and give her a different color dry erase marker to answer.

- Virtually anything she is working on in school (cursive writing, spelling, and more) may be practiced using these erase boards.

Tips:

- Before starting any practice session, try giving your child two minutes to draw or write anything she wants on her board. After the two minutes, have her clear the board and get ready. Giving her the "free" time at the beginning will help her to better focus on the *math* when you begin.

- Does she have a short attention span? Watch closely for signs of boredom. If needed, stop and take a one-minute break and let your child doodle for a brain break.

- Try to limit the board's use to academic work so her interest level doesn't diminish from overuse.

- Use many different colors of dry erase markers to keep interest flowing. (There are even neat-smelling ones!)

#198
Story Problems

Minds, like parachutes, only function when they are open.
~Anonymous

Story problems don't have to be confusing! After all, in real life, that's mostly what we're faced with. Rarely are we presented with situations where we are given only the necessary numbers and told precisely what to do with them. More often, we are given much more information than we need and must sift through it to determine what is relevant. Then, we must decide what to do with it.

Children can be helped to do this when working through a story problem by following a few simple steps that help to break it down into manageable chunks. Try it with every problem by having your child determine these answers:

- What is the question? (Underline it!)

- Which are the important numbers? (Circle them!)

- Which operation will I need to use? (addition, multiplication, etc.)

- What do I expect the answer to be? (Estimate)

- Now do it!

- Does my answer make sense? Is it close to my estimate? Does it answer the question that was being asked?

Talking through the problems with your child can be an enormous help at first, too. When he hears how *you're* thinking through the problem, it is a good model for him. Ask him how he is thinking through it, too. The more the process is discussed orally, the quicker he will internalize it and be able to do it himself.

See our website for a step-by-step guide for solving story problems.

#199
The Family That Cooks Together...

I think careful cooking is love, don't you? The loveliest thing you can cook for someone who's close to you is about as nice a valentine as you can give.
~Julia Child

Asking your child to help you with cooking or baking not only makes her feel important but also gives her practice in important life skills. Let her help you set the temperature for the oven, check the timer, and measure ingredients when you cook or bake. Fractions come to life and have concrete meaning when you bake!

An older child can be challenged to make *1/2* of a pancake recipe or *double* your favorite cookie recipe.

Try this recipe for making a fun playing dough:

You will need:

2 cups of flour

2 cups of water

1/2 cup of salt

2 tablespoons of oil

2 tablespoons of cream of tartar

Food coloring

1. Put flour, salt, cream of tartar and oil into a medium pan.
2. Mix food coloring and water in a separate bowl and add to first mixture.
3. Cook over medium heat, stirring until ball forms.
4. Knead as soon as possible and store in the refrigerator or a baggie.

It's so much fun to play with, perhaps you'll want her to triple the recipe and share with family and friends!

Pancakes, Pancakes by Eric Carle has a fun recipe (for pancakes!) in it and is a good book to read to go along with this activity.

#200
Measuring

The measure of who we are is what we do with what we have.
~Vince Lombardi

Have you made the playing dough from Idea #199? If not, try it today. You and your child will enjoy making it and playing with it!

When you are done playing with the dough, you can use it to practice measuring with a ruler. Here are just a few suggestions to practice measuring with your playing dough:

- Make the longest playing dough "snake" possible and measure it in inches and centimeters.

- Try to estimate and make a snake that is six inches long, a foot long, and so forth. Measure to see how close you got. Then make it four inches shorter. Measure it now.

- Make an 8 cm snake and ask your child to make one twice as long, half as long, etc.

- Ask him to cut a 12-inch snake in thirds or fourths to practice fractions.

- Older kids can be challenged to measure to the nearest quarter of an inch.

Jim and the Beanstalk by Raymond Briggs and *Much Bigger than Martin* by Steven Kellogg both talk about measuring and are good ways to introduce this concept to your child.

#201
Body Math

To keep the body in good health is a duty...
otherwise we shall not be able to keep our mind strong and clear.
~ Buddha

Few things interest children more than learning about themselves. Use this to your advantage to increase your child's math skills. Below are some ways to practice math and have your child learn cool stuff about her body:

- It is said that you are as tall as the length of your arms from fingertip to fingertip across your chest. Help your child measure herself and see if it's true for her. Then, have her measure you and the whole family. If it does not hold true for someone, use subtraction to find the difference.

- Have you heard that your feet are as long as the area between your wrist and your elbow? Help your child measure both and let her calculate if it's true for her. If not, subtract to find the difference. Don't forget to have her measure you or others in your family.

- How tall is your child? Measure her and then figure out how many more inches or centimeters she'd have to grow before she is as tall as Dad, Mom, etc. How about calculating how many more inches she would have to grow to be 6 feet tall?

- Tell her your height and have her figure it out in inches. (i.e. 5 feet 4 inches = 64 inches) Then try the other family members.

- Show her how to take her pulse. (On the side of the neck is usually the easiest for children to find.) Count her heartbeat for 15 seconds. Challenge her to find the number of heartbeats she would he have in 30 seconds, 45 seconds, one minute, all day...

- Ask her to run in place for one minute; then, have her check her heartbeat again. Try having her compare her running heartbeat to her heartbeat sitting still. How much faster is the running heartbeat than the sitting-still heartbeat?

- Encourage her to watch a family member and count how many times he or she blinks in 30 seconds. Challenge her to calculate approximately how many times he or she would blink in 1 hour, all day…

- Which bone is longer: her thigh bone or lower arm bone? Estimate the difference then measure and find the actual difference.

The amount of math you and your child can do together is only limited to your imagination. I bet she can think of more math to do related to her body. Don't forget, many of the activities from above can be graphed! (Another good opportunity to practice graphing.)

The Children's Book of the Body by Anna Sanderman and Ian Thompson is a great body book for younger children. *How the Body Works/100 Ways Parents and Kids Can Share the Miracle of the Human Body* by Steve Parker is a great way to introduce this topic with older children.

#202
Cereal Box Math

The mind is not a vessel to be filled but a fire to be kindled.
~Plutarch

There's a multitude of math waiting on your child's cereal box or favorite snack box. Here are just a few questions to ask older children:

- If there are 120 calories in one serving, how many calories in two or three servings?

- How much more Vitamin C is there than Vitamin A?

- If you need 100% of vitamin B6 in a day and your cereal only gives 10%, how much more do you need?

- Pour a normal bowl of cereal. Then, pour the cereal into a measuring cup. How many servings do you *actually* eat in a day?

Try these with younger children:

- Count the number of vitamins this cereal contains.

- How many times is the name of the cereal written on the box? Look everywhere!

- Compare the amount of sugar to that on another box of cereal (or another food). Which has more? How much more?

- Look at the vitamins, percentages, and any other part of the nutritional information. Which ingredients make this cereal especially nutritional?

#203
Bug Off!
(Game for +, −, ×, ÷)

I like a teacher who gives you something to take home to think about besides homework.
~Lily Tomlin

Materials: a new fly swatter; flashcards or notecards.

1. Hand your child the fly swatter and tell her she's going to practice math. Already she's interested and ready to enjoy this game to help improve basic math facts in addition, subtraction, multiplication, or division.

2. Place cards with the answers to math facts she is working on in school or struggling with, face up, spreading them fairly far apart. Then, simply ask a question such as, "What is 3x4?" and have her slap the fly swatter on the index card with the correct answer.

Variations:

- Use another fly swatter and play the game with her. Take turns or race each other.

- Let her play with a friend (with supervision!).

- Have her teach a sibling (younger or older).

- Time her. Challenge her to improve on her time.

- Let her quiz you. She can ask the questions and you find the answer. She'll have to tell you if you're right or wrong so she *will* be learning. Remember, you learn 90% of what you teach someone else!

- Want to make it harder? Write the *equations* on the index cards. You would say, "The answer is 6." She'll have to swat the "2x3" or "5+1" card depending on the operation she's practicing.

- Don't forget to switch the index cards around often.

What Comes in Twos, Threes and Fours? by Suzanne Aker is a nice book that can help introduce the concept of multiplication.

#204
High There!
(Game for Place Value)

Some infinities are bigger than other infinities.
~John Green

Materials: ten note cards numbered 0-9, and for each player three more note cards labeled "hundreds," "tens," and "ones" laid out next to each other in that order.

Objective: To create the largest number possible or (if playing with others) the largest number of all.

This is a game that will help your child practice place value. Your child can play it alone or with up to two other people. To play with others:

1. Shuffle the number cards and place them face down in a pile.

2. A child chooses one card and places it under one of the place value cards, based on its value. For instance, if a 1 is chosen he would probably chose to place it in the ones spot, knowing another card he chooses will likely be higher. If a nine is chosen, he will probably know that placing it in the hundreds spot will make his number the largest possible.

3. The other players, in turn, choose a card, too, and decide where to place it according to its value, the other cards left, and whatever other cues they can use; this continues until all players have created a three digit number.

4. All players read their 3-digit number aloud and compare them. The player with the largest number is the winner.

Variation:

- Older children can be challenged to create the largest 4-, 5-, or 6 digit number. You can use the same set of ten number cards. However, instead of each child picking a number and keeping it, one child at a time picks a number and everyone writes it down secretly on a piece of paper, with columns labeled with place values, in the place they think best for making the largest number possible. Another player chooses a number and so on until all places are filled. Everyone will have the same numbers, but they may be in a different order. Compare to see who has the larger one.

- If your child is playing by himself, he can tell if he's "won" by determining whether the number he made really *is* the largest possible with the three digits he picked from the pile that time. If not, challenge him to rearrange them so the number is the largest it can be.

How Much Is a Million? by David M. Schwartz might be a fun book to read to help reinforce the idea of place value.

See our workbook available for purchase online for a High There worksheet.

#205
Create the Largest Sum
(Game for Place Value)

The essential thing in life is not conquering but fighting well.
~Pierre de Coubertin

Materials: Index cards

Objective: To create the highest possible answer (sum) to a 2-digit addition problem.

You can use the same 0-9 number cards that you made for "High There" for this similar game. Playing this game can help reinforce place value skills as well as 2-digit addition. Again, your child can play this by herself or with one other player. Tell your child the goal is to create a 2-digit addition problem by placing two numbers on top and two numbers directly below. Shuffle the cards, and place them face down in a pile.

To play alone:

1. Have her choose a card and decide in which spot she thinks it will produce the highest sum. (For instance, if she picks the 8 or 9 she'll probably want to put it into one of the tens positions. A 1 or 2 would probably go in a ones spot.)

2. Continue playing until four cards have been placed into position.

3. Have your child add the two 2-digit numbers and determine the answer.

4. Now look at the numbers. Is there another way to rearrange them so that she could create a larger sum?

Variations:

- Play together and take turns choosing cards until you both have four cards in place. See who has the larger sum. Could either of you have made it larger? How? Do it!

- Use blank cards as placeholders (already set up) on which to put each number card as it is drawn.

- Have a piece of paper sitting underneath the addition equation on which to write the answer.

David M. Schwartz also wrote *If You Made a Million*, another good book your child may enjoy while reviewing place value.

See our workbook available for purchase online for a game board for this game.

#206
Dollar Dash
(Game to Practice Counting Money)

There are people who have money and people who are rich.
~Coco Chanel

Materials: two one-dollar bills; pennies; quarters; dimes; nickels; two dice; a paper laid out sideways, divided into 5 columns: **Dollar, Quarters, Dimes, Nickels, Pennies**—in that order.

Objective: To use counting and trading up or down to "dash" from one penny to one dollar.

This game is great for practicing counting money and for 2-digit addition readiness. Played in reverse, it will give your child excellent practice for *subtracting* larger numbers as well.

To play:

1. Take turns rolling both dice, counting the number shown, and adding that many pennies to their column. (Because a penny is worth 1.)

2. Repeat this procedure until you have five (or more) pennies in your ones column. Now, trade in five pennies for one nickel (because a nickel is worth 5) and place the nickel in its column on your mat. (Extra pennies stay in the ones column.)

3. When a player gets two nickels, he can trade them for a dime and place the dime in the dime column.

4. When a player gets a combination of 25 cents (perhaps two dimes and one nickel), he can trade those coins in for a quarter.

5. Keep taking turns rolling the dice, adding pennies, and trading when necessary until one player has four quarters to trade in for one dollar—he dashed to the dollar! He then places the bill in its column and wins!

Variations:

To practice subtraction, play in reverse by starting with the dollar and subtracting for four quarters or ten dimes first, and then immediately a dime for ten pennies when the dice are rolled.

Anno's Mysterious Multiplying Jar by Masaichin and Mitsuma Anno, deals with adding larger and larger numbers (and the concept of multiplication) and could be used before an activity like this game.

See our website for a mat set up for this game.

#207

Go Fish!
(Game for +, −, ×, ÷)

> *Many men go fishing all of their lives*
> *without knowing that it is not fish they are after.*
> *~Henry David Thoreau*

Materials: index cards (as many as you have facts to practice plus the same number for the answers to those).

Objective: To make matches of a math fact and its answer.

This game can be made to practice just about any area of math, especially the basic math facts in addition, subtraction, multiplication, and division. Write one fact on each card and its answer on another. Remember to have your child help you make the cards!

Here's how to play:

1. Begin with a shuffled pile of facts in one spot and a shuffled pile of answers in another.

2. Each player selects three fact and three answer cards. (In the beginning, you may want to start with two of each. Little hands hold four cards easier.)

3. Everyone checks to see if they have a match already in their hand. (A match is a fact and its answer.) Matches are set down together by the player. It's a good idea to have everyone say the number sentence aloud as they do this: "6 x 7 = 42" to help verbally reinforce the fact for memorization.

4. For each turn that follows, the player first fills up her hand by taking any facts or answers needed to get back to 3 of each.

5. She then asks another player for one of two things: Either an *answer* to a fact she holds in her hand ("Do you have a 6?"), or a *fact* that matches an answer she is holding ("Do you have a fact that has the answer of 12?").

6. If she gets a card (a match) from another player, she gets to ask someone for another card. This continues until she does not get a match from another player. That player tells her to "Go Fish," and she selects a card from either the fact or the answer pile in the middle. If a match is made now, she lays it down, but her turn is over. Play continues the same for all other players.

7. The winner is the one with the most matches when the cards are all gone.

Variations:

You could play with "open hands" in the beginning, or always with younger children. To do this, place the cards face up in front of you while playing instead of holding them in your hand. This is not only easier for little hands, but also it allows your child to see your cards and use some critical thinking skills while determining the best one to ask you for. (It can also allow *you* to make a not-so-good request to her and therefore allow her to get ahead.)

Another good book dealing with the concept of multiplication is *Bunches and Bunches of Bunnies* by Louise Mathews.

#208

This Means WAR!
(Game for +, −, ×, ÷)

> *War does not determine who is right - only who is left.*
> ~Bertrand Russell

Materials: deck of cards or index cards

Depending on your child's skill level, you could play this game with a regular deck of cards or with any type of math facts your child needs to practice such as the ones you've made to play Go Fish! This game works well for addition, subtraction, multiplication, or division. Even the answer cards are helpful here because your child can continually see those numbers and become familiar with them as answers.

To play is easy:

1. Shuffle and deal out all of the fact cards (and answers if you desire) so that every player has an equal pile.

2. At the same time, all players flip up their top card for all to see. Whoever has the largest answer or number wins that hand and collects all cards shown. It's a good idea to have everyone say the number sentence aloud as they do this: "36 divided by 4 equals 9." (If you are using a regular deck of cards, flip up two cards each time and add, subtract, or multiply them. You can make all face cards wild cards and let the player choose which number it will be!)

3. Play continues until all cards have been turned up. The players count the cards they've won, and whoever has the most is the winner.

4. In the event two players turn up the same answer (remember even a "6" card and a "3 x 2" card are the same), a "War" is called. Each player then places one more card face down next to their original and a third face-up next to that. Simultaneously, the players flip over the middle cards and add up the answers to all three together. Now, the player with the largest sum collects all six cards to keep! (Or, it can be simply the middle card flipped up that determines who wins.)

Variation:

- Practice *greater than* and *lesser than* (traditional War) by simply comparing the cards flipped up. The greater number wins.

- If one particular skill needs practicing (like x4s), you can use a regular deck of cards. Pull out one of the 4s, and set it by the piles. Each player flips up one of their cards and multiplies it x4. Whoever has the highest product gets both cards. This way, you are practicing x4s repetitively.

- To practice all multiplication, addition, or subtraction facts, deal each player two piles of regular playing cards. Each player flips two at a time and multiplies them together (or adds/subtracts). Whoever has the highest answer gets all four cards.

- To practice fractions (either simply what the numbers mean for beginners, or how to compare them for upper elementary kids), flip up two cards. Place the smaller one above the larger one to create a fraction. Talk about what each fraction means. Draw them out if needed to show what they are worth. Whoever has the largest fraction wins the pair.

You could read *Amanda Bean's Amazing Dream* by Cindy Neuschwander to further reinforce the concept of multiplication.

#209

Near-Knowns
(Game for +, ×)

Playing games that are fun and exciting helps keep kids turned on to math. (And they don't even realize they are practicing those same old math facts!)

Materials: a deck of regular playing cards

Here's another game that children love and that can be used to practice basic math facts, specifically the doubles.

Knowing your doubles facts in both adding and multiplication can be extremely helpful. When they are memorized, they can be used to help figure out facts *near* the doubles. For instance, if your child has memorized 7 + 7 = 14, then he can also quickly figure out that 7 + 8 must be 15 because it is one more than 7 + 7; therefore, the answer is one more than 14. With multiplication, for example, if 6 x 6 = 36 is memorized, then your child can be helped to see that she can use that to figure out the nearby fact of 6 x 7. If 6 x 6 is 36, then 6 x 7 is 36 + one more group of 6, so 42.

Likewise, +9s are usually tough for kids. However, +10s are much easier. Kids can easily learn that 10 + 6 = 16, 10 + 8 = 18 etc. You can point out to her that +9s are near +10s, but just one less. So when she sees 7 + 9, she can think "7 + 10 is 17, so 7 + 9 is one less: 16!"

Here, again, you can use a simple deck of cards to reinforce these doubles facts. To play, begin a game of War, but for each card turned over, just double it! For instance, if you flip up a 5, say, "5 + 5 is 10." If you are multiplying, say, "5 x 5 is 25." After a few rounds of this game, many of the doubles facts are sure to be memorized!

See our workbook available for purchase online for a worksheet for practicing this activity.

#210
Pop Top Math
(Game for +, −, ×, ÷)

It's easier to go down a hill than up it,
but the view is much better at the top.
~Henry Ward Beecher

Materials: plastic tops from pop bottles and index cards or flash cards

Objective: to match answers to their math facts

Start saving the tops off your pop or water bottles for this fun activity! Use flash cards or index cards with any basic math facts your child needs to practice. With a permanent marker, write down the *answers* to the equations on the top of the pop tops.

To play:

1. Place as many fact cards as you think your child can handle on the table (or floor) face up, spreading them slightly apart. It is better to start small and have success. Success feeds interest!

2. Lay the pop tops in a line in order from least to most.

3. Say, "go," and have your child pick a fact, think of the answer, and then find its pop top. He'll place the pop top on top of the corresponding equation.

4. Continue until all pop tops are placed on facts.

Variations:

- Play with him. Split up the tops and see who can finish placing the tops on the correct equations first.

- Use a timer and see how long it takes him to put the tops correctly in place. Repeat the game and encourage him to try to beat his last score. In between rounds, practice any facts that seemed particularly tough.

- Play with a friend.

- Teach a sibling (younger or older) the game.

Tips:

- Make sure to switch the index cards around often so he can't just memorize what goes where!

- Keep track of the incorrect answers and start the next game by reviewing them. Don't use only the problems he is struggling with. Put some easy ones in there to encourage him, and let him feel successful.

The Doorbell Rang by Pat Hutchins is a funny book to read; it deals with the concept of division in a very basic and yummy way. (You'll probably want to make chocolate chip cookies together afterward!)

#211
Roll of the Dice
(Game for +, −, ×)

Just play. Have fun. Enjoy the game.
~Michael Jordan

Materials: two dice, paper, pencil, calculator (for younger children)

Objective: to be the first to reach 100 points (or other agreed upon number) by rolling the dice.

Sometimes the best part of playing a game, for children, is rolling the dice or spinning the spinner. Use your child's love of dice to play this game that helps practice addition, subtraction or multiplication.

To Play:

1. Everyone playing picks a number from 1 to 6. That number will be his or her *unlucky* number.

2. The first person rolls the dice. If her unlucky number does not show up, she adds the dice together and writes the sum down on paper.

3. Now, she has a decision to make: keep rolling or pass the dice to the next person. If she keeps rolling, she adds the amount on the dice to the *original* amount on the paper. She can continue to roll the dice and add the amount to her total, or she can be safe and pass the dice to the next person and protect the points she has accumulated. (Perhaps draw a line to show where one turn stopped and another began.) However, if she rolls her unlucky number on one of the dice, she loses all points accumulated *during that roll.* If she rolls the dice and her unlucky number is on *both* dice, she loses *all* points and has to start again at zero. The first person to reach 100 points wins.

Example:

Susan's unlucky number is 2. On her first roll she has a 1 and 5. She writes 6 on her paper. She decides to roll again. She rolls a 3 and 6. She adds 9+6 and writes 15 on her paper. She decides to pass the dice and not be too greedy. (She may want to draw a line to designate where she stopped.) The next time it's Susan's turn, she rolls a 4 and 5. She adds 15+9 and writes 24 on her paper. She rolls again and gets a 2 and 3. Since 2 is her unlucky number, she loses all the points she's accumulated on that turn (up to that line she drew). So she loses the 9 points and goes back to 15 points. If she would have rolled double 2s, she would have lost all points and had to start again at zero!

Variations:

- Allow younger children to add the dice together for each roll, but use the calculator to add it to their total.

- To practice multiplication, multiply the two numbers on the dice and add that amount to the previous amount.

- Need subtraction practice? Start at 100 and subtract down to zero. (The first person to reach zero wins.) If you roll doubles of your unlucky number, this way you would go up to 100 again.

- You can find dice with many more sides (ie. up to 9, 12, 20...) to practice larger facts.

See our workbook available for purchase online for a game board for this activity.

#212
Concentration
(Game for +, −, ×, ÷)

Each day of our lives we make deposits in the memory banks of our children.
~Charles R. Swindoll

Materials: index cards or flash cards, note cards with answers

Objective: to match math facts with their answers

This traditional matching game can be modified to practice any basic math facts. You will just need cards with facts on them and cards with the corresponding answers on them. Again, use facts that are particularly difficult for your child and need extra practice. (It sure doesn't hurt to throw in some he knows, too, so not every single one is hard!) You may use the same cards you've already made for other games, too! Experiment to find a comfortable number with which to play. Around 24 may be a good place to start.

To play:

1. Shuffle all cards and lay them face down in rows. (Such as four rows with six cards in each).

2. Have your child turn over two cards. If they match (one card shows an equation and the other shows its answer), he gets to keep the cards. If they do not match, the cards are turned face down again in their rows.

3. Play continues until all matches are made.

Variations:

- Time your child playing alone. Reshuffle the same cards another time, and see if he can beat his previous time.

- Play with another player, taking turns trying to find matches.

- For younger players, make two separate places for facts and answers so each pick he is sure to get one fact and one answer.

You could read *Moria's Birthday* by R. Munsch to bring up discussions about division and even place value.

#213
It's a Cake Walk
(Game for +, −, ×, ÷)

Materials: index cards or flash cards

Objective: to walk around, finding answers to math problems

Some children are very good visual learners. They only need to *see* information, and they can understand. Other children are auditory learners. By simply listening to information, they can comprehend. Many children, however, are kinesthetic learners. These children need to move around or touch physical objects to help them understand. If you have a kinesthetic learner at home (or even if you're just looking for another fun way to help your child practice math), try this game to get her moving and touching and increasing her comprehension of any basic math facts.

To play:

1. Place index cards or flash cards with answers to whatever math problems your child is working on or struggling with in a big circle on the floor. Spread them apart like the numbers in a traditional cakewalk.

2. Have her start in the middle of the circle while you call out a question such as "What is 2x4?" (You can also use flashcards.) Have her walk over as quickly as possible and stand on or by the index card with the correct answer.

Variations:

- Play with two or three people, and see who can find the answer the quickest.

- Have her time herself. How fast can she find the answer to five or ten problems? Have her play again and try to improve on her time.

- Write the *equations* on the index cards and say, "The answer is 8." She would then have to find and walk to the equation that equals 8 such as 2+6 or 2x4.

- Keep it interesting by asking her to hop or skip or gallop to the answer.

- How about giving her a break and let her quiz you! You will find the answers, but she will be learning also because she will have to tell you if you are correct, thus reinforcing the facts she is trying to learn.

#214
The More Things Change... ("New Math")

> *With the new day comes new strength and new thoughts.*
> *~Eleanor Roosevelt*

Today, many elementary schools are teaching adding, subtracting, multiplying, and dividing differently than how many parents learned it themselves. They are teaching it, sometimes, in several different ways to try to reach all learners and to get kids ready little by little. It can be frustrating when your child comes home with adding homework and you try to help by saying "Carry the one" and he looks at you like you just spoke another language. He's never heard of "carrying." Your way may now be considered the "traditional way" of teaching.

For adding, a popular new method is "Partial Sums."

For subtracting, a popular new method is "Partial Differences."

For multiplying, some popular new methods are "Partial Products" and "Lattice."

For dividing, a popular new method is "Partial Quotients" or "Ladder Division."

Of course, it is extremely difficult to help your child if the way the teacher teaches it is different from how you would. It is also confusing and frustrating to teach your child the "traditional" way, only to have him go to school and see it done differently. So, to help you out, we've included step-by-step instructions in the Appendix for how to teach each of these methods. The field of education is always changing, and new methods are always being sought and very well may find their way into your child's homework. If so, don't fret. Try searching the Internet for the concept, or even ask his teacher for instructions. Remember, teachers want concepts to be reinforced at home so they will be happy to send you info!

See also our workbook available for purchase online for step-by-step guides to these.

#215
...The More They Stay the Same (Strategies for + -)

> *If you don't like something, change it.*
> *If you can't change it, change your attitude.*
> *~Maya Angelou*

In the previous idea, you read about the fact that the way teachers teach math concepts to your child might be different from the way you learned how to do them yourself. However, some things never change. Here are a few basic concepts to reinforce with your child that will help her to become stronger in math:

- It is important to transition from counting on her fingers to using mental math (visualizing the math in her head). One way to reinforce this is by using a number line for a while. She can actually count on or back by moving her finger across the numbers to "see" the adding or subtracting.

- Use counters for tough math. They are fun and incredibly helpful for visualizing. Just like training wheels, they won't be necessary forever. She will ditch them when she is ready.

- Another great way to help her is by showing her how to visualize the standard configuration of numbers 1-10. Dominoes represent a perfect and natural way to see and memorize the way numbers look as dots. You can make up games with them, too, by putting the standard configurations on flash cards and playing some of the games in this Part. Once she memorizes that 5 means 4 corner dots and one in the center, she can "see' it in her mind and use that to add or subtract instead of her fingers.

- *Counting On* is a great strategy for adding. It simply involves saying the larger of the two numbers in your head and then counting up the other number. Again, doing this less on fingers and more using mental math is desirable. For example, 12+ 4 would sound like, "12... 13, 14, 15, 16; my answer is 16." This helps your child see that she doesn't need to count up to the first number but rather just say it and count on.

- For subtraction, there are really two strategies that should be considered. In both, though, you are finding the difference between two numbers. If the two numbers are far apart or the number being subtracted is small, *Counting Back* is best. Say the first number aloud, and then count down the other number of steps. For example, 18-3 would sound like, "18... 17, 16, 15; my answer is 15."

However, if the second number is close to the first, sometimes *Counting Up* is a much faster solution. For example, for 17-12, you might start with the 12 and count the number of steps it takes to get up to 17 (keeping track, using mental math). Say, "12... 13, 14, 15, 16, 17; it took five steps so my answer is 5." Try some problems both ways to show your child that, either counting up or down, the answer is the same!

#216
"Conversion Crazy"
(Converting Fractions into Percents and Decimals)

*A man is like a fraction whose numerator is what he is
and whose denominator is what he thinks of himself.
The larger the denominator, the smaller the fraction.*
~Leo Tolstoy

A number can be represented in many different ways. For instance, ½ can also be expressed as .5 or 50%. In upper elementary school, children are asked to convert fractions to percentages and to decimals. This often tends to be confusing to kids at first. The more your child "plays" with fractions and talks about what they mean, the more he will understand them. Try the following activity to make it all a little more fun!

1. Give your child a deck of cards with the Jokers and face cards removed. This leaves the aces (1s) through tens. Have him randomly choose two cards. Place them on the desk with the little number above the larger number. He has just made a fraction. Discuss what this fraction means. Sometimes, relating it to a pizza or candy bar helps it become more real. (For example, if he turns over a 4 and a 10 he has made 4/10. Talk about what 4/10 means. You might say it represents a pizza that is cut into 10 equal pieces and he ate 4 of them. This is less than half of the pizza because 5 pieces would be half.)

2. Now, see if the fraction can be reduced. If so, reduce it. For example, 4/10 can be reduced to 2/5.

3. Next, turn this fraction into a decimal. This can be done by using a calculator or with paper and pencil, dividing the bottom number into the top number (4 divided by 10 = .40). Discuss how much .4 is worth. Relate it to 4/10 to show how they represent the same amount. Usually, fifth-graders learn to do this on paper, but fourth-graders use a calculator.)

4. Now, turn the decimal into a percent by simply moving the decimal over two places to the right to create 40%. Again, discuss how much this is worth, perhaps relating it to a test.

Of course, your child will be doing a lot of converting, but perhaps having picked out the numbers himself will make it slightly more fun.

Variations:

- Let a beginner try rolling two 6-sided dice to get the two numbers for his fraction. The options will only be 1-6, which nicely limits the fractions he could make.

- There are also apps for Smartphones that have dice with varying amounts of sides. If you have one, have him roll some multi-sided dice to create his fraction.

See our website for a sample worksheet to help you organize this activity.

#217
"Hidden Treasure"

You must be the change you wish to see in the world.
~Mahatma Gandhi

Idea #20 explains how to play an original game we created. In that idea, we suggested the many ways to use this game. The beauty of this game (besides being fun and highly motivational) is that you can use it to reinforce so many different things. Many Parts in this book have a "Hidden Treasure" idea so check it out!

Math is no exception. Just place the facts your child is working on in the box and follow the directions. If you play this game with your child, when you pick a fact out of the box, you can model any helpful hints or ways that you remember it. For instance, if you pick out 9+5, you might say aloud, "Well, I know 10+ 5 is 15, and 9+5 is only one less, so the answer must be 14." If you get a subtraction fact like 18-16, you might say, "I don't want to count back 16 times, so I think I will count up from 16 to 18 since they are close; they are two steps away so the answer is 2." This thinking out loud lets your child hear how you problem solve and will help her learn to think that way herself. Of course, she wants to win the game so she may be more motivated than by simply practicing with flashcards alone.

See Idea #20 for instructions on how to play "Hidden Treasure."

Part 8
Science Fun

INTRODUCTION: This Part begins with general scientific principles that are taught in elementary school like observing and classifying and using the scientific method. We have also included easy and enjoyable activities that your family can do together that focus on some common science concepts and use the principles from the beginning of this Part. The emphasis is on *finding the fun in science* in and around your home. We hope this combination will help bring science into your home and make it real and meaningful to your child.

Every state develops its own science curriculum. Most schools have the entire curriculum for each grade posted online. Ask your child's teacher what they will focus on for the year, or go online and type your school district's name and "science curriculum."

The activities you read about and do here will no doubt give you lots of other ideas for creating unique activities on your own. Go for it! Young children often love science because of the endless possibilities and hands-on opportunities it offers. Capture their excitement now and let *them* invent their own experiments as well. If they learn to enjoy science now, they will likely hold onto their enthusiasm as scientific *lessons* become more involved in the future.

#218
Become a Collector

Science is organized knowledge.
~Herbert Spencer

Remember that children learn best by *doing*. Science makes that easy! Two of the first science concepts your child is taught in school are to observe and classify objects. In science, observing means to look at an object very closely and notice the small details and nuances that make that object unique. After observing several objects, your child may be asked to classify them. Classifying objects simply means to group them according to their similarities.

In the very early years, children are given various shapes of different sizes and colors and are asked to classify them. A kindergartener could classify the objects a few different ways. He may choose to classify them according to color (all the red shapes together, yellow shapes together, etc.) or by size (all the small shapes in one pile, large shapes in another, etc.) or by shape (all the circles in one pile, squares in another pile, etc.).

Classifying doesn't end in the early years. It becomes more challenging in the upper elementary grades. For example, children learning about the different characteristics of various animal groups (mammals, reptiles, birds) may be asked to observe the characteristics of a variety of animals and decide how to classify each animal.

You can help your child become adept at observing and classifying at a young age by encouraging him to start a collection. A collection can be anything that he enjoys looking for and keeping. Nature offers many suggestions. He could have a collection of:

- rocks;

- leaves;

- shells;

- insects;

- coins; or

- game cards.

As your child's collection grows, encourage him to practice his sorting and classifying skills. For example, young children could sort a collection of rocks by size, weight, or shape, and older children could classify the rocks into the different types of rocks (igneous, meta-morphic, and sedimentary).

Your child can also help you around the house as he sharpens his classifying skills. He could:

- help you sort and organize (classify) your junk drawer;

- sort and classify a box of photos to be put into a photo album; and/or

- sort clothes out of the dryer and classify into groups (mom's, dad's, mine, and so forth).

Imagine practicing an important science skill *and* getting a once-dreaded chore done, too!

#219
Getting Closer

We still do not know one-thousandth of one percent of what nature has revealed to us.
~ Albert Einstein

As we go about our daily lives, we see the important things, usually the big things, but how often do we, as grown-ups, stop and look closely at anything? Here's an opportunity to get down and see the wonderful things the world has to offer in a different way, close up, with a magnifying lens.

Magnifying lenses can be inexpensive and very fascinating. Even simple print in the news-paper takes on a new look when observed through a magnifying lens. Try having a variety of lenses (different sizes, various magnifying powers) available, and then go out with your child and discover how interesting things look up close. Try looking at these:

- insects: even dead bugs can give clues about the wonder of nature. For example, look for pollen dust on the body of a dead honey bee, find an insect's three body parts, and so on;

- the different parts of the flower;

- dirt—yes, dirt!—and what is in it;

- the veins in various leaves (compare them);

- a bean seed (dissect it);

- a bean seed after being soaked between two pieces of paper towel for a day;

- a feather from a bird (compare different birds' feathers);

- a drop of water on a clean surface;

- the skin on your hands;

- an eyelash;

- a single strand of hair; and/or

- an onion skin (try putting a drop of food coloring on it for best results).

Just going out and looking for objects such as these can be an adventure if you make it one. Make a list of items, and turn the outing into a scavenger hunt for them. Bring a special collection box or bag. Afterward, your child may enjoy keeping an "Up Close" section in a science journal (Idea #224). In the journal, she can write the details of her observations or draw what she sees through her magnifying lens.

See our workbook available for purchase online for a sheet to help you organize this activity.

#220
Stop and Smell the Roses

You can complain because roses have thorns,
or you can rejoice because thorns have roses.
~Ziggy

It's all in the way you look at things, or maybe in how you observe them. Using your five senses is an integral part of science. Observation, of course, relies on them. How can you help your child become more aware of using his senses? It's easy. Try an activity such as this one.

Take a walk together as a family early in the morning or late in the day. Bring a paper bag or bucket to collect special treasures you may find. As you are walking and talking, discuss the things you:

- **See:** Look up, down, inside of and under things. Try seeing the same old things in a new way today.

- **Hear:** Stop for a moment. Listen for the obvious and the subtle. Try to mimic the sounds you hear.

- **Smell:** Don't forget to use adjectives to describe your olfactory observations. What does that pretty flower smell like? How *does* your child describe the smell of dirt, the summer breeze, etc.?

- **Feel:** Discuss things that you can touch. How long has it been since you've felt the rough bark of a tree, rolled in the grass, walked barefoot in the sand?

- **Taste:** This one may be trickier. Help your child find some edible outside items. If you can't find any, try bringing a snack along and discovering how great it tastes outside.

When you get back home, make a collage together of the things you collected with your child. Try writing a poem about what you observed (Ideas #131 and #132).

It doesn't matter if you try this activity in the country or in the city, at a park or in your own backyard. What's important is the observation and using all five senses. Of course, spending time relaxing together is always great, too!

See our workbook available for purchase online for a sheet to organize this activity.

#221
"Hidden Treasure"

The brighter you are, the more you have to learn.
~ Don Herold

Hopefully you have used the game, *Hidden Treasure*, for reinforcement of many different subjects (Idea #20). Now, you can use this fun, motivating game to increase your child's science knowledge as well.

Try using science words and terms your child talks about or brings home from school on her homework assignments as cards for the game. You could also ask your child to bring home her science book and look it over together for science terms to add to your *Hidden Treasure* game, perhaps putting the term on one side and its definition on the other.

Involve the whole family in playing the game with science facts and terms. As you become familiar with the information your child is learning, you can find other opportunities during the day to ask her about what she's learned and check for comprehension. Younger siblings can get a head start on their science knowledge, and older siblings could always use a bit of review, too!

#222
What If...?

In all things it is a good idea to hang a question mark
now and then on the things we have taken for granted.
~ Bertrand Russell, English mathematician and philosopher

You probably do some sort of problem solving every day. Scientists, too, are always problem solving and questioning themselves and the world around them. They start with a problem or question and then begin to search for the answer. When trying to uncover all of life's unanswered questions (such as a cure for a disease), they gather all the facts they know are true and then begin to wonder "What if?" So begins the experimentation. (See more about the Scientific Method in the next idea.)

You can help your child begin to think like a scientist by helping him create an experiment for something he is curious about. When your child starts to experiment, he too begins with a problem or question. For example, he may want to find out how to make his plant grow taller. Then, he begins to find the solution by trying all of his "What ifs." *What if I placed it in a different location? What if I added nutrients to the soil?* And so on.

Help your child start thinking like a scientist. Play the "What If" game. Start by asking general questions that he can answer verbally such as the following:

- What if the dinosaurs came back?

- What if the Earth suddenly no longer grew grass?

- What if no one recycled anything anymore?

- What if the sun only shone for 1 hour a day?

- What if the rain only fell twice a year?

Then be on the lookout for science "What ifs" around your own house. For example:

- What if you forgot to feed the dog for a few days?

- What if you never did your homework?

- What if Dad just quit going to work?

- What if we just left the doors wide open every day?

- What if we got rid of all our watches and clocks in the house?

- What if TV was banned in our city?

- What if the power went out and did not come back on for a month?

Playing the "What if" game can help your child prepare for when he begins trying experiments on his own. He will understand that there are many ways to try to solve his problem or answer his scientific question; he just needs to experiment to discover which one is best! Besides, it's also a fun way to pass the time when you are driving in the car, standing in line, or out on your scavenger hunt.

Let your child make some of his own "What ifs" for you to answer, too!

#223
The Scientific Method

Somewhere, something incredible is waiting to be known.
~Carl Sagan

In the previous activity, you read about thinking in terms of *What if..?* Scientists do that all the time, but there are several more steps a scientist must take in order to determine answers. Many times they are able to perform experiments in order to get answers. You can offer opportunities for your child to do the same.

Experiments are so much fun for children! They offer hands-on opportunities to "play" with science. Of course, you will often do experiments at home just for fun and without much fuss. Occasionally, however, you could employ the scientific method in your experimentation. Although it sounds intimidating, it is not. It just makes sense. The scientific method is a thorough, logical way to work through an experiment. You can write all of the following information down on paper, simply discuss it, or do a combination of the two, writing down whatever you feel is necessary and discussing the rest. Here are the steps:

1. **Question:** Formulate a question that you have wondered about. What would you like to find out about? Write it down. (An example would be, *Is oil lighter or heavier than water?*)

2. **Hypothesis:** Make an educated guess as to the answer to your question. (*I think that oil is lighter than water.*)

3. **Procedure:** Write down the steps that you will take in order to complete the experiment. You should also make a materials list so you know what you need and be sure you have all ready before you begin. (*Materials list: 1 cup water, 1 cup oil, tall glass. Procedure: 1. Pour water into glass. 2. Pour oil into glass. etc.*)

4. **Results:** Measure and record what happened in your investigation. Was your hypothesis correct? (*I was correct. The oil was lighter than the water and therefore floated.*) Be sure to emphasize that even if her hypothesis is incorrect, she has still learned something! It doesn't mean she was wrong, just that the experiment proved something she hadn't known before.

5. **Conclusions:** Evaluate what you have learned or discovered as a result of conducting this experiment. Talk about what it means and how you might use this knowledge again in the future. Create any new questions. (*I learned that oil is lighter than water, and therefore floats on top of it. I wonder what else is lighter than water?*)

Your child will most likely be using the scientific method at school when working on experiments. It is used on many standardized tests now as well. The more opportunities your child has to participate in activities that use these steps, the more familiar she will become with them. Many other ideas in this Part offer ways for you to try this at home and practice using all of the steps.

See our website for the steps to print out.

#224
Science Journals

I cannot teach anybody anything, I can only make them think.
~Socrates

A great way to help your child comprehend something (such as a science topic) is to have her write down what she has learned. Since science experiments are so much fun, children often love to do them. (*All* the time!) Creating a science journal is a great way to promote scientific understanding and a perfect opportunity to have your child practice her writing skills in an authentic way.

Simply use a spiral-bound notebook or gather loose sheets of paper to add to the center section of a Duo-Tang Folder. It is a great way for her to organize her thoughts and ideas. She can use it to *plan* the experiment on paper (using the scientific method, Idea #223), and she can record her findings afterward. Many children also love to include illustrations, which is another good way to sum up what she's learned. Younger kids can try only the illustration at first and dictate the words to you.

When she has learned something new in science at school, you could encourage her to write a few sentences about it in her science journal at home. To inspire her, you might tell her you'd like to learn about it, too, by reading what she wrote. Read her entries over together. Add in important details that may have been left out. Of course, if you have done a scientific activity at home together, she can write about that, too.

Many standardized tests your child will take in school are now using the concept of writing about science. After the children complete an activity or experiment, they are asked to write about the steps involved in the process, their findings, and conclusions. What a great way to help her practice important skills in a meaningful way. Besides, it is just another way to build a bridge between school and home and stay connected to what your child is learning in school all day.

#225
Weather or Not

Nature is painting for us, day after day,
pictures of infinite beauty if only we have the eyes to see them.
~John Ruskin

This first part of this Part gave you some general principles of science and some generic ways to reinforce scientific skills. The rest of Part 8 will focus on specific areas of science and offer ways to have fun with it. Let's begin with the weather!

The weather always gives us plenty to discuss and affects most of us at least some of the time. It's there every day, rain or shine, to offer you plenty of scientific ideas to discuss with your child, too.

Isn't it hard to believe that there is the exact same amount of water on the earth (and in its atmosphere) as there was back in the days of the dinosaurs? Many children have a difficult time understanding that even when water disappears from sight, it is really just in another form somewhere else. Here is a super fun science activity that helps kids understand the water cycle in a firsthand way. Make your own rain in a bag!

Here's how:

1. Have your child draw a picture on a zip-close baggie with permanent markers. Include in the picture a sun and clouds at the top, a tree, and a lake going all the way across the bottom fourth of the baggie.

2. Fill the baggie with water to the top of the "lake" and seal tightly.

3. Tape the baggie to a window that receives much sunlight.

4. Watch and see what happens. As time goes by, the sun heats up the liquid (water) and air inside the baggie. The water evaporates (rises up as a gas) until the "clouds" can't hold any more water. Then it condenses back into a liquid and "rains" back into the lake. This process repeats endlessly just as it does on Earth. Notice you never add water to the baggie or take it out, but that it just moves around (sometimes more in the "lake", sometimes more in the "clouds").

Here are some other ways to help your child understand the water cycle:

- Try going online or to a library to find more information to read about the water cycle.

- What else could your child use to create his own example of the water cycle?

- Have him write what he learned (Idea #224) or tell someone what he did, what happened, and why.

- Could he make one of these rain-in-a-bag experiments for someone else and explain to them how to use it?

- Research different *types of clouds* (start with cirrus, stratus, and cumulous), and make an example of each with cotton balls.

- Chart the weather outside for a month. Tally the number of sunny and rainy days.

- *Evaporation Race.* Place one half-cup of water on a plate or in a bowl. Place it outside in the sun. Do the same with another plate or bowl, and place it on your kitchen table. Together, predict which will evaporate first and by how long. Set a timer. Check every hour or so. Record your results.

#226
Plant Parts

A weed is no more than a flower in disguise.
~James Lowell

Children can easily recognize plants. Your child can probably identify a variety of them, but can she identify all of the basic parts? Here are ten fun activities to try with your child (and whole family!) that will help make a plant's structure understandable in hands-on ways:

1. Discuss the *function* of each part. The best way to do this is by observing a plant your child is familiar with either in or around your home. Don't forget that trees are plants, too, just on a larger scale. Begin by asking your child what she thinks each part would do by observing it. Here's a guide:

    a. Leaf: makes food with help from the sun.

    b. Stem and trunk: like a big straw, they carry water and minerals from the roots to all parts of the plant and hold it upright

    c. Roots: like smaller straws, they hold the plant in the soil and send water from soil to stem.

    d. Flower: grows fruit and seeds for new plants.

    e. Seeds: allow new plants to be grown.

    f. Fruit: holds the seeds.

2. Eat the different plant parts. You can either do this as you encounter them (*"Hey, these carrots are roots!"*) or purposely set out to gather a few from each category. Here are those six main parts usually discussed in school and some options you could try:

    a. Leaf: lettuce, cabbage, spinach

    b. Stem: celery, rhubarb, chives

    c. Root: carrot, radish, onion, beet

    d. Flower: broccoli, cauliflower

    e. Seed: pea, peanut, sunflower seed, pumpkin seed

    f. Fruit: apple, tomato, peach, banana

3. After your family samples a variety of the parts, have your child ask everyone what her favorite part is to eat. Make a tally chart. Who else could she ask? Make a graph of her results, and decorate it with real and drawn plants. (See Part 7 for graph and tally chart info.)

4. Experiment! Carefully split the stem of a white carnation lengthwise about 6 inches up from the end. Place one-half of the stem in a glass of water with red food coloring and the other half in a glass of water with blue coloring. Have your child draw a picture of what she predicts will happen to the white carnation up above. Watch it for a few days. In just a few days you'll all be amazed!

5. Dissect a plant part such as a fruit, seed or flower. Use a magnifying lens to observe what's inside.

6. Plant a seed. Tape a seed to the inside of a clear cup. Fill with dirt. Water it a little each day, and watch as the roots sprout and the stem shoots out. Keeping it on the side of the cup like this allows you to see what you would miss if the seed were buried in the middle of the dirt.

7. What is your state flower? Research it.

8. At dinner tonight, begin a discussion of the different ways we use each plant part. (For instance, we eat them; we use the stems of trees for lumber and paper, and so on.)

9. Make up some *Plant Part Riddles.* "I take nutrients and water from the roots to the leaves. What am I?" Now have your child make up some for you.

10. Have your child record some of these experiments and her discoveries in her science journal. Don't forget to include illustrations.

See our workbook available for purchase online for a page that organizes this activity.

#227
Seed Experiments

To see things in the seed, that is genius.
~ Lao-Tzu

Planting seeds and then observing and recording the growth of plants is always fascinating for young children and another good way to bring science into your home. If it's possible, consider helping your child plant a real garden in which he can truly enjoy the "fruits" of his labor. Here are some easy and rewarding foods to grow:

- pumpkins;
- tomatoes;
- carrots;
- potatoes;
- green beans;
- peas; or
- anything he shows an interest in!

If it is not possible for your child to grow his own garden, he might enjoy the following seed experiment which gives evidence to the importance of water and light to living things.

You will need:
- three clear cups;
- potting soil; and
- bean seeds.

1. Fill three clear cups about 3/4 full with potting soil and place a bean seed in each cup just under the soil.

2. Place each cup in a different location. For easier recognition, have your child label each cup A, B, and C. Place the cups as follows:

    a. Place cup A in a location without any light (such as a dark cupboard), and do not water it.

    b. Place cup B in a sunny place, but don't give this plant water.

    c. Place cup C in the same sunny place but provide this plant with water on a regular basis.

3. Predict what will happen to each seed and why. It may be helpful for your child to draw a picture of what he thinks will happen to each. Your child will quickly see how important sunlight and water are to a plant's survival.

Older children most likely know that sunlight is important to plants, but does it have to be *sunlight* or will *any* light do? To test this question your child may want to try the above experiment with different variables. For example, try placing all three plants under different light sources. Cup A could be in direct sunlight, cup B under a lamp, and Cup C under fluorescent light. Whichever experiment you do, encourage your child to keep an observation chart or journal to record what he notices. Provide him with the resources he may need to understand the results of his experiment (encyclopedias, resource books, and Internet sites).

It is very satisfying for most children to plant something and watch what happens. Perhaps it's the fact that they are able to be a part of bringing something to life. If your child simply enjoys nurturing and watching something grow, he is sure to enjoy planting a narcissus seed. These flowering plants grow amazingly tall very fast. It's great for little ones who want to see something quickly. Older children will also enjoy watching the plant grow quickly and can use a measuring tape and graph paper to record the plant's growth as it grows inches in a matter of days.

Variation:

- If an outdoor garden is not possible, try growing some herbs inside. Complete kits can be found at nursery stores and are easy to do. How fun to use them later in a recipe together!

- Soak another of the seeds that your child is using for this activity in a wet paper towel over night. Carefully break it apart to see what's inside. Use a magnifying lens. Draw what you see.

#228
Bring Space Closer to Home

Shoot for the moon. Even if you miss, you'll land among the stars.
~Les Brown

Many children are fascinated with space. Like dinosaurs, it is obscure to them since they cannot actually touch it or be in it. Or can they? Here are ten fun ways your family can help make space (and some of the stuff in it) more relevant:

1. Do some research together at home, at the library, or via the Internet to discover the answer to some of these seemingly easy, but thoughtful questions:

    Why is a year 365 days long? Would a year on another planet be the same length? Why is a day 24 hours long? What's the significance of 28 days on Earth? What's the difference between rotation and revolution?

2. Read *Papa, Please Get the Moon for Me* by Eric Carle to introduce your child to the phases of the moon. Have your child sketch a picture of the moon tonight in her science journal. Each night, watch and draw the moon. Note the differences. Discuss whether the moon *actually* changes shape as it appears to do. Learn the names of the different phases (from new moon to full), and record them in the journal. If you have a window in the right place, you could even "trace" the shape of the moon each night (at the same time each night) on the window with soap! Then, you will even be able to track its movement through the sky over the month. (It washes off easily!)

3. Read *The Magic School Bus Lost in the Solar System* by Paula Cole for fabulous facts in a fun and kid-friendly text.

4. Cut about 11 large circles from lined paper to record three main facts about each planet, the sun, moon, stars. Staple them together with a cover to create a Space Fact book or tie a string to each and hang them in order from a hanger to create an instant mobile.

5. Create a poster of all the planets. Use neon-bright crayons to color the planets in order from the sun on white construction paper. Wash over them with black watercolor paint to create an interesting project. Decorate with glitter for stars. What could you use to show the number of moons for each planet?

6. Now, use the first letters in the planets' names to create a mnemonic device for remembering their order. (See Idea #334 for more information on how to do this.)

7. Lay outside on a clear night and look for constellations in the sky. How many can you name? What's your favorite one? Why? Learn more about it. Look again in a week or a month. Is it still in the same place? Can you find any other planets up there? (Venus and Mars are often visible.)

8. Have your child write his opinion, trying to convince others, of whether he believes there is life somewhere else out there. Have your whole family do this, and then share your ideas with each other.

9. Read *Draw Me a Star* by Eric Carle. Have your child practice drawing his own 8-pointed stars! Predict how many he could draw in one minute. Time him. How many did he draw? What's the difference between his estimate and actual number? Let others try. Tally the number others make. Make a graph, and decorate it with stars.

10. Have your child keep a learning log in his science journal to write about everything he learns.

See our workbook available for purchase online for planet activity pages.

#229
Reusing and Recycling Fun

We do not inherit the earth from our ancestors,
we borrow it from our children.
~Haida Indian Saying

As you are sorting through things that may be recycled, think about whether that object could be used for science purposes. Many science experiments can be conducted using things from around the house that were going to be thrown away. Here are just a few ways to turn common household objects into a science experiment:

1. Use a plastic bag, old string, and any object with weight to create a parachute. Make a few parachutes, each one a different size and with a different object (for weight). Discover what happens when you toss the objects and their parachutes when the surface area of the parachute is bigger or smaller or the object heavier or lighter.

2. An old 2-liter bottle can be used to make a "tornado." Fill it with water, and put an object inside the bottle. Put the cap on tightly, turn the bottle upside down, and spin it quickly around and around in a circular motion. Turn it right side up, and watch the object inside get caught in the tornado inside the bottle. Now, go recycle that 2-liter.

3. About to throw away a raw potato because it grew sprouts? Have a straw? Before you recycle both, challenge your child to try to pierce the raw potato with a straw. In the first attempt, don't let her cover the top of the straw. In the second attempt, have her put her thumb over the opening at the top of the straw. She'll be surprised at the results! See if she can figure out why that happens.

Ask your child to come up with some experiments using old or about-to-be-recycled things from around the house. You'll be amazed at the creative ways she uses what she has to make her own science experiments.

When it's time to recycle bottles that can be returned for money, perhaps your child can do something else for nature. Encourage her to save up that money to buy a tree, and then plant it together.

Reusing and recycling is not only good for the environment, but also it's good for the mind!

#230
The Birds and the Bees

One can never consent to creep when one feels an impulse to soar.
~Helen Keller

No, this activity isn't about *that*; it's about things that fly! Today, we're going to show you how easy it is (especially in science) to create your *own* questions, find your *own* answers, and have fun together while doing it. Let's begin, however, with some birds and some bees—and a few bats.

1. In Idea #143, there is a description of a Venn diagram. You can make one by tracing something circular. Search with your child to find just the size you need, or copy one from our workbook online.

2. Choose a topic such as things that fly. Now choose two things within that category to compare and contrast, such as birds and bats. (If you use these two, try reading *Stellaluna* by Janell Cannon for an adorable story filled with facts and fun about a bat that thinks she's a bird.)

3. Gather as a family, and use pencil to write in facts everyone knows about birds and bats, being careful to put them in the correct spot. (Just true of birds? Just true of bats? True of both birds and bats?)

4. Now, do some research. Find more facts to add to your diagram. Look through books, the encyclopedia, and the Internet; talk to friends or family who may know about them; even observe them firsthand if possible. You could even get out the binoculars and spy on some birds or visit a museum to get a closer look at bats. Change any facts that you find to be incorrect. You might focus on physical characteristics, habitats and homes, food, life cycles, etc.

5. Make more Venn diagrams according to your child's level of interest. Within this category you could also try two flying bugs, birds and bees, an airplane and a helicopter, butterflies and moths, even birds and airplanes.

Variations:

- Try with a *3-circle* Venn diagram! For example: birds, bats and bees.

- Use topics your child is studying in class. For instance, if his current science theme is plant life, you might compare and contrast flowers and weeds.

- Include detailed illustrations around your Venn diagrams. What exactly *do* bird feet look like? What shape are a bat's wings? What colors are on a bee?

- Depending on your child's interest, extend your fact-finding to include writing about a favorite topic. Help him turn his facts into sentences to create a paragraph, a report, or even a book about what interests him most.

- Catch some things that fly. Fill a Frisbee or bucket with water and leave it outside for a day or two. Observe and discover the various things that fly into it.

- Who was James Audubon? Do some research, and pretend to interview him; write about what you learn (Idea #168). If you and your child learn about him together, one of you could pretend to be him!

See our website (Idea #143) for ready-made Venn diagrams.

#231
What's the Matter?

We boil at different degrees.
~Ralph Waldo Emerson

Matter is everywhere, but what exactly *is* it, anyway? Matter is something that is observable with some of our five senses. Matter has weight and takes up space. It is all around us. To help your child understand the concept of matter, as well as its various phases, here are some facts to share and activities you can try:

- Discuss what is and is *not* matter. (For instance rocks, milk, and air *are* matter; ideas, words, and feelings are *not*.) Make a chart of what you come up with. Look around your home, even take a walk or a drive to find examples around you. Further organize the chart into the various phases of matter such as solids, liquids, and gases. Work together as a family on this activity. As a reminder, here are definitions of the three states of matter:

  - **Solid** matter keeps its shape. Examples: table, computer, and book.

  - **Liquid** matter has no distinct shape of its own but rather takes on the shape of the container it's in. Examples: water, juice, pop.

  - **Gases** have no particular shape at all and spread out to fill the containers they are in. Examples: air, helium, vapors. A filled balloon helps to show children that gas *is* actually a form of matter because they can see the balloon expanding.

- Water is the perfect example to use for many of these experiments. It is easy to change so that you can see all three states.

- Conduct experiments to change states of matter. (Note: Matter changes states when heat energy is added or removed from the object.)

  - **Melting** means changing from a solid to a liquid. A fun experiment is to have a race to melt two ice cubes. Place each on a plate. Have your child decide how she will make her ice cube melt the fastest, and you do the same. Predict what will happen, and watch the ice melt.

  - **Freezing** or **solidifying** means changing from a liquid back to a solid. Try freezing juice in your ice cube tray. Once juice begins to freeze, stick a toothpick in the center of each. You will have a fun experiment to eat in a few hours.

  - **Evaporating** means changing from a liquid to a gas. Boil some water in a pan. Watch the steam coming up. Discuss where it is coming from and why.

- **Condensing** means changing from a gas back to a liquid. Now, put a dry lid on the boiling pan of water for a few minutes. Take it off. Shake it, turn it. Discuss how the droplets got there. Another great experiment to show condensation is to fill a glass of colored water with many ice cubes. (Making colored cubes is a good idea, or use juice and your juicy cubes!) Place the filled glass in a warm place and watch what happens. Discuss why and how water is forming on the *outside* of the glass. (Having colored water on the inside helps to prove to kids that the water isn't just seeping through the glass to the outside because the water on the outside is clear.) This experiment helps kids see, too, that there is water in the air. (The scientific explanation: The air is cooled as it passes by the glass so it condenses on the outside.)

- Remember that not all matter responds the same way to changes. (See Idea #233 for more experiments.)

See our workbook for an organizer for this activity.

#232
What on Earth?

Find your place on the planet. Dig in, and take responsibility from there.
~Gary Snyder

Help your child learn the order of the planets from the sun by creating an acronym using the first letter of each planet. Here is the order of the planets from closest to the sun to the farthest: Mercury, Venus, Earth, Mars, Jupiter, Saturn, Uranus, and Neptune. (Scientists now consider Pluto not to be a planet). When Pluto was considered a planet, a popular acronym to remember the order was My Very Energetic Mother Just Served Us Nine Pizzas. Now that Pluto is no longer considered a planet, sit with your child and have fun making up new acronyms with the eight planets. If your child creates it, he's more likely to remember it!

You can help him get an idea of how far away each planet is from the sun with this activity.

1. Use adding machine tape, and roll it out until it is about 20 feet long. Lay it on the floor or other hard surface.

2. At the left end of the paper, have your child draw the Sun and label it.

3. Using a ruler or yardstick, measure the following distances from the sun for each planet and draw and label each planet:

   a. Mercury: Draw Mercury about 3 inches away from the Sun.

   b. Venus: Draw Venus about 5 inches away from the Sun.

    c. Earth: Draw Earth about 7 inches away from the Sun.

    d. Mars: Draw Mars about 10 inches away from the Sun.

****** Draw a belt of asteroids between Mars and Jupiter. **********

    e. Jupiter: Draw Jupiter about 34 inches away from the Sun.

    f. Saturn: Draw Saturn about 5 ¼ feet away from the Sun.

    g. Uranus: Draw Uranus about 11 feet away from the Sun.

    h. Neptune: Draw Neptune about 16 ½ feet away from the Sun.

4. Look at books or the Internet to see the colors of each planet (and check for rings and other characteristics); have your child use colored pencils to color each planet.

5. Find a place in your home to display it. It is a great visual to understand how far away planets are from the sun. Use the strip to discuss how the distance away from the sun affects temperature and why life like ours on Earth cannot exist on those other planets.

#233
Ideas for Using the Scientific Method

*The most exciting phrase to hear in science,
the one that heralds the most discoveries,
is not 'Eureka!' (I found it!) but 'That's funny...'*
~Isaac Asimov

Of all the advancements in TV today, many of us say that being able to skip over commercials is our favorite! However, as you are thinking like a scientist lately, there can be some fun in watching those commercials. Many of the experiments you have been reading (and will read) about in this Part can be done quickly with minimal preparation and with materials you probably already have in your home, but if your child is enthusiastic about science and seems to love these quick and easy experiments, you might want to capture his excitement and try some more involved experiments. One fantastically fun and authentic way to do this is to put the claims made by those commercials to the test by using the scientific method. (See Idea #223 to review the procedure.) Here are a few ideas to suggest to your child:

- Which brand of battery really does last the longest?

- Which type of gum blows the biggest bubbles or has a flavor that lasts the longest?

- Which brand of toilet paper actually has the longest roll?

- Which cereal stays crunchiest the longest. Which bran cereal has the most raisins?

- Which brand of paper towel absorbs more?

- Which brand of baggie holds the most?

- Which brand of cola do most people really prefer?

- Which pen does write the longest?

Try one of these or make up your own as a family. The possibilities are endless!

Don't forget to help your child plan the experiment the first few times. You may want to be involved throughout the steps as well, depending on your child's age and familiarity with the steps of the scientific method. Now is a good time to discuss two other things as well.

The first is that, in science, things are not always exact and experiments don't always work out exactly as we'd like them to every time. That's okay. That is why it is important to make a detailed plan of how you will carry out the experiment so that if things don't work out, you know exactly where to make some changes for next time, and if things do work out, you will be able to explain to someone exactly how you got those results.

The second is that you can help minimize discrepancies by trying to predict the effects any variable may have. Variables are unexpected things that can affect the outcome of your experiment. Attempting to determine and eliminate them before your child begins the experiment will help make his results more reliable. That's why planning the procedure of the experiment (in writing on paper) can be extremely helpful. He can read or show it to a few others and receive input on ways he might improve his steps even before beginning. If he wants to be able to state his findings as a fact, he will need proof, and a well-planned procedure is a great start.

Tips:

- Using at least three different products in his experiments will help make his results more authentic. Your child should be sure to apply exactly the same test to all of the products involved in exactly the same way.

- If your child is young, you can do the writing portion (taking dictation) of the scientific method. It will be very beneficial to him to see how the written part is essential to help organize the experiment and describe outcomes.

- When you do watch TV or flip through a magazine, be on the lookout for the promises some ads make, and suggest your child try it for himself.

These ideas are usually perfect for science fair demonstrations and experiments for school, too!

#234
Bath Tub Science

99% of the water on the earth is undrinkable because 97% is in the oceans-salt water.
2% is frozen fresh water in the polar ice caps.
Only 1% is drinkable fresh water.
~The Magic School Bus Waterworks by Joanna Cole

You don't have to visit museums (although that is a great idea!) or be in a classroom to do fun science experiments. Science is as close as your own bathtub. Even the youngest of children can experiment here by filling various containers to compare volumes and watching things float and sink. No matter what your child's age, have her put on her bathing suit and jump on in. (Of course, she could also try them in the sink and not get wet!) Try some of these fun ideas to get you started.

1. Play "Sink or Float." Give your child a variety of objects. Have your child predict first whether they will sink or float, then let her try it. Try to choose some that may not be found in the bathtub normally. (Of course, be sure they're waterproof!) What fun it is to watch Dad's old shoe float or Mom's coffee mug sink to the bottom! Now switch roles and let her find things for you to predict and experiment with. You can use modeling by talking out loud through your reasoning. (Hint: Density, not weight, determines whether an object sinks or floats in a substance. You may wish to read more about this, but an easy example is that a huge boat will float while a marble will not.)

2. Fill three glasses (be sure to use the same kind) with a different amount of water. Tap gently with a spoon or something hard from the tub and hear the different sounds they make. Why is this? Discuss it. Create a tune or two together!

3. Offer your child two (or more) different containers. (The more different in shape, the better!) Discuss volume and predict which of them will hold more water. Try it by filling one and pouring its water directly into the other.

4. Mix primary colored bath tablets (such as red, yellow, and blue) into the bath/sink water, predicting first what color you will make. Choose different combinations during each scientific bathtub/sink experience.

5. Make a boat out of tinfoil. Predict how many pennies you will be able to put in it while it still stays afloat. Try adding pennies until it sinks. Count them. How close were you? How could you rebuild your boat to make it hold more pennies? Try it!

Tips:

- Go put your suit on, too, and join in on the fun.

- Try these activities with friends and family in a wading pool on a nice sunny (hot) day.

See our workbook for an organizer for this activity.

#235
More Water Fun

Every dewdrop and raindrop had a whole heaven within it.
~Henry Wadsworth Longfellow

Of course you don't have to be *in* the bathtub to have some water fun. You can also just fill up the tub and experiment with your child kneeling beside it or fill up the kitchen sink, a big bucket, or a bowl. Try one of these activities. Just find some water and have fun!

1. Fill a glass with water to the brim. Slowly slide pennies into the water, one at a time. Watch the water level rise above the brim! Discuss how surface tension makes this possible.

2. Use those pennies again. Using an eyedropper, carefully place one drop of water at a time onto a penny. Predict how many will fit on before falling off. Again, surface tension is the reason this is possible. Try it again. Did you fit the same amount of drops? Remind your child that scientific experiments are not always perfect. Sometimes results vary. Can you determine the reason *these* results may vary?

3. Actually *see* the surface tension with this experiment. Pour water onto a light-colored plate. Now, sprinkle pepper onto the surface of the water. Carefully squeeze a drop of dishwashing liquid or touch a bar of soap to one spot on the edge of the water. Watch the pepper flee from the soap to the other side of the plate. You have just broken the surface tension of the water! Discuss how this experiment supports why people use soap to wash dishes.

4. Pour 1/2 cup of water into a clear glass. Now add 5 tablespoons of salt. Stir well, and leave the mixture in a safe spot where it can sit undisturbed for a week. Predict what will happen to the salt and to the water. Watch daily as the water slowly evaporates into the air leaving the salt behind.

5. Reinforce your sink and float experiment with this activity. Clean out an empty plastic pop bottle. Fill 1/3 of it with water. (Using colored water works nicely.) Have your child predict what will happen when you add equal parts of cooking oil and then syrup to fill the other 2/3 of the bottle. Which liquid will be the heaviest, the lightest? A variation is to use slightly less of each liquid and to add small items to the bottle, such as a cork, rock, or glitter. Predict where each of these items will end up. Glue the cap on tightly, and your child can carry around his experiment and explain it (and sinking and floating) to everyone he meets!

6. Take out two ice cubes, and lay them on plates. Place a few tablespoons of salt onto one of the ice cubes. Leave the other one alone. Set them both in the same place undisturbed. Predict what will happen to each of the cubes as they melt. Check in on your experiment every ten minutes. Can you measure and record the results? Discuss how this experiment helps to explain why people throw salt onto icy sidewalks and roads in the winter.

7. Make a mug of hot water and put in 10 drops of red food coloring. Fill a mug with cold water, and add ten drops of blue food coloring. Now, gently pour them, one at a time, into a large, clear glass. Watch carefully and predict what will happen. At first, the colors do mix, and the water becomes purple. After a few minutes, though, the hot (red) water rises, and the cold (blue) water falls. Note: This experiment works best with extremely hot and very cold water. Be careful not to let children too close to the hot stuff!

8. Sitting down together as a family, make a list of 100 ways water is used.

See our workbook available for purchase online for several water fun activity organizers.

#236
Kitchen Chemistry

The joy of discovery is certainly the liveliest that the mind of man can ever feel.
~Claude Bernard

Just as the bathtub might have provided an unexpected place to learn about science, your own kitchen can also give you and your child with a place to experiment. Here's a few fun ways for your child to be a scientist right in her own kitchen.

1. Try writing an invisible secret message in lemon juice. Then, carefully hold it next to a heat source, or brush it with an iodine and water mixture, and see what happens!

2. Make raisins dance! Add some raisins to a clear glass of water. Now, stir in some baking soda and see the results!

3. Make a volcano in a mug! Add baking soda to a mug. Now, add vinegar. Watch the results! (This works well if your child ever has to make a volcano for class; she can make it erupt, too!)

4. Blow up a balloon without your mouth! The mixture above works well for other things, too. Add baking soda to a long-necked bottle. Be ready with a balloon that fits tightly over the neck of the bottle. Drop in vinegar, and quickly seal the balloon over the bottle; watch the gasses produced fill up the balloon for you!

5. Make some crystals. Place a few charcoal bricks in an aluminum pan. Pour food coloring over the charcoal. Now, place a solution of the following over that: 6 Tbs of salt, Bluing, 6 Tbs of water, 1 Tbs of ammonia. Let it sit in a warm place, and watch the crystals grow.

6. For an edible crystal, make rock candy! Fill a glass or a jar with a sugar water solution, adding as much sugar as the water will hold. Tie a string to a pencil, and lay it across the opening of the glass so that the string falls into the mixture. Set the glass somewhere where it won't be jostled. Watch as the sugar crystals climb the rope! Play around with food colorings and flavorings, too.

7. Create magic milk! Pour milk on a plate so it covers the plate. Add a few drops of food color to the middle. Take a cotton swab, and dip it into dishwashing detergent (liquid). Touch (don't stir, just touch) the swab to the middle of the plate, and watch what happens to the colors. Work together to find out why!

8. Create a chemical reaction with grape juice! Pour two glasses of purple grape juice in clear cups. (We recommend doing this outside to avoid accidental spills and stains!) In one cup, add lemon juice. Watch what happens to the grape juice when an acid (lemon juice) is added. (It should turn red). In the other glass, add two spoonfuls of baking soda (base). When you add a base (baking soda) to an indicator (grape juice), it should turn green. Help your child read more about bases and acids to find out why this happened.

#237

Egg-citing Egg-speriments

Education is learning what you didn't even know you didn't know.
~Daniel J. Boorstin

Have you ever thought of eggs as being especially scientific? Well, perhaps not, but eggs *can* actually provide many opportunities for learning, such as experimentation, scientific discovery, and real family fun! Round up your family, "break" out the eggs, and give these super-fun *egg*-speriments a try:

1. Place a raw egg in a deep bowl of vinegar, which is an acid, and ask your child to predict what he thinks will happen. Wait a few days; then, observe and discuss. (Within a few days, the acidic vinegar will dissolve the calcium in the eggshell, causing it to thin and become translucent. If you carefully hold the egg up to a light, you should be able to make out the parts inside! Kids will delight at the new, rubbery feel of the egg, too! Does the egg look bigger now? Why do you think this could be? Pop it open. Smell it. See if you can figure out why.

2. Offer your child a raw egg and a hard-boiled egg. Challenge him to guess which of the eggs is raw and which is hard-boiled without shaking them. Now, try spinning one of the eggs on its bottom. Does it spin upright well? Try the other egg. How does this one spin compared to the first? Ask your child why he thinks they spin differently. Tell him hard-boiled eggs spin well. Can he tell which one is the raw egg and which is hard-boiled now? Find out why this is true.

3. Gather up a raw egg and lots of *stuff*! Tell your family that you are going to drop a raw egg off of a ladder (or out a window etc.)! After the "EEEWWW!"'s, tell them the mission: to create a "shuttle" for the little "astronaut egg" so that he can remain safe on impact. (Let your child be the leader of the operation.) Now, set off together to figure out how to build it. Construct it together. Put the egg inside, and give it a try. Did he survive? (If he did, talk about why.) If he turned out more like Humpty Dumpty, brainstorm ways to make the shuttle safer for him. Try it as many times as needed to bring the little astronaut egg back down to Earth safely.

4. Place a peeled, hard-boiled egg on the greased mouth of a glass bottle with a wide bottom. Carefully light a piece of paper on fire, and gently place it in the bottom of the bottle. Quickly set the egg back in the mouth of the bottle. Ask your child to predict what will happen. (As the paper burns, it produces a gas. As the gas cools, it creates a partial vacuum in the bottle. The air pressure outside is so much stronger than inside now that it actually pushes the egg inside!)
   Extension: For an older child, you could present this experiment as a challenge. Give him the egg and the bottle, and ask him to figure out a way to get the egg inside without ripping it or even touching it after it has been placed in the mouth of the bottle.
   CAUTION! Never allow children to light the match or come too close to the flame.

5. Make an egg graph together as a family. Poll people as to how they like their eggs prepared: hard-boiled, fried, sunny-side up, scrambled, or poached. Tally answers and create an egg-shaped graph based on the results. (See Idea #189 for graphing hints.)

6. Fill a glass with water and carefully drop in a hard-boiled egg. (It should sink.) Discuss the density of the egg being greater than the water. Allow your child to predict how he could get this same egg to float here. (Try adding a few teaspoons of salt at a time and gently stirring the water. Eventually, the egg will begin to float because you changed the water's density and eventually made it greater than the egg's density so it could float.)
   Hint: Colored eggs work nicely for this activity because you can still see the color through the salty water.

7. Carefully break open a raw egg onto a large plate. Allow the whole family to look at all of the egg parts. Observe closely with the magnifying lens. Study the broken shell, too. Discuss how you could find out what each part is called and what it is for. Find out together. If you are comfortable with it, allow your child to touch the parts with his fingers for a real kinesthetic experience.

CAUTION! Be sure to wash hands carefully after handling raw eggs. Very young children should be supervised well.

Tips:

Use the scientific method, written or oral, with many of these activities.

See our workbook for several egg-citing worksheet organizers.

#238
Simple Machines Made Simple

The squeaking wheel doesn't always get the grease. Sometimes it gets replaced.
~*Vic Gold*

The six simple machines are the lever, wedge, pulley, wheel (and axle), inclined plane, and the screw. They, alone or combined in the bigger machines they make up, help to make our lives easier. Although they may be taught only once or twice in elementary school, they are the foundation for many other areas of physical science and technology (and many other classes to come). They may also seem foreign and abstract to many children. Here are ways that you can make learning about simple machines meaningful and easy:

1. Find examples of each simple machine around your home. Make a chart. Tally your finds. For instance:

   - Lever: Fork, screwdriver, scissors, shovel…

   - Wedge: Knife, nail, axe, doorstop…

   - Pulley: On a flagpole, vertical blinds, crane…

   - Wheel and Axle: Toy cars, your car, roller blades..

- Inclined Plane: Ramp, steps, ladder...
- Screw: Screws, some spiral chair spines...

2. Discuss how each is used and could be used.

3. Pick a job to do that uses a simple machine. Discuss how that job could be done without the use of simple machines.

4. Use many or all of these simple machines to make a project together as a family. You could do something big like build a tree fort, something useful like make a bug box, or something silly like create an object simply for fun and to practice identifying and using simple machines.

5. Create your own experiment using an inclined plane. Use a board, and elevate it by propping up one end with several books so it becomes an inclined plane. At the bottom of the board, place a Styrofoam cup (the closed part of the cup should be touching the bottom to the board). Choose several balls with different masses/ weight. Take turns rolling the balls down the inclined plane, and use a ruler/yardstick to measure how far each ball moves the Styrofoam cup. Discuss how the mass of the ball affects the distance the cup moved. Change the height of the inclined plane and repeat the experiment. How does the height affect the distance the cup moved? Have your child create a graph showing the results.

#239
Physical Changes

We must always change, renew, rejuvenate ourselves; otherwise we harden.
~Goethe

Physical changes may sound fancy, but they are really quite simple. They are changes in the size, shape, or appearance (of an object) only. (No new substance is created.) Try these fun-filled, family activities that will help your child understand physical changes:

1. Experiment with popping popcorn. Try the old-fashioned way: Pour regular corn kernels into a pan and watch them expand and change! Can you still find parts of the old kernel in the fluffy white one?

2. Light a candle, and watch with your child as the wax melts. It's still wax, just in a different shape. Now, try it with an ice cube. Set it out to melt; then, discuss how it is the same as and different from its frozen state.

3. Can you think of more experiments that show a physical change for the following actions: break, crush, condense, dissolve, evaporate, mix?

Brainstorm together as a family, and give them a try. Alternatively, you could give each person a few and challenge him or her to create a demonstration to show the rest of the family.

As with most things, the more you play around and have fun, the more interested your child will be in it. The more he is interested, the more he will remember.

#240
Fun with Bubbles

Wisdom begins in wonder.
~Socrates

Have you ever looked at a bubble really closely? Bubbles, at an instant glance, look clear. However, if you take a closer look, you'll see that bubbles actually go through a variety of colors before they pop.

For some bubble fun, you will need bubble solution, a straw and black construction paper. Pour the bubble solution in a bowl. Swirl the straw in the bubble solution, and gently blow out the straw onto the black construction paper. If you blow carefully and gently, the bubble will "stand" on the paper. Carefully observe all the colors in the bubble, and after it pops, write down all the colors you noticed. If your whole family is participating, who can blow the biggest bubble? Who can blow the smallest?

Repeat the experiment several times. (You won't have to convince your child—it's fun!) You will begin to notice that every bubble has many different colors. Just like the colors of a rainbow are always red, orange, yellow, green, blue, indigo, and violet, do the colors of the bubble always appear in the same order until it pops?

What are the colors, and in which order do they appear? Well, you're going to have to try it to find out! Get everyone involved. The whole family will enjoy this activity. The more people looking for the pattern of colors the better! The colors appear and disappear very quickly! Have fun!

See our workbook available for purchase online for some bubble fun.

#241
Science Game

Blessed is the man who keeps in touch with his child's heart.
~Chinese Saying

Here's a game of tag, full of science fun. This science game is sure to please elementary children of all ages. You can play this game with just three people but more people will increase the fun.

1. Have your child create a "predator/prey" list. Divide a piece of paper into two columns. Label one column "PREY" and the other "PREDATOR." In the predator column, he should write the names of animals that *eat* other animals. In the prey column, he should write animals names that *are eaten* by other animals. The predator and prey going across each line should be a true predator/prey relationship. (For example, if your child chooses her first predator to be a lion, then the prey across from lion should be something a lion eats such as a zebra.) Here's what her list may look like:

PREDATOR	PREY
Lion	Zebra
Human	Deer
Cat	Mouse
Owl	Snake
Frog	Fly
Snake	Frog
Hawk	Rabbit

(Notice that some predators can also be prey!)

2. Evenly separate the children playing into two lines, and have them face each other (like in "Red Rover").

3. Now begins a science form of the game "tag." You or your child can start by looking at the list and choosing one predator/prey relationship. (As an example, let's say he chooses "frog/fly.")

4. Point to one of the groups, and say, "You are frogs." (They do not know yet whether they are going to be the prey or the predators.)

5. Now, the other group must play close attention because if they are going to be the *prey*, they will need to run away from their predators (the frogs) without being caught (tagged)! If it turns out they are the *predator*, they must run after the other team (the prey) and try to tag them before a previously designated safe zone is reached.

6. Now, tell the other team what animal they are. ("You are flies.") Everyone must quickly decide who is the prey and the predator in this situation, and either chase or be chased!

7. In the frog/fly example, the group designated "fly" (prey) would run away from the "frogs" (predator) before getting tagged.

Being tagged does not eliminate a child from the game. Each child returns to the line after each predator/prey is called. The children playing can take turns being in charge and naming each group predator or prey.

Note: Before you start the game remind children of the safety rules in tag. A tag is a light touch and not a hard push! Sometimes, children need to be reminded because of their enthusiasm for the game!

#242
Tips on the Science Fair

Discovery consists of looking at the same thing
as everyone else does and thinking something different.
~Albert Szent-Gyorgyi, 1937 Nobel Prize Winner

There comes a time in nearly every child's life when she has to make up a project for the science fair. Perhaps you've already been to one. If so, you have undoubtedly seen the ones that you know the child did herself and the ones where it looks like the parents did all the work. If your child comes home with the challenge of contributing to the upcoming science fair, think about the goals of the project and what you want her to get out of it. Of course, your guidance is helpful, but be careful to let it be her project and not yours. Here are some ways to ensure that:

1. If she already has an idea, great! If not, offer some suggestions, but let her choose. Look online or go to the library if she are stumped for ideas. Be sure to help her choose something she is capable of doing. A fifth-grader can take on a tougher project than a kindergartner. See Idea #233 for some ideas.

2. Once she has the idea, make a few lists. For one, make a materials list of things she will need to complete the project. List the steps she will take from beginning to end, and decide when they need to be done. See Idea #223 for the scientific method, which can give her a terrific way to organize the steps.

3. Work together to get all the materials and organize them. Having a tri-fold poster board is a nice touch to any project. You can include pictures and other important info on it for the visitors of the science fair to easily see. It can also help explain what is going on, in case it is not so obvious.

4. When it comes time to begin the process, make sure your child takes the lead. You can help her, certainly, but let her tell you what to do. Ask her, "How can I help?" Instead of decorating the poster board yourself, ask her how she wants it done. Care more about the fact that she is doing it on her own than what the finished project looks like. If you have suggestions, this is a good time to share them, but instead of telling her what to do, perhaps say, "When I have to do that, sometimes I like to..."

5. When the project is finished, be sure she tries it out a few times at home to make sure everything works. It is easier and a whole lot nicer to work out kinks at home. That way, things will run smoothly at the fair.

By letting her do the work, you will know she understands what she has created. If you have guided her but let her do the choosing and put in the effort, she will stand there proud to show off her project. While you may look around and see more glamorous projects done by other students (aka parents), you will probably enjoy her proud smile more!

See our workbook available for purchase online for an organizer for the scientific method.

#243
Backyard Science

Keep your face to the sunshine and you cannot see the shadows.
~Helen Keller

Even your own backyard can provide you and your little scientist a place to explore. He can:

- collect bugs (Idea #244);

- find different plants, collect them, dry them out, and make a book of plants;

- make his own weather station using a thermometer for temperature, a cup to measure rainfall, a wind vane to determine wind direction, and a journal to keep daily track of the weather;

- start a compost pile;

- grow a garden (vegetables or flowers);

- look at the night sky and draw the constellations;

- place a black cloth and a white cloth (preferably of the same material) out in the sun; leave for ½ hour, then feel them. (Can he explain the difference?); and

- create an evaporation experiment outside using two glasses of water, one with salt and one without.

The possibilities are only limited to his (and your) imagination. Science is back in your backyard. Go and enjoy it!

#244
You Bug Me!

Read nature, nature is a friend to truth.
~Edward Young

Did you know that three out of four creatures on Earth are... BUGS? (Insects, to be exact.) It pretty much doesn't matter where you live, chances are you have access to bugs, some of the most fascinating things on Earth to kids. Bugs are usually quite easy to find. You might look inside on windowsills or outside in bushes or trees, under rocks, in the dirt, in car grilles, around lights at night, in compost heaps, on flowers or plants, in dead wood, tree stumps, sappy trees, fields, swamps, anywhere. Whichever kind you find, bugs provide a great opportunity for hands-on, authentic, (and *free*) scientific discovery. Here are some skills you can practice with your child while having fun with bugs:

1. Observe a variety of bugs close up. Get down on the ground (or up in the tree, into the pond, etc.) with a magnifying lens and some bug-collecting tools such as nets and tweezers. (Colanders make good strainers in pond water.) Use sugar water, fruit, or meat as bait if you'd like, and see if you attract different bugs than you readily found on your own.

2. Classify the bugs you find into groups such as insects and spiders. What qualifications do the bugs need to meet before they fit into their category?

3. If your child is interested in collecting bugs, you could either encourage her to narrow her focus and try to find many of the same bugs or to find as many different kinds as she can. Decide how to organize and label them.

4. Build a bug box to carry bugs in. (Equip it with soil, twigs, water, some foliage from its habitat, and a screen for breathing air.) In a pinch, an empty yogurt container is a good bug carrier if Mom's plastic bowls are off limits.

5. List the characteristics of the insects: three body parts, two wings, six legs, and so on.

6. As a family recycling project, construct a bug-collecting net from old pantyhose and a wire coat hanger.

7. Research and illustrate the life cycle of a butterfly. Compare it to the moth's.

8. Find and then compare and contrast a honey bee, wasp, and hornet using a triple Venn diagram (Idea #143).

9. Predict, count, tally, and graph the types of bugs found in various places around your home. Try a shaded area vs. sunny area, day vs. night, on a piece of fruit vs. meat.

10. Read a variety of bug books. Go to the library and check out a few. Try *The Icky Bug Alphabet Book* by Jerry Pallotta for starters.

11. Have your child write about and illustrate the bugs she finds in her science journal (Idea #169).

12. Challenge your child to invent her own new bug, using some of the things she's learned about bugs through her discovery. Can she classify it according to its characteristics? She could draw and write about it in her science journal, too.

Tips:

You might want to wear bug spray as protection while hunting for certain kinds of bugs! Gloves may also come in handy. Of course, take precautions against getting stung!

#245
Things to Do at the Zoo

It is not so much what is poured into the student,
but what is planted that really counts.
~Unknown

Going to the zoo is fun! You can also make it an educational experience, too. Here are a handful of ways to find the science in the zoo:

1. Predict and record what animals you will see at the zoo. Check off the animals as you go.

2. Have your child take pictures of some of his favorite animals. When you get home, study the photos and discuss why the zookeepers created its habitat like they did. Research the animal in the wild. What does it have in the wild that it also has at the zoo? Is anything missing? Why?

3. Have him think of his favorite two animals. Can he combine them and create one new animal? What would it be called? What would it eat? Where would it live? Illustrate it, and label its characteristics. Tell why it has certain features and how it uses them.

4. Go to the zoo in search of and take note of several animals he feels are especially fantastic for some particular trait. Have him combine at least two of the animals together to create one supreme animal. (Think about strongest legs, best defense, best camouflage, most powerful jaws, and greatest hearing or eyesight.)

5. Make it a family challenge. Have everyone create the "best" animal, and then share. Discuss reasons why each is good. Is there a "winner"?

6. Could he build this new animal or his favorite animal out of household items?

7. Take time to read the information with or to your child that is usually posted outside of each exhibit. He may not remember everything, but he's bound to absorb more information by hearing about the animal and looking at it, too.

8. Play "Who am I" after visiting the zoo. On the car ride home or even as a game another time, you can ask questions like "I'm a mammal; I love swimming; I live in the Arctic. Who am I?"

See our website for some zoo fun organizers.

#246
Mystery Insect: The Life Cycle of an Insect

Here's an opportunity for you and your child to observe all four stages of the life cycle of an insect right in your own home. Here's what you'll need:

- plastic (see through) cup;

- plastic wrap;

- rubber band;

- Corn Flakes cereal; and

- mealworms (from pet store—they use them for feeding other animals).

To Do:

1. Fill the plastic cup ¾ of the way with the Corn Flakes.

2. Add 4-6 mealworms.

3. Cover the cup with plastic wrap, and secure it with the rubber band.

4. Poke several small holes in the plastic for air.

5. Add a tiny piece of moist paper towel every three days or so for moisture (not too much, though, or the cereal will get moldy).

6. Place the cup in indirect sunlight.

The mealworms are in the larvae stage of the life cycle. In this stage, they will live in the flakes and eat them, too! Every few days, your child should empty the cup carefully onto a paper plate and spread the flakes around to find the mealworms. (They are similar in color to the flakes). She can measure the mealworms and write the measurements down in her science journal (Idea #224) or on just a piece of paper. While the mealworms are out, she can count the number of segments each has and watch the way they move. Get a magnifying lens, and look at them close up (and draw them). Try different things, and observe them. What do they do if you put an obstacle in their way (go around? crawl over?)? What if you blow lightly on them? Cover them up? Put a drop of water next to them? (Do they go near it or away from it?) How do they feel crawling on your finger?

When she's done looking at them, have her carefully pour the flakes (you do not need new flakes) and the mealworms back into the cup. She can add a small piece of moist paper towel or a tiny piece of carrot for moisture.

Have her pour out the flakes and the mealworms every few days to measure, observe, and record her observations. It won't be long before she starts to notice they are getting shorter and fatter. She will also notice that they molt and leave behind their old skin. Not long after that, they will start to go into the pupae stage. They stop moving and almost look dead, but they are not. Be patient. Soon, the color will change, and the metamorphosis will take place. They will enter into the last stage of the life cycle (adult) and become insects. What kind? You'll have to do it to find out!

Part 9
Social Studies Today

INTRODUCTION: Part 9 contains activities and ideas to help make social studies more relevant to your child. At the lower elementary school level, social studies generally focuses first on the local community and family. In upper elementary school, the focus is broadened, and children will learn about the states, the government, and the history of their country, as well as other cultures and other parts of the world. Every state develops its own curriculum for social studies. Your child's teacher will let you know what they will focus on for the year. Most schools have the entire curriculum for each grade posted online. Use the search box on the Internet and type your school district's name and "social studies curriculum." Chances are you will find it. If not, don't be afraid to contact the school and ask where you can find it.

The world is turning into a global village, and it is our responsibility to make sure we are raising children who are knowledgeable about the world around them; social studies can help achieve that. At the same time, in order to get your child interested in social studies, you will need activities that help your child *discover* history, not just memorize facts. This Part will provide activities that will get your child involved and interested in learning about the world around him.

In this Part the ideas start close to home, focusing on your family history. If children can see the importance of their neighborhood and their own family history, they are more likely to recognize the importance of their state or country's history. Then, there are more activities to help bring the world a little closer to home and make learning social studies more interesting, relevant and fun.

#247
Creating the Environment

First comes thought; then organization of that thought,
into ideas and plans; then transformation of those plans into reality.
~ Napoleon Hill

What is it about the library that makes people want to sit down quietly and get to work? It's the atmosphere. The library is full of books, reference materials, tables and chairs, computers, proper lighting, and helpful people; all of this creates the proper atmosphere for learning and working. Creating the right atmosphere in your child's workspace, too, invites your child to learn and can make it so much more enjoyable.

Consider your child's workspace. She probably has paper, pencils, markers and other office-like supplies on her desk. Now, look around her workspace while you consider the subject of history/social studies. Are there any maps hanging on the walls? Does she have access to a globe or reference books with maps? Do you have the newspaper delivered? Is it accessible to her?

If you want history to be important in your child's life, show it by creating an environment where she feels immersed in the subject. Start by talking to her teacher about her social studies curriculum for the year. What will they be studying? Once you learn that, you will know what the two of you will want to put around her workspace to provide her with the tools she needs to be successful throughout the year.

#248

"Hidden Treasure"

Education is learning what you didn't even know you didn't know.
~Daniel Boorstin

As you read about in Idea #20, the game "Hidden Treasure" is an easy and fun way to practice just about anything! Social studies is no exception. If you aren't sure how to play, go back and read the directions. Basically, you are placing cards in a special box and taking turns pulling out a card. Questions/terms on the cards are read to each other, and points are earned for correct answers. For what to write on the cards, try:

- states and their capitals;

- presidents and their terms or major accomplishments;

- any names of famous people in a current chapter and their major accomplishments;

- the Amendments in the Bill of Rights and what each allows;

- any dates in a chapter and their significance;

- any terms in a chapter and what they mean; and

- types of landforms and what they look like.

#249
A Family Timeline

You will never find time for anything. If you want time you must make it.
~ Charles Buxton

If you find getting your child interested in people or events from a long time ago is difficult, try this activity which brings history a little closer to home. Talk to your child about how history is happening every day in your family. Discuss how families change: a new baby is born, the family moves, a grandparent moves in, and so on.

Have her create a list of all the events in her life she can think of as far back as she can. Then, have her interview family members to record other important events that have happened within the family and add it to her events list. Use butcher paper (cut to one foot high by six feet long) to create the timeline. If you cannot find butcher paper, tape together several 8 1/2" x 11" sheets of paper. Have her create her time line starting with the earliest event she's recorded on her list and continue on to current events in the family.

What a great way to make history personal and interesting for your child! She may even want to spruce up the time line by adding photos, drawings or other mementos that coordinate with each event. Put the timeline in a place where everyone can see, enjoy, and talk about their family and all they've experienced so far.

See our workbook available for purchase online for a timeline template.

#250
Family Traditions

Family traditions counter alienation and confusion. They help us define who we are;
they provide something steady, reliable and safe in a confusing world.
~Susan Lieberman

What makes your family unique? Every family has traditions and celebrations they do every year that are special to them. Perhaps your family vacations at the same place every summer. Do you do something special for each person's birthday? How about the holidays? These traditions can be recorded by your child. Perhaps he'll want to videotape each one as they happen throughout the year or he can interview someone in the family for each tradition and videotape the interview.

Another option could be to create a memory book where, on each page, he can write a detailed description of each tradition, what happens, where it happens, who usually participates, etc. This book can be typed and printed out or hand written. He can add photos or hand-drawn pictures to make the book even more meaningful. The memory book can be displayed prominently for everyone to read and enjoy. As new traditions emerge, they can be added to the book. It will be an ongoing project that will be even more meaningful as he grows older; he can look at the book and see how he captured the history of your family in the memory book.

#251
A Family Newsletter

If the family were a boat, it would be a canoe
that makes no progress unless everyone paddles.
~ Letty Cottin Pogrebin

Creating a Family Newsletter is another way for your child to realize that history happens every day, and, as a bonus, she will be working on her writing skills in a fun way. The newsletter can be handwritten or word processed or a combination of both. Have your child think of a title for the newsletter. Then, have her think about major family events that have happened in the last year and make a list of them. If you have a calendar in the message center where everyone writes important things down, you may want her to consult the calendar to help jog her memory. She can also talk to other members of the family and ask them what they remember most about the past twelve months.

Have her choose the most important events to include in the newsletter and think of catchy titles that make the reader want to read the article. This might be a good time to look through a newspaper and read all the titles of the different articles. Help her notice how those titles work to catch the reader's attention. Once she's picked her events and their titles, she's ready to begin writing the articles. Younger children can dictate their words to you or a sibling, while older students can write on their own. Many word processing programs, like Microsoft Word, have a newsletter template that will make creating it so easy and fun. She can add hand-drawn pictures or insert clip art. If newsletter templates are not available and she wants to type it, she can just create two columns and insert text boxes where needed. Let her experiment with it. Chances are she'll amaze you with what she creates. With the computer lessons given in elementary school these days, don't be surprised if she has ideas you hadn't even known how to do!

Many families send out newsletters like this at the end of the year to family and friends to keep them updated on the important and interesting events in their lives. However, she may be so proud of her newsletter that she may want to post it at home right away or send it off to loved ones. If that's the case, let her! Challenge her to keep a journal of all the important events from now on, and perhaps she can do a bi-annual or quarterly newsletter to share.

#252
Getting Personal

*To look at the paper is to raise a seashell to one's ear
and to be overwhelmed by the roar of humanity.
~Alain de Botton*

If you haven't introduced newspapers to your child, now is a good time. Most children's worlds are very small. It's not too early to open their eyes and see that the world involves more than their school and neighborhood. Of course, there are articles in the newspaper you may not want your child to read so be sure to preview the newspaper and choose the articles you want to focus on. Start by opening his eyes to what is happening locally and make the news personal to him. If an article covers something he feels particularly passionate about, encourage him to express his ideas.

Perhaps the city is considering putting a dog park in the neighborhood. If he agrees and feels strongly that this would be a great idea, have him write a letter to whoever is in charge (or a letter to the editor) and explain his reasons why he supports the idea. Perhaps he may read that a favorite restaurant is closing and feels strongly that it shouldn't. To whom can he write? Encourage him to express his ideas and reasons to the appropriate person. You never know, he may even get a response from his letter writing. What a great way to show that his opinion and ideas are important. Children have many opinions and it's important that we listen to them and encourage them to start thinking for themselves.

Remember, newspapers don't have to be in paper form. Online newspapers are available for cities all over the world. Perhaps he would be interested in reading news articles from other states where relatives may live or other places he's always wanted to visit. Reading appropriate news articles can broaden your child's horizons and make him aware of the world he lives in. What a great way to prepare your child to be a responsible, involved, and caring adult.

#253
Get Involved!

*Never doubt that a small group of thoughtful,
committed people can change the world.
Indeed, it is the only thing that ever has.
~Margaret Meade*

In a previous activity, you encouraged your child to voice her opinions and state her views on issues that are important to her or her family. While writing a letter about something she is passionate about is a great start, there's another way to become involved in the community more regularly: volunteer! Your child probably knows how lucky she is. If you sit on her bed with her and look around her room, there is evidence everywhere of how lucky she is to have what she has. She probably realizes that not everyone is as lucky as she is, but does she realize that some children her age go to bed without food every night and go through holidays without gifts?

If she wants to help other people, help her find ways to do it. What is she interested in? Think about these:

- If she loves animals, many humane society shelters will let the two of you walk dogs or bake homemade treats to help feed the sheltered animals.

- Even if your family does not regularly attend church, their bulletins/ websites list various ways to help those in need. Most of the time, volunteers would contact the place in need and not the church.

- Does your school need sprucing up? Get together with some neighborhood families and clean up the playground or plant some flowers in front of the school.

- She might even consider donating some of her toys or clothes to those in need.

- Call the local senior center and see if they would welcome a child to come read to some elderly people. Paint a picture or write a poem for them.

- Could a local doctor's office use some gently read books your child has outgrown?

- Sometimes there are opportunities for kids to come in to the local library to read to younger kids.

There are many opportunities to help make the world a better place. All she has to do is look for them!

#254
Give Some Direction

Lack of direction, not lack of time, is the problem.
We all have twenty-four hour days.
~Zig Ziglar

Reading and interpreting maps is an important part of social studies. Before reading maps, your child should understand direction. A great way to make it fun is to have him make his own compass. Here's how.

Materials: small bowl, a needle, a cork or a packing peanut, a magnet (one from the refrigerator may work).

1. Fill the bowl halfway with water and set it aside.

2. Hold the needle by the eye. Rub the magnet down the needle *in one direction* about twenty times. This will magnetize the needle.

3. Place the cork in the water so it floats. Carefully center the needle on the cork. If you use a packing peanut, push the magnetized needle through the top of the packing peanut until it's centered. Place the packing peanut in the bowl of water (needle should not be touching the water).

4. Watch as the needle starts to turn. It will stop when the tip you magnetized is facing due North. To test to make sure the needle is working, gently blow on the needle so it moves. You should notice the needle moving back to its original due North position.

Depending on your child's age and his experience with direction, you may need to explain cardinal directions. The four cardinal directions are north, south, east and west. They are represented on a compass rose and look like this:

Children often forget the correct placement of the four directions. A fun way to help them remember is to make a silly sentence with the four letters. Always start with N for north, and then move to the right (like a clock moves), thinking of four words. Each word should start with the letter N, E, S, and then W. For example, a very popular sentence is "Never Eat Slimy Worms." He will have fun making up his own crazy sentences, and he will be more likely to remember it if he creates it himself.

One of the nice things about this homemade compass is that it's so easy to take with him. The next time he goes somewhere, whether it's a walk to the park or camping or to a friend's house, he can take the makings of his compass with him and set it up easily by just filling a bowl with water (or even using a pond or puddle of water if it's deep enough). If it's been a while, he may need to re-magnetize the needle for the best results. Either way, he's sure to have fun creating and using his very own compass.

#255
Making Maps

A good plan is like a road map: it shows the final destination
and usually the best way to get there.
~ H. Stanley Judd

It's much easier for children to understand maps and their importance if they've actually created a map themselves. It's usually best to start by mapping something very familiar to her, like her room. Tell her she gets to create a "bird's eye view" map of her room. Explain for a bird's eye view, she should start by imagining she's a bird flying over her room. What would it look like from above? (It may help to have her stand on a chair to actually get a feel for it.) Where is the bed, dresser, closet, etc.? Have her draw each major object on a piece of paper. Depending on her age, it can be very simple, with objects marked by boxes, rectangles and circles, or more detailed (and/or more to scale) for older children.

When she's finished her map, have her bring the compass she made in activity #254 into her room so she can find which way is north. Once she finds north, she can add the cardinal directions and the compass rose to her map.

Have fun with directions in her room. Consider hiding something (like a favorite toy or stuffed animal) in her room and giving her directions to help her find it. She can hold her map with compass directions on it as you give directions such as, "It's about two steps north; now three steps east; turn to the south"—until she finds it!

See our workbook available for purchase online for a birds-eye view sample.

#256

Seen Around Town

There's only one interview technique that matters... Do your homework so you can listen to the answers and react to them and ask follow-ups. Do your homework, prepare.
~ *Jim Lehrer*

How well does your child know his city or town? Talk about what he's noticed in the area on previous trips into town. What does a city need to function? Ask him questions to help him realize what he may have forgotten such as *Who helps keep us safe?* or *Where can people go to get food or buy things they need? Where are the government offices?* Have him make a list of all the places and businesses he can think of. Then, take a walk or drive around town, and have him write down (or better yet, take pictures of) the places he may have missed. There are likely to be a few places he's never noticed before! He can sort them into categories: Do they provide goods or services?

This is a perfect opportunity for him to find out about what makes a city run. Have him choose a few places he is interested in and find out if they are willing to let him come in and interview someone about what they do. Perhaps he can tape record it, take pictures, or even get a tour. This is a great way to start to understand what it takes for a city to run smoothly and provide what the people living in the city may need. If he understands how his city or town works, he will be more likely to understand bigger ideas like how the government runs.

See our workbook for an organizer for this activity.

#257
Making Sense of Maps

*Maps are essential. Planning a journey without a map
is like building a house without drawings.*
~Mark Jenkins

In activity #256, your child got to know more about her city or town. She's now more familiar with what is in her town, how it runs and the many important goods and services it provides to the people. Now, have her use her knowledge of her city to improve her map skills. She's already made a simple map of her room in activity #255, but most of the maps she'll look at in elementary school will be more detailed and complicated. They usually have:

- a title;

- different colors;

- a compass rose (to show orientation); and

- different symbols to represent important parts on the map in a "legend."

She can use the same bird's eye view technique she used to map out her room to make this map of her town. Remind her to imagine she's a bird flying over her house. Have her close her eyes. Can she see her street? The school at the corner? Her friend's house? The police station? A park? If she's having trouble imagining what this may look like, have her look on the Internet for a bird's eye view of a small neighborhood. When you think she understands, she is ready to create a bird's a eye view of her own neighborhood or town. Here is an example:

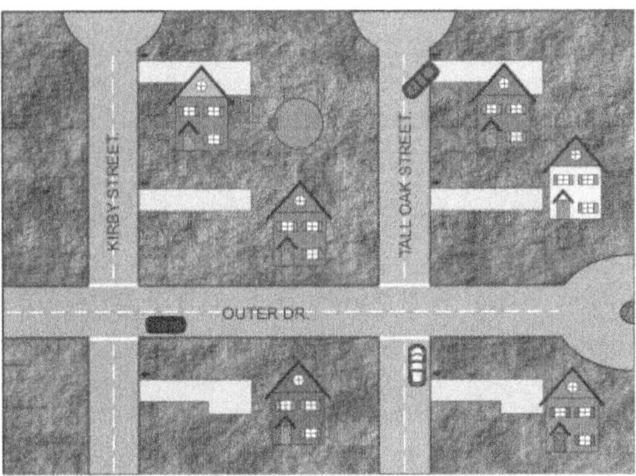

A poster board works well for this activity. Have her start by drawing her street (two lines about an inch apart with the street name in the middle). Before she can draw the street, though, she should use her compass to find out which way her street runs (north and south or east and west). She should draw it on her poster board and then add the compass rose to make sure the street is drawn in the correct direction. Next, have her draw in the surrounding streets, making sure she checks her compass rose and that the streets face in the correct direction. She can continue to build out from her street until she has a good representation of her neighborhood.

Older children can be challenged to draw the town or a bigger part of the city they live in instead of their neighborhood. They should also be encouraged to create symbols for different objects on their map and add them to the legend. (i.e.: Hospital, Police, Railroad Tracks, Lakes, Schools, Parks, Forests…)

Have her check to make sure each of the following elements is on her map:

a. a title: "My City" or "My Neighborhood," etc.;

b. symbols: have her use symbols to represent various things on her map and add those symbols to the legend;

c. map key/legend: a box containing all the symbols she used and an explanation of what they are next to the symbol; and

d. a compass rose to show the cardinal directions.

By making her own map, she will begin to understand the importance of maps and will be less likely to skip over the maps she will see in her social studies books. Authors put them there to give a visual representation of what they are saying, but kids often skip them because they don't understand them. Once she has made her own, she will have a much greater understanding of reading someone else's!

See our workbook for a sheet to organize this activity.

#258
Host a Scavenger Hunt

Do not go where the path may lead,
go instead where there is no path and leave a trail.
~Ralph Waldo Emerson

In a few previous activities in this Part, your child has had practice in understanding maps and creating them. In this activity, he can take all that hard work and have fun with it. Encourage him to create a scavenger hunt in his neighborhood or city/town.

In a scavenger hunt, the participants are given clues to various places and are asked to get something from that place to prove they've been to the right place. Your child can create clues for local establishments that are on his map for his friends and/or family. He can photocopy his map for all the participants to help them. He may want to first stop by each place he's considering using to make sure they are willing to participate. For example, if the library is on his map, he could write a clue such as *Find the place where you can travel to faraway places without ever leaving your neighborhood. Take a picture with one of the people working there.* For a restaurant clue he could have them bring back a menu; for a dentist office he could have them bring back a sticker, etc. The possibilities are only limited to his imagination.

He could put a time limit on the hunt, and when everyone meets back, the person or group with the most correct answers to the scavenger hunt is declared the winner. There doesn't even need to be a prize. Everyone will have so much fun following his map and the clues to complete the hunt, they'll want to do it again!

#259
Latitude and Longitude

I can't change the direction of the wind,
but I can adjust my sails to always reach my destination.
~ Jimmy Dean

When your child needs to find a word in a dictionary, she can't start until she at least knows the first letter. It would be next to impossible to find one word in a huge dictionary if she didn't know where to start. The same is true when finding locations on a map or globe. Maps can be huge, and globes can be difficult because of their shape. That's why we use a system of lines called "latitude" and "longitude" to help identify where places are located. It may help her remember which lines go in which direction by having her memorize this saying: *"Longitude lines go up and down, latitude lines go round and round."* If she draws these lines herself, she is more likely to remember them.

Some fun ways to practice drawing these lines is by drawing them on a pumpkin, balloon, orange, softball, or anything she can find that is basically a sphere. The direction of each line and how to find where the lines meet at a location is all your young elementary school child needs to know for now. If she's ever played a game like "Battleship," she may be familiar with following a line of latitude and a line of longitude and finding where they meet. You can label the longitude lines with letters (A, B, C) and latitude lines with numbers (1, 2, 3). She can practice finding A5 by using one index finger for A and one index finger for 5 and bringing them together to find the location where they meet.

Older children can use maps and globes to notice how the lines are labeled (with degrees and cardinal directions). Have her use the map or globe to find a place on the map. Start by providing her the latitude and longitude numbers and have her follow the lines to where they meet. For example, *"What would you find at 43° N, 103° W?"* (Of course, she'll know her cardinal directions from activity #254.) Once she seems to understand, switch things around, and have her find the latitude and longitude to some of her favorite places. You could ask her to find the latitude and longitude for her state, country, a mountain, or a body of water. Then let her quiz you, a friend, or another family member. She can give the longitude and latitude, and you will have to find the location she's picked out. She will enjoy being the teacher, and she will be learning in the process.

If she'd like to make a game of it, try playing Latitude and Longitude Bingo. She can create the bingo cards by putting the names of her favorite places in each square. Then, she would put the latitude and longitude of each place on a card, fold it, and put them all in a bowl. As she pulls out each card, she'll name the latitude and longitude, and each player (equipped with a map) will find the corresponding location. If a player has that location on their map, he or she can cover it and be one step closer to a Bingo. Whether your child is creating the game or playing the game, she'll be learning so much and not only about latitude and longitude. She'll also become very familiar with maps, globes, and locations of various places around the world.

See our website for a ready-made Bingo gameboard.

#260
A Puzzling Idea

Our whole life is solving puzzles.
~Erno Rubik

If you want a fun way for your child to study geography, try making a puzzle. Whether he's learning about the states or the world, it's easy to create a magnetic puzzle for him to practice. Have him print out an illustrated printable map from the Internet (or use an actual map if you don't mind it being cut up). Put the map on magnetic paper; then cut out all the shapes. If you don't have a magnetized white board, the refrigerator works well. (You can also glue the map to poster board instead if you don't have magnetic paper.)

Make a game of the puzzle by seeing who can create the world (or states or whatever the map is about) the fastest. Once your child becomes comfortable with the puzzle, use paper to cover the names of the states/countries. Have him say the name of each state/country as he puts it all together. If you have a small magnetic whiteboard, it's a great activity to take along with you on a long car ride.

#261
Make a Time Capsule

Lost time is never found again.
~Benjamin Franklin

Creating a time capsule is a fun way to record your child's history. It's her way to let people in the future have a good idea of how she lived and what was important to her at the time. Here's how to do it:

Have her place items that tell about her life into a container with a good seal on it. Help her choose things that represent milestones in her life. If she doesn't want to put her beloved things in the capsule, she can take a picture of important objects, places, things, and people and include them in the capsule. She may want to include headlines from current papers, advertisements/slogans she feels are important to her generation, book titles she loves, and music she listens to for a start.

Once she's gathered her items, have her show them to the family and explain why they are important. It's also a good idea to have her write a note with the date on it to include in the capsule. While most time capsules are buried, hers doesn't have to be. She can put it in a secure location to be opened at a later date. She doesn't even need to leave it for the too-distant future. If it's stored long enough, she may even forget about it. Wouldn't that be a fun graduation or wedding gift to give to her? Or, imagine her opening up a time capsule she made when she was eight when she has children of her own. Everyone will enjoy looking at the items she chose to represent her life so many years ago.

See our online workbook, available for purchase, for a sheet to organize this activity.

#262
Current Events

Those who never learn history are condemned to repeat it.
~ Unknown

History is being made every day. Help your child become aware of what is happening around him by making it a point to look at current events together. Even local news stories can have an impact, not only on your family but also on the world. Consider having a contest: *Who can find the most important article of the week?*

Articles can be found in a newspaper, online, or in a magazine. Each person can discuss their article and its importance using the 5 W's found in most news articles. Each person can tell Who, What, Where, When, and Why to try to prove why their article is the most important. Then, post the articles on the message center where everyone can vote. You can even put a world map on the message center and have each person put a pin in the place where the article takes place.

He's not only staying current, but he's also getting practice identifying important places on the map, both great skills that will help him in class and in the future.

See our workbook for a sheet to help organize this activity.

#263
Becoming "Cultured"

A people without the knowledge of their past history,
origin and culture is like a tree without roots.
~Marcus Garvey

Have you talked to your child about her heritage? If not, now is a great opportunity to start the conversation. Children are often much more interested in learning about different cultures if they have some connection to them. Have her pick a country her ancestors are from and research it. She could research and learn about these:

- food;

- clothing;

- dance;

- holidays;

- what people do in their free time;

- music;

- the type of money they use;

- the religion(s) they practice; and

- traditional stories from the country (folktales, tall tales, etc.).

Find a way for her to represent all she has learned. Depending on her age and what she may need to practice, perhaps she can:

- write a paragraph about it (Idea #173);

- write a 5-paragraph essay about it (Idea #156);

- draw a picture and label things;

- write a poem or song about it (Idea #132);

- write a letter to a real or imagined relative living there;

- create a poster board with pictures and small captions; or

- write a letter to other family members that share the same heritage about what she found out.

#264
Symbols and Flags

Symbols are miracles we have recorded into language.
~ *S. Kelley Harrel*

Every country and state is unique, and each showcases its individuality in many ways. One fun way to find out about a state or country is to look at flags. State flags, in particular, have many symbols that represent history and culture. Have your child look at his state flag (or the flag of any state or country) and try to guess what each picture, word, symbol, or color means.

After he's made his guesses, have him research the meanings behind the symbols and pictures on the flag to see if he was right. He is bound to find out many interesting facts about the history of his state or country as he researches. He may even be motivated to create a family flag. He can brainstorm all the things that make his family unique. Have him share his creation with the family. Perhaps his flag can be incorporated throughout the year on correspondence between family members. Maybe each family member could do the same, and then you can all compare what each of you chose to include on your family flag and why! What a great way to showcase his wonderful family and its history.

See our workbook for a blank flag template.

#265
Living History

Study history, study history. In history lie all the secrets of statecraft.
~*Winston Churchill*

Children love to act and reenact things they've seen and done. Why not put that talent to use by having your child reenact certain events she's studying in social studies. Perhaps family and friends can join her as she recreates history at home. Whether she simply tells the actors what to do or actually writes a script, she is reinforcing all the knowledge she's gained through studying. Also, by acting out events, she is cementing them in her mind.

Each event that is acted out will be a piece of history she will find hard to forget. This works particularly well with events that are tough to understand. If she can invent a play about it, she has truly learned about it. How fun when you and the rest of the family also participate! (On next week's test on the Boston Tea Party, she is certain to recall Dad yelling "No taxation without representation" and understand why he was so adamant about it!)

#266
What a Relief!

Even before you understand them, your brain is drawn to maps.
~Ken Jennings

When your child is studying different terrains (mountain, tundra, ocean, river, forest, etc.), creating a raised relief map (a 3-dimensional representation of terrain) is a great hands-on activity to show what he knows. Here is what he'll need:

- large piece of cardboard, heavy poster board, or thin piece of wood;

- several cups of salt;

- several cups of flour;

- food coloring; and

- water.

Below are the directions for creating the map.

1. Trace the state or country on the cardboard/poster board or wood.

2. Mix salt and flour using 2 parts salt to 1 part flour.

3. Stir in enough water to make a smooth, heavy paste.

4. Divide the paste into as many parts as you have terrains. (For example, if your state has only three types of terrains, divide the mixture into thirds.)

5. Add a different color food coloring to each part (each terrain type will be a different color.)

6. Use the colored mixtures to form the different terrains in the correct regions.

7. Don't forget to include a color-coded map key for the different terrains.

How interesting, and what a good learning tool, to look at your state in 3-D!

#267
Art Reflects History

A picture is worth a thousand words.
~Napoleon Bonaparte

Art history *is* history. Art from the past is a great learning tool to discover many things from history. Through books and the Internet, we have access to art from a thousand years ago! Show your child art pieces from the time period she is learning about. Many things can be determined by looking at art:

- She can see the type of clothes worn during that time.

- Through clothing, she may also be able to possibly determine temperature/climate and geography.

- She can find some of the activities or hobbies popular during that time.

- She can use problem solving skills as she discovers how things have changed and evolved over time.

All of this provides a connection to the past and is a reflection of history and culture. Perhaps she might even be encouraged to create her own art piece that she feels represents the current time period. History can truly come alive through art!

#268
Put Yourself in History

If you would understand anything, observe its beginning and its development.
~Aristotle

Whether you're trying to help your child with a subject being taught at school or you are trying to teach him about a particular event in history, the following activity will help get your child to think about and understand it more thoroughly.

Whatever situation you are presenting to your child, help him to think about it hypothetically first. Give him the scenario and ask, *"What would you do?"* For example, if he's learning about pilgrims who came to America on ships, have him close his eyes and imagine himself there as you give details about why they wanted to leave England. You could add pictures or videos to reinforce the ideas. Have him give his ideas of what he would have done if he had been there. Younger children are more likely to give improbable answers, but that's okay. Accept all answers, even the improbable, because just getting him to think about the choices the people in history had to make is making him an active, engaged learner. Older children can write down their thoughts or defend their ideas verbally.

When all ideas are exhausted, that's when you can start helping him discover what the people long ago really did to solve the problem. Having him think about it from a more personal standpoint first, though, will help him understand it much, much better.

#269
History is in the Bag!

If you don't know history, then you don't know anything.
You are a leaf that doesn't know it is part of a tree.
~ Michael Crichton

Here's a great, hands-on way to reinforce what your child has learned after a topic has been covered in class or by you. All you will need is a bag and some creativity!

Let's say she's just finished learning about the underground railroad and Harriet Tubman. Let her:

1. Find or make at least ten different objects to represent what she's learned. For example, she might gather a monopoly house, a picture of a tree with a symbol carved on it, a Lego person (to represent Harriet), a toy train, a picture of people hiding, a toy lantern, etc.

2. Put all these items in the paper bag.

3. Begin to tell the story of the underground railroad, using the props for visuals. She might start out by pulling out the train and saying, *"First of all, the underground railroad was not a train at all."* Then, she would put the train down on a table and pull out the monopoly house. *"It was actually a series of houses used to help slaves escape to freedom."* She would continue to tell the story of slavery and of Harriet Tubman until all the pieces are out. She can ask her audience if there are any questions. If there seems to be many questions or confusion from the audience, she should consider adding additional pieces or pictures to the bag to make sure she's accounting for all the main ideas.

What a great way to study for a test and remember what she's learned!

#270
Postcards from the Past

Whether you think that you can, or that you can't, you are usually right.
~Henry Ford

After learning about a particular time in history or a particular event, your child can create a postcard to capture the time.

To do:

1. Cut a piece of poster board to postcard size or a little bigger. (Bigger especially works better for younger children whose handwriting is not refined.)

2. Draw a picture on the front depicting something particularly important from that time and place.

3. Have him decide to whom he will write the postcard. A real, historical person would be great. Make up an address for him or her using a real city.

4. Have him write on the back of the postcard as if he were truly living during that period in time. For example, if he learned about the Oregon Trail, have him write to someone as if he were really traveling on the trail. He could include details he learned like what he had to eat, what he didn't have that he wanted or needed, sickness that may be affecting the family, and much more.

This is a great culminating activity to show all that he's discovered while learning about a particular time in history.

See our workbook for a blank post card template.

#271

Make a Game of it

It is not that I'm so smart. But I stay with the questions much longer.
~Albert Einstein

Sometimes, children are required to memorize certain dates, names, events, and places. This type of memorization can turn many children off learning. It may be unavoidable, but you can help by making a game of it.

Take index cards, and use information from her book, notes or handouts to help her learn. For example, if she's learning about the presidents, one card can have a name such as "Abraham Lincoln" and another card could have one or two facts about him such as "16th president" and "helped free the slaves." Show her the cards, and when she's comfortable with them, shuffle and deal them out (five a piece) like a game of "Go Fish." You could read one of your cards, and if she has the match that goes with it, she gives it to you. If not, you draw from the deck.

You could also play a memory game with the cards by placing all cards face down on the table. Have her flip over a card and read it, then try to find the other card with information that matches. If she makes a match, she keeps both cards. If she picks two that don't match, both cards get turned back over, and it's your turn.

Ask your child for more ideas about how you can use the cards to study. Chances are she'll learn more and have a lot more fun playing games than just memorizing facts.

#272
Interactive Geography Games

Any fool can know. The point is to understand.
~Albert Einstein

The Internet has many websites that make learning Geography a game for children. There are, for example, websites that give a blank map and ask you to click on a particular state or country such as http://www.lizardpoint.com/fun/geoquiz/. Other websites, such as http://www.reachtheworld.org/geogames/, challenge by timing how quickly the different locations can be identified. Players are racing against time and trying to improve their time each time they play. Some sites use games children already know, like Tetris, and relate the game to geography such as http://www.mapmsg.com/games/statetris/.

There are so many more websites for interactive practice of geography. Simply have your child type "interactive geography games" in the search box and let him click around and start learning! (Even if those specific websites are no longer available, doing a search will surely bring you to others.)

#273
An Historical Timeline

Let him who would enjoy a good future waste none of his present.
~Roger Babson

Your child will learn so much about history in school that it may be hard for her to keep it all straight in her mind. What came first, the French and Indian War, the American Revolution, or the Civil War? She will learn about each of these events, and more, but it's important to piece them all together and have a solid idea of when important events happened in history.

One way to do this is to organize all these events by creating a timeline of historic events. If she's done activity #249, she's already had experience with creating a timeline. While that activity may have been easier because it was about her family, this one might be more challenging but very important to help her organize what she's learned about her country's past.

Consider using 8 ½" x 11" pieces of paper and the wall space around her workspace for this project. Like a wallpaper border that circles around the middle of a wall, the timeline could wrap around her workspace walls as she adds more and more events to it. Each paper could represent approximately 20 years of history. For a younger elementary student, this timeline would be very simple and may only have a few things written on it. As she gets older, the timeline will fill up as she learns more and more each year in elementary school. The historic timeline is an ongoing project that will grow with your child. It will be a great visual representation of what's she's learned in social studies every year.

Variation:

If sticking the timeline on the wall is not possible, attach pieces of paper together with clear tape. When she is done recording on it for the day, fold it up accordion-style and stash it. It will fold up to be the size of one piece of paper.

#274
Debates

Tell me and I forget, teach me and I may remember, involve me and I learn.
~ Benjamin Franklin

Your child has debating skills even if he doesn't know it. How many times have you said "No" to something and had to listen to reasons why you should change your mind? Being able to look at two sides of a problem and intelligently argue in favor of one side is a great skill. Through a proper debate (2-sided and calm, versus a temper-tantrum or argument!), your child can learn listening skills, analyzing skills, problem solving skills and speaking skills, just to name a few. You can help him put those skills to work in the area of social studies.

Take an event from social studies he's been learning about in school and have him choose a side to debate with a friend or family member. In order to debate something, he will have to truly understand it inside and out. Arguing his point of view helps him to verbalize what he's learned and commit it to memory.

For example, if he's studying the American Revolution, he could choose either to debate for the colonists or for the King of England. Remind him that he doesn't have to agree with what he's debating. He just needs to present the pros of his side and the cons of the other side with intelligence. Should the colonists rebel and break away from the King? Does the King have a right to tax their goods? Once he decides on his argument, have him jot down the main points he wants to get across. He will learn to listen to the other person's point of view and be able to address each point with examples he's written down and dispute with intelligence.

Who knows? Perhaps even future frustrations that arise in your family may be solved more peacefully with some practice with a true debate!

See our workbook for an organizer for this activity.

#275
Famous People

Study the past if you would define the future.
~Confucius

Your child will learn about many famous people in her elementary years. One way to make learning about famous people fun is to let her know that after she has learned about an assigned famous person, you will interview her as if she is that person.

If, for example, she reads about Amelia Earhart, she can dress and act as Amelia. (What could she find to wear?) You can ask her questions as if you are a reporter for an important newspaper or magazine back in that era. She can tell you all about herself, how she struggled for approval because she was a woman, how she persevered and flew on paths that few men would dare to do, etc. You can write down what she's telling you, but you may have more fun videotaping it so your child can play it back. Every time she watches herself as Amelia, she will be cementing the knowledge in her head. With this activity, she will learn facts and stories about important people in history that she will likely never forget.

#276
History and Literature

You cannot open a book without learning something.
~Confucius

When most people consider reading about history, they imagine reading a dry, boring, and thick history book. It doesn't have to be that way. There are many fiction books for children that are based on historical facts. In these books, called historical fiction, students can enjoy reading and learn stuff at the same time!

For example, in *The Magic Tree House* series by Mary Pope Osborne, each book is based on an historical event that the fictional characters travel back in time to attend. Even though the book is fiction, the facts, (certain famous) people, and events represented in the book are accurate. Children will enjoy imagining themselves traveling back in time to important historical happenings. Your child won't even realize she is learning about history when she is reading historical fiction.

Ask your child's teacher for popular books for your child's age. Below are a few books about history or other cultures.

For Younger Children:

- *When I Was Young in the Mountains* by Cynthia Rylant

- *I Will Come Back for You: A Family in Hiding During World War II* by Marisabina Russo

- T*he American Girl* series by various authors

For Older Readers:

- *Johnny Tremain* by Esther Forbes

- *Little House on the Prairie* series by Laura Ingalls Wilder

- *The Adventures of Huckleberry Finn* by Mark Twain

- *Roll of Thunder, Hear My Cry* by Mildred D. Taylor

- *Number the Stars* by Lois Lowry

Part 10
Spelling Strategies

INTRODUCTION: In this Part you will learn about ways you can encourage good spelling with your child as well as some specific strategies for practicing school spelling words.

Often, in school, an emphasis for spelling is placed on learning a select group of words for the spelling test at the end of the week. Children are not always taught that the main goal for spelling in the elementary years should be to learn *how* to spell. Acquiring a broad set of skills while they are young helps children know how to spell a lot of words, to become good spellers, and to be able to use what they already know to spell new words when needed.

How can you help your child learn how to become a good speller? What are some ways to motivate kids to practice their spelling words each week? How can you be sure they have the tools they need to figure out how to spell new words on their own? In Part 10 you will read about many ways to help your child learn how to do these things. You will read some important information about research in spelling, some ways to encourage good spelling skills, and a bunch of quick and fun strategies to help motivate your child to practice those school words.

Some children are just naturally good spellers. Others really need some support and tools to use. Some may always struggle, but you *can* help. This Part shows how.

#277

The Goal of Spelling

Whatever is worth doing at all is worth doing well.
~Lord Chesterfield

Of course, it is important for your child to do well on the spelling tests at school. Presumably, the words he has brought home for the week are carefully chosen and appropriate for his grade level. Therefore, it is obviously necessary to practice them as much as needed. The question remains, though: is he really *learning* them, or is he just practicing enough to get through the test, only for those words to then just drift out of his memory? Passing the weekly test shouldn't be the main goal for your child's spelling. It is possible for some children to get a lot of support at home and do well on every spelling test but continually not spell those, and similar words, correctly in their daily writing. When asked those spelling words a few weeks or months later, they may not spell them correctly.

If this sounds like your child, you may want to rethink the way you help him practice his spelling words and begin to provide him with more opportunities for authentic writing at home. (See Parts 5 and 6 for a wide variety of ideas.) The important thing to concentrate on when you are practicing spelling words is not to put all of your focus on your child memorizing this group of words but to develop skills that will last a lifetime. Focusing on the way words are put together, common word parts, and vowel sounds in particular, will help your child acquire skills needed to be able to spell those words later on, too. He will also be able to use that knowledge to spell new, similar words when he encounters them.

#278

Use the Message Center

My life is my message.
~Mahatma Gandhi

Are you still using your message center (Idea #6)? Putting your child's spelling list there each week will let the whole family know which words she is studying at all times. Perhaps this will encourage an older brother or sister (or babysitter, grandma, or other person) to help her practice. Seeing them all the time will also help her to remember to practice.

Here are some general tips for studying spelling words:

- Daily review works the best for long-term results. The more she practices, the better she will become at spelling these words. Cramming the night before the test is not nearly as effective long term as a little practice time every day. Not all practice has to be boring! Instead of saying, "Spell *declaration*," with the response being, "d-e-c...," try some of the much more fun ideas in this Part.

- Go over the words quickly when she first brings them home to discover which words are the trickiest and highlight the ones she consistently knows. As she practices, she will see the highlighted ones growing and feel a sense of accomplishment. And—there is no sense practicing the words she already knows!

- If she consistently knows how to spell all the words on the list each week, you might talk with her teacher to arrange a more sophisticated list for her or at least some challenge words.

- If she consistently does well on tests but does not spell according to grade level in her writing, more repetition is not necessarily going to help. Again, some ideas in this Part will probably work better. Let your child explore language and play with words as much as possible to increase spelling skills in natural ways. Children will discover many spelling rules for themselves through authentic reading and writing experiences and a variety of educational games.

#279

"Hidden Treasure"

Truth is the property of no individual but is the treasure of all men.
~ Ralph Waldo Emerson

Probably one of the most beneficial (and easiest) ways to play *Hidden Treasure* (Idea #20) is to practice spelling words and skills. Put each word on a note card and drop the cards in the container. Take turns reaching in and pulling out a word for another player to spell.

How many you use for each game depends on your child's skill level and enthusiasm. About 20 to begin with should work great. Keep words from past lists that remain difficult for him, and remove those he has mastered. Then, the next time you add more words, there will still be several left from before to practice as well. This continuous review should help with long term learning beyond the end-of-the-week test.

You could play each week with:

- all of your child's spelling words;

- just the words that he is having trouble with;

- new words and leftover words that remain difficult;

- challenge words that his teacher or you have provided;

- a group of high-frequency words from a grade level list (his teacher can give you one);

- words you have seen misspelled in his writing (keep a growing list until you have about 20); and/or

- a specific group of words fitting a category he needs to practice (such as short vowels, "tion" words, silent "e" words, etc.).

Don't hesitate to involve the whole family. (Read about the ways to make it fair when playing with advanced spellers like you!) Offer hints to your child (such as, "*Night* rhymes with *right,* so use that to help you spell it.") if he struggles to spell a word. Remember that the goal of *Hidden Treasure* is to help your child have fun while mastering spelling skills so do anything you can think of to make it enjoyable as well as educational.

See our website for more detailed instructions on how to play!

#280
The Stages of Spelling

Life isn't a matter of milestones,
but of moments.
~Rose Kennedy

Spelling skills are not necessarily directly related to grade level. There will be spelling skills worked on and expectations in each grade level, but, in general, it is a developmental process with common stages. Children all begin at one end of the spelling continuum and progress at their own pace toward the other. Below are the common stages of spelling and indicators of what a child in that stage would look like. See if you can determine where your child is by looking over her writing carefully. Then, take a look at the next stage to see where she is headed.

1. Preliminary Spelling:

    - Children are becoming aware that print carries a message.

    - They use writing-like symbols (or approximations of letters) to represent written language.

    - Their writing is not readable by others.

    - They do not understand sound-symbol relationships yet.

2. Semi-Phonetic (Sound or Invented) Spelling:

    - Children are developing an understanding of sound-symbol relationships.

- They may represent a whole word with one, two, or three letters, using mostly initial and final sounds, usually consonants, such as "kt" for *kitten.*

3. Phonetic Spelling:

   - Children can make almost a perfect match between letters and sounds although letters are chosen without regard for conventional letter patterns.

   - They represent all substantial sounds in a word.

   - Spelling attempts are more meaningful ("sounded out") and more like standard spelling such as "wacht" for *watched.*

4. Transitional Spelling:

   - Children use letters to represent all vowels and consonant sounds in a word ("holaday" for holiday).

   - They still have difficulty recognizing if a word "looks right."

   - They have a rapidly growing bank of learned words.

   - They are beginning to use spelling conventions like double and silent letters.

5. Independent (or Conventional) Spelling:

   - Children have become aware of the many patterns and rules that are characteristic of the English spelling system.

   - They use a multi-strategy approach to spelling new words.

   - They can recognize when a word doesn't look right.

   - They have a large bank of words that they can automatically recall.

Remember, even if your child is above or below the desired spelling stage for her grade, the important thing is to progress. Hopefully, knowing that there are several stages (and, of course, stages in between the stages) will ease your mind and also let you actually see the progress as you start to see skills in the next stage develop.

#281
Sound Spelling

Dew knot trussed yore spell chequer two fined awl yore mistakes.
~Brendan Hills

Children are full of great ideas. Even the youngest of children have so much to say and many a story to tell. Just because they may not be perfect spellers doesn't mean they can't actually write for themselves. You can encourage even a very young child to write wonderful stories, all on his own, by showing him how to use his own "sound spelling."

Sound spelling (sometimes called "invented" spelling) is simply the most phonetic way a child can think of to spell a word. Children are taught to "spell it so you can read it." For instance, if he is struggling to write "bright" in a story, he should be encouraged not to give up but to try his best. He should say the word aloud and listen for all of the sounds. He should try his best to segment out all of the sounds he hears and try to figure out what letter(s) to use to represent those sounds.

Here are some ideas and tips:

- You could tell your child to "Write down the letters you hear yourself saying." (He might write *brit.*)

- Encourage him to think of words that he *does* know how to spell that rhyme with the one he is stuck on. Could that word help him spell this one? (If he knows *night*, he could use that *ight* pattern, *bright.*)

- After he is done writing his draft, ask him to go through his story and circle any words he would like help spelling. This is often a very complex skill. Children do not always want to and aren't always able to find their own mistakes. It takes practice. Go over his story with him, helping him spell any of the words he has circled. Say the words together, and show him how you write what you say and point out any patterns or rules that may be helpful. "The *ight* make up the *ite* sound in this word." Some teachers like to call the "correct" spelling "book spelling." Teachers can say (and you can, too!) something like, "The book spelling of *bright* is b-r-i-g-h-t." This sometimes just sounds nicer than saying, "You spelled the word *bright* wrong."

These ideas should help your child naturally move toward conventional spelling if done with consistency and patience. Because it takes a long time to master conventional English spelling, children will naturally write many words they haven't yet learned how to spell while they are young writers if they are allowed the opportunity to sound spell. Research has proven, too, that children who are encouraged to use sound spelling write longer and better first drafts than children who only write words they know how to spell. Just like your child babbled before he learned to talk, and stumbled as he learned to walk, he will most likely sound spell before he learns to be a conventional speller.

#282
A Spelling Dictionary

Infinite patience brings immediate results.
~Wayne Dyer

Patience is required to learn to become a conventional speller. (Some of us are still working on that!) One of the ways you can help your child become a good speller is to have her keep a list of words she *does* know how to spell. A regular list would keep growing and soon become out of control as your child grows as a writer and a speller so one clever way to organize her bank of known words is to create a personal spelling dictionary.

To do this:

1. Buy a regular notebook or make something even more useful with a binder. (Put about 30 pages of loose-leaf paper in it to start.)

2. Label each page with one letter A-Z. You may want to give the most common letters a few pages each. (This is where the binder is more practical because as you find you need more room for any particular letter, you can simply insert more pages!)

3. Leave a few blank pages in the back.

4. Now, begin entering words. Obviously, a very young child can start by entering all of the few words she does know how to spell and add more as she learns them. An older child, however, would have an overwhelming task to try to do the same. She may want, instead, to add only:

   - her new spelling words from school each week;

   - words she finds herself trying to spell in her writing and can't, (i.e. words she's sound spelled); you may want to help her select some;

   - challenge words provided by her teacher, herself, or you; and/or

   - grade-level high-frequency words.

The pages in the back could be used to:

   - group like or rhyming words with the same pattern;

   - collect "Million Dollar Words"—great words she intends to use in writing (Idea #183);

   - record key features of the roots in words (e.g., for *geography*, "geo=earth");

   - provide definitions; and/or

- include anything your child finds helpful!

Her spelling dictionary could be kept at her study space and will provide her with confidence as well as a quick reference the next time she's writing.

Variations:

- Add any mnemonic devices (e.g., for *principal*, "My <u>pal</u> is the princi<u>pal</u>;" see Idea #334), spelling rules, or hints next to an entered word to remind her how to spell it.

- If she enjoys working on the computer, she can create her dictionary using a program like Microsoft Word. She can create a folder on her desktop and call it "Spelling Dictionary." In the folder, she can create a page for each letter of the alphabet, definitions, million dollar words, rhyming words, etc. She can even use clip art to include pictures which may help her remember words and definitions.

#283
High Frequency Words

Think twice before you speak,
because your words and influence will plant
the seed of either success or failure in the mind of another.
- Napoleon Hill

There are too many words in our language to count! So, how do you know which words your child should know how to spell? To help you out, every grade level has a list of words called "high frequency words" that are common for that developmental age/stage. Most teachers will include those words in the weekly spelling lists, sometimes wherever they fit in, sometimes just a few per week, or sometimes all at once. However it is done in school, you can ask your child's teacher for the list and practice the words with her at home.

These high frequency words really should be memorized. They are called "high frequency" for a reason; they do show up in kids' writing often. Therefore, they should be spelled correctly. Try posting tough ones on note cards at the message center (Idea #6) or on the fridge where your child can see them several times a day. Put them on his mirror or on his ceiling so he can "study" them in bed! Find fun places to hang them up; the more he sees them, the more quickly he'll learn them.

There are many other ideas in this Part to help you find fun ways to practice these and other spelling words so practicing doesn't have to be boring anymore. Read the ideas, try them out, and find a few favorites. Your child will be glad he put in the effort to forever memorize each grade's high frequency words.

#284
Using a Thesaurus

Impossible is a word to be found only in the dictionary of fools.
~Napoleon Bonaparte

Perhaps when you were young and didn't know a word, you had to look it up in a dictionary. Today, kids have the ease and availability of the Internet to look up any word they need almost anywhere and anytime, but did you know, she can find more than definitions in an online dictionary?

Websites such as www.webster.com work as a thesaurus as well as a dictionary. A thesaurus entry does not give the definition of a word. Instead, when your child types in a word, she is given a list of other words (synonyms) for that word. It's a great tool to help make your child's writing more interesting. For example, instead of using the word *walk* in a story, your child can use the thesaurus and find many interesting synonyms such as *amble, saunter, stroll, promenade, hike, march,* and *traverse.*

If she knows how to use an online thesaurus and dictionary, she may be more likely to use it than a traditional printed one. And if she gets used to using one, she is more likely to spell words correctly *and* create much more interesting writing pieces as well!

#285
Making Words: Spelling Strategy

I have not failed. I've just found 10,000 ways that won't work.
~Thomas Alva Edison

Children love to play games. They love a challenge, and they will love improving spelling skills (although they probably won't realize they *are*) when they play challenging games with words.

Making Words, created by author Patricia Cunningham, is a perfect game for elementary children learning the conventions of standard spelling. Kids will be manipulating individual letters to create small words and eventually one large word with all of the letters. It is a hands-on activity that encourages children to look for patterns in words and focus on individual vowel and consonant sounds. To play, all you need is a few sets of the ABCs printed on index cards with upper case letters on one side and lower case on the other, or the magnetic letters people sometimes put on refrigerators.

1. Choose a word that contains letters with which it is fairly easy to create smaller words. Choose a word appropriate for your child's spelling skills. He should be able to spell at least a majority of the little words and have a possibility at getting close to the big, original word. (For example, *stamp* for young spellers, *Christmas* for middle level spellers, or *declarations* for more advanced spellers.)

2. Make a list of as many words as you can think of that can be made with the letters in your big word. For example, for *stamp: am, Pam, at, amp, Sam, as.* Ms. Cunningham has several books out that have already done this for you. She has chosen large words and has found all the little words that can be made with its letters. However, if your child is having a particular problem with a certain spelling pattern such as *-ai*, you may find yourself wanting to pick out your own word at his level with that pattern in it. There are websites that will unscramble a word for you and give you all the possibilities!

3. Pick out the letters needed to spell the large word and give them to your child in either a scrambled order or in alphabetical order. (Note that you may need to give two or more of the same letter if needed.)

4. Allow your child a minute to look over the letters and move them around a bit. (You may want to challenge your child to create some small words on his own before beginning.)

5. Tell your child you will be asking him to create several small words with the letters, gradually building up to larger words. Finally, he will try to use *all* of the letters to create one large word.

6. Say one of the smallest words, and ask him to build it using only the letters you gave him. (Beginning easy builds self-confidence.) He should use the lowercase letters and can flip a card over if a capital letter is needed.

7. Continue from small words to the largest words. Praise correct spellings. Review any incorrect with your child carefully. (Gently show him what the word says that he *did* create and work with him to change it into the correct spelling.)

8. When he has spelled all of the smaller words, challenge him to use all of his letters to create one large word. You can give some hints or just ask him to look for letters that he thinks may go together and work from there. Give him as much time as he wants. Some kids like to try and try and others get frustrated quickly.

Variations:

- Place a few sets of magnetic letters on a cookie sheet in alphabetical order. (The letters will stick!) Kids love to move them around to form words.

- You can write all of the smaller words on index cards and, afterward, have your child sort them in different ways: by number of letters, vowel sound, etc. The more they play with the words, the better they will spell those words later on their own.

See our website for examples of Making Words.

Try this website to find all the little words inside a big word you might choose: http://www. solverscrabble.com/solver/

#286
Games & Puzzles: Spelling Strategy

> *To acquire knowledge, one must study;*
> *but to acquire wisdom, one must observe.*
> *~Marilyn Vos Savant*

You know that playing games is a great way to not only have fun with your child but also to help him practice his skills. Here are a few ideas for word games you can make up:

1. Make a Word Search. There are websites that let you enter the words and it makes the word search for you! Let your child enter the words for added practice. (This is an example of such a website: http://puzzlemaker.discoveryeducation.com/WordSearchSetupForm.asp.) If you want to really make your child search carefully, enter some "slightly wrong" words, too. For instance, if *elephant* is a word, enter that word correctly, but also enter "elefant" or "elephent", too. Then, as he is searching he will really have to scrutinize if it is the one he wants or not.

2. Play Hangman with his words. This works better when there is a large list or it is review time. Little kids, however, can still have fun playing when the list is shorter.

3. Make a crossword puzzle with clues to each word. Again, there are websites that make this very easy to do. (Try: http://www.puzzle-maker.com/CW/).

A little bit of time put in by you can sure make a fun and motivational way to practice spelling words!

#287

Pretty as a Picture: Spelling Strategy

Every day we should hear at least one little song, read one good poem, see one exquisite picture, and, if possible, speak a few sensible words.
~ Johann Wolfgang von Goethe

If your child is creative, maybe a good drawer, another fun strategy for practicing spelling words can be to have her draw a picture and "hide" the words in the picture. A word can become the trunk of a tree, the stripes on a tiger, or a reflection in a pond. The whole time she is planning and squeezing in the letters of each word, she is practicing its spelling without really even knowing it! Now, have her give the picture to you and see if you can find the words!

Sometimes, a list of spelling words is particularly tricky because it contains two different spelling patterns that are very similar. For instance, perhaps she has a list of 20 *long a* words: ten words have the *-ai* pattern and ten have a silent e. Not only does she have to learn how to spell each, but she also has to remember which pattern belongs to each word. Pictures, here, can be helpful, too. Here's how:

1. Split the words into two groups according to their pattern. Read all of the words in one group and draw a picture that includes all of them. Perhaps, depending on the age of your child, she can also write a silly story using all of them.

2. Now, do the same for the other list.

3. You end up with two separate pictures and maybe two separate stories that link all of the like-words together. Now, when she hears a word, if she is not certain of its pattern, she can recall the picture (and/ or story) it is in and link it with another word in there that she does know for sure and, therefore, know its pattern, too!

Here is an example with just a few words:

Tail Sail Pail Main

Captain Joe flew the main sail while his dog knocked over the pail of fish with his tail. (Draw a picture to show this.)

Tale Sale Pale Mane

Let me tell you a tale of a sick, pale lion whose mane was all shaggy. He went to a hat sale to buy a hat to cover it up. (Draw a picture to show this.)

Now, when asked to spell *main* she might recall it being in the same picture as *sail* which she knows is *-ai* and therefore spells this *main* correctly, too.

#288
Silly Sentences: Spelling Strategy

I'm not young enough to know everything.
~James Barrie

Young children do know so much. Even if your child is struggling to become a good speller, chances are he *does* know how to spell many words. The trick is to get him to realize this and to help him become an even better speller in fun ways that don't seem like regular school learning. A fun way to increase spelling skills is to write some "Silly Sentences" for him.

To do this, simply write him a message on a piece of paper, on a wipe-off board, or at the message center, containing some spelling mistakes. Begin with a few simple mistakes on high-frequency words for young spellers. Try many tricky ones for more advanced spellers. Use school spelling words and misspell them, or use any words your child frequently writes and misspells. Most kids like to know how many mistakes there are. He will not give up after finding and fixing three things if he knows you made ten errors! Since kids love a good challenge, you might say, "I wrote you a message but, oops! I made ten mistakes in it!" Kids love to be the teacher and find parents' mistakes!

Now, challenge him to edit your message. Let him use a special pen, a colored pencil, anything to make editing fun and so that he can see his edits easily. He should read each word carefully, checking it for spelling and fixing it when he finds an error. It's helpful to be close by as he works on it so you can help if needed by offering hints like, "The end of that word sounds like the beginning of *chair* and you know how to spell that word." Don't forget to go over it when he's finished to clarify any difficult words and praise him for a job well done.

Another fun way to practice is to turn the tables and have him write some "Silly Sentences" for you (or someone else) to edit. Sure, he will be doing the spelling (and misspelling) at first, but after you are done (and have "missed" a few mistakes for *him* to instruct *you* on), he will have to be the final editor to determine whether you are correct. Therefore, he will have to know how to fix each one!

See Idea #159 for more info, and see our website for two examples of Silly Sentences.

#289
Chant and Clap: Spelling Strategy

Success is the sum of small efforts—repeated day in and day out.
~Robert Collier

Just as efforts must be repeated to achieve success, so must many new things be repeated in order to be learned. Spelling is no different. For children who have a tough time with spelling, or for any child who encounters a difficult word, orally repeating the letters in the word may be a helpful strategy for memorization. Add in some tactile support, and you have a recipe for success. The Chant and Clap method, or a variation of it, may help your child.

To use it:

1. Choose a word that is difficult for your child to spell. For example, *multiplication*.

2. Have him chant (say) the letters in the word aloud as he claps, once for each letter. You can help him even more by pointing out known parts of the word, or breaking it into syllables so that, as he chants the spelling, he is saying *groups* of letters instead of just individual letters, further aiding in memory, like this: *mul* (pause) *ti* (pause) *pli* (pause) *ca* (pause) *tion*.

3. Have him chant and clap each word three times and then move on to another difficult word.

Variations:

- Have your child place a faint dot under each letter of the word as he chants its spelling.

- If clapping is too noisy or hectic, have him tap two fingers on his arm as he chants each letter.

#290
Break it up! Spelling Strategy

If we can really understand the problem,
the answer will come out of it,
because the answer is not separate from the problem.
~Jiddu Krishnamurti

When faced with the challenge of spelling certain words, especially long ones, it helps to have a few tools in your "spelling toolbox." One of these strategies goes along with the principle of breaking large tasks into smaller, more manageable, ones. Try breaking larger words into smaller ones.

For instance, the word *caterpillar* might be tricky for a second grader to learn, but if you show your child how the word is made up of smaller parts, or "chunks," that she already *does* know how to spell, it will automatically become easier.

Here is an example: *cat er pill ar.*

She may already know how to spell *cat* and *pill* and be familiar with the *-er* chunk. After she realizes this, she only needs to listen for those word parts as she thinks about spelling the whole word.

You might also try:

- Breaking compound words down into the two original words (e.g., *snowflake* into *snow* and *flake*)

- Pointing out a pattern a tough word might have like others she knows.

- Circling all of the vowels in the word to emphasize where and what they are.

- Finding words that rhyme with a tough word.

- Noting any prefixes or suffixes on a root word; for instance, *international* isn't so tough when you point out the prefix *inter-* and the common suffix *-al* around the root word *nation*.

#291
Using Steps: Spelling Strategy

Faith is taking the first step even when you don't see the whole staircase.
~Martin Luther King, Jr.

Another easy strategy for practicing his spelling words is a 6-step strategy. It's a nice one because your child can do this by *himself!* Here are the steps:

1. Fold a piece of paper in half lengthwise. Open it back up. Copy a spelling word along the left-hand side.

2. Say the word aloud.

3. Spell the word aloud as you look at it.

4. Close your eyes, and spell it aloud. (Open them and check it.)

5. Fold the paper over the word to cover it up. Write the word again on the folded part without looking.

6. Open the fold, and check it.

It's that simple! Getting your child used to practicing in this way can set him up for a lifetime of good study skills because he can use this strategy or one similar to it for studying lots of things on his own. You might try writing these steps on a notecard and posting it somewhere that your child can easily find when needed.

#292
Mnemonic Devices: Spelling Strategy

Each day of our lives we make deposits in the memory banks of our children.
~Charles R. Swindoll

We are all well aware that many words in the English language cannot be spelled phoneti-cally. There are patterns that puzzle even the best spellers. When faced with words that just "don't make any sense," creating fun, mnemonic devices can be helpful.

Mnemonic devices are little phrases or rhymes that are used as a memory tool. You may recall in math class learning the order of operations (parentheses first, then exponents, multi-plication, division, addition, subtraction) by using the mnemonic device of "Please excuse my dear Aunt Sally." The first letters in that sentence correspond with the first letters, in the same order, of the operations. You can also do the same thing with spelling.

For example, the word *laugh* is not phonetic and, therefore, can be tough for kids to learn to spell. Try making up a funny sentence like "I would la<u>ugh</u> if I saw <u>ugly</u> gorillas <u>h</u>ugging!" The *u* in *ugly*, *g* in *gorillas*, and *h* in *hugging*, spell out the tough part of the word: *-ugh*. If your child practices this funny sentence, she can then remind herself of it any time she needs to spell that word, like on her test. Here's a few more just so you get the idea:

- If the *-or* in *author* is tough, try, "Would you rather be the author of a book *or* the illustrator?" Emphasize the *or* so she will remember there is an *-or* at the end.

- If the *u* in *hurt* is tricky, try, "Are U hurt?" Emphasize the *u* so she remembers it is a *ur* word.

- If the *ie* is tough in *piece*, try, "I'd like a *pie*ce of *pie*!" She'll remember that *piece* starts with *pie*.

- If the *o* in *people* is tough to remember, try drawing the O big and turning it into a person's head. This might help her visualize the *o*.

- "You h*ear* with your *ear*."

- "Never bel*ieve* a *lie*."

You get the picture! Have fun making up whatever funny, weird, silly thing works for her. You can certainly help her with some, but the more she develops them herself, the more she is likely to remember them! She could keep a list of the ones she makes up in her Spelling Dictionary, too! (See Idea #282.)

#293
Tactile Ideas: Spelling Strategy

You can learn from a child's curiosity,
You can learn from a rain, rather than waiting for a storm,
You can learn from a tree, better than forest.
Understand the virtue of small things before doing great things.
~ Emma Brynstein

For young kids, the more you can incorporate several different kinds of learning while practicing spelling words, the better. Many kids learn best by seeing the words. Some learn best by hearing them. Probably, you are already doing this with your child, but there is a third kind of learning, tactile, that is also quite helpful for learning how to spell. This involves simply getting your child moving in some big or small way while spelling. Here are some fun examples:

1. Close your eyes, and tell your child to spell a spelling word out by writing it with his finger on the palm of your hand. Can you guess what it is?

2. Pour sand on an old cookie sheet or plate. Have your child write the words with his finger in the sand. (Hint: If he loves this idea and wants to use it every week, try a long, flat container with a lid. Then, you can just keep the sand in it, and it won't spill out!)

3. Try that same idea, but instead of sand, try shaving cream or flour!

4. If it's snowy out, fill up a spray bottle with colored water, and spray the words into the snow.

5. Put a set of magnetic letters on the fridge or a cookie sheet, and spell one word at a time. (You may need more than one set of letters!)

6. Get a ball of string or yarn. Cut about eight pieces into 5-foot long sections. Spell out his spelling words (one letter per strand) on the floor, and let him walk on them as he spells them out loud. Let him spell them out for you to walk on!

7. At snack time, use mini pretzel sticks to spell out the words. Then, eat 'em! (Can he use traditional-shaped pretzels, too? This is trickier. He'll have to nibble each into the correct letter!)

8. Round up a few handfuls of something like pennies or buttons. Have him use them to make the letters in the spelling words.

#294
Ransom Notes: Spelling Strategy

There are only 3 colors, 10 digits, and 7 notes;
it's what we do with them that's important.
~Jim Rohn

Here is another fun way to bring several different learning styles into the practicing of spelling words. Make a ransom note! Well, not really of course, but something like it. It's quite simple:

1. Find an old newspaper or magazine that you don't mind being ripped up.

2. Have your child pick a spelling word that she is having trouble with and look for the letters in that word in the magazine. (Hint: headlines usually work best because the letters are bigger and easier for little fingers to cut out.)

3. Glue the letters in the right order on a piece of paper to spell out the word!

This works best not necessarily with the entire list, but with just the words that she is stuck on. The time this takes your child to search for just the right letter, cut it out, and glue it in the correct order is sure to help her memorize its spelling.

#295
Read My Mind: Spelling Strategy

A word to the wise ain't necessary—it's the stupid ones that need the advice.
~Bill Cosby

Another fun game to play with spelling words is called "Read My Mind." This is a motivating game for kids who may be having trouble with spelling due to a lack of awareness of letter sounds and groups. It can easily be tailored to fit any child's spelling level. You can play with your child's entire spelling list from school each week, save only the most difficult words each week, or choose words he misspells often in his writing. Ten to twenty words is usually a good start, depending on your child's age and ability level. Try it, and find out.

To play:

1. Write each word to be used for the game on an index card (one word per card). Arrange them all on a table face up for your child to see.

2. Secretly choose one of the words, and write it down for only you to see.

3. Challenge your child to "read your mind" and guess the word you've chosen. Tell him that you will give him five clues to help him out and he will make a guess after each clue. Your first clue should always be the most general, such as, *"It's one of the words laid out here."*

4. Have your child say the word card he thinks it is, and place the word card next to him. This first guess really is just a wild guess, of course, because he has no clues as to what it is. If he gets it now, did he really read your mind!?!?!?

5. Now give him another clue such as, *"The vowel in the word makes the short* a *sound."* Your child should look carefully at the word in front of him that he had chosen first. Does it meet the new criteria? If it does, he can keep it. If it doesn't, he should choose another of the words that does and put back the other.

6. Do the same for the last three clues, getting more specific each time in order to narrow down the choices until by clue 5, there is only one possible word. After each clue, your child should either keep the word he had chosen previously or choose another one that meets all of the clues.

7. When all five clues have been given and he chooses his final answer, show him the word you chose. Was he correct? How long had he "read your mind"? Did he have that one set aside the whole time? Did he just choose it with the last clue? Praise him for a job well done either way!

The clues you give can be tailored to meet your child's specific needs. If beginning sounds are troublesome, focus on those: "My word begins with the *th* sound" or "The word begins with *ch.*" The clues can include any feature of the words that you want your child to focus on and become more aware of such as number of letters, vowel sounds or combinations, beginning or ending letter(s) or sound(s), or "My secret word finishes this sentence: ..."

Variations:

- Your child could turn over any words that do not fit the criteria each time a clue is given to help him visually narrow down his choices each time. (This helps you, too, by seeing if he's missing any.)

- You could have your child write down the word he chooses each time after a clue given. This will give him even more practice spelling the words he needs help with. On the next line, he can either write the same word (if it is still possibly the secret word) or write a new choice.

- Let your child choose a word (and give you the clues), with you trying to read his mind. He will still need to pay close attention to the letters and chunks of each word and do a lot of problem solving and analyzing of the words to think of just the right clues to give you. It is so fun to see if he can stump you!

#296
What's in There?: Spelling Strategy

What lies behind you and what lies in front of you,
pales in comparison to what lies inside of you.
~ Ralph Waldo Emerson

Here's a way to turn part of Making Words (Idea #285) into a family activity. Gather the whole family for a round of "What's in There?"

To play:

1. Choose a word with lots of letters. It could be a holiday word if one is coming up, a place your family recently visited, or any word you can think of. Write the word nice and big on a piece of paper. For instance, *Valentine's Day*.

2. Now try to come up with as many words as you can think of using any of (and only) the letters in that word. i.e. *let, vine, said, ladies, evident, island*. Jot all of your words down on a piece of paper. See who can come up with the most! Who can come up with the biggest word? Did anyone find a word that no one else found?

Hint: For younger kids, you can give them the letters in the word written out one per card, or give them the correct magnetic letters, so they can physically move the letters around. Older players do not get this advantage!

Variation:

Try the opposite! Choose a small word like *sand*. How many words can you think of that have all of those four letters in them. For example, *thousand, dancers*? This is much trickier and is best used with good spellers.

See our workbook for a sheet to organize this activity.

#297
Alphabetizing the Words: Spelling Strategy

In order to succeed, we must first believe that we can.
~Nikos Kazantzakis

Here is another short and simple way to practice spelling words. Have your child put his spelling words in alphabetical order. Younger kids may need help, but it is a skill used all through the elementary years so, even if you are teaching it to him first, it will be easy when finally brought up at school. If he already knows how, this is good reinforcement. It is also helpful because, in order to do it, your child will really have to analyze the letters in each word, and as he is doing it, he is also practicing the spelling of those words!

It doesn't even have to end with his spelling words. Alphabetizing anything around the house like DVDs or music collections can help him better understand the concept and start to see the patterns in many words. Objects without words on them can be a nice challenge to alphabetize. For example, if you asked him to put his toys, cars, animals, etc. in alphabetical order, he would have to think of the beginning sounds and visualize the spelling of the object in his head, which will help him remember it.

#298
It's Rhyme Time! Spelling Strategy

> *Outside of a dog, a book is a man's best friend.*
> *Inside of a dog it's too dark to read.*
> *~ Groucho Marx*

Another strategy for improving spelling is to look for patterns in words. As your child becomes more familiar with word patterns, she will be able to spell new words in the future using those patterns. Rhymes are usually high interest and can therefore provide some great opportunities to practice spelling without even realizing it. Here are a few fun ideas to try with your child:

1. Rhyme Times (also sometimes called Hink Pinks): These are riddles with 2-word answers. First, think of two rhyming words like *funny* and *bunny*. Now, create the question using other words for your rhymes, such as "What do you call a rabbit that tells jokes? (A funny bunny!) "What is a large feline?" (A fat cat!) Make some up for your child and, of course, let her make some up for you!

2. Couplets: These are two sentences about the same thing that rhyme at the end. Many times they have the same number of beats per line. For example:

    Summer vacation is so much fun!

    I like to swim and also run!

    or

    I have two cats, one mean, one nice.

    Both of them like to chase fat mice.

Your child can use her current spelling words or patterns that are giving her difficulty to create her own Hink Pink or Couplet. She will have fun creating them and won't even realize she's practicing her spelling.

See our workbook for a sheet to organize this activity.

#299
The Long and Short of It: Spelling Strategy

Building a better you is the first step to building a better America.
~ Zig Ziglar

Spelling is a very visual activity. The more your child works with tough words and ex-amines a word's letters and parts, the better he will understand how to spell it. A fun way to practice spelling tough words is to pay attention to the height of the letters, to notice those individual letters in a different way. He will be spending several enjoyable minutes looking closely at those words, which will aid in mastery.

To try this strategy:

1. Choose a word that your child has trouble with.

2. Trace the word with straight lines, creating boxes of one of three different shapes around each letter. You will have some short boxes around the short letters (a, c, e, i, m, n, o, r, s, u, v, w, x, z), some will be tall and upward (b, d, f, h, k, l, t), and some will be tall and downward (g, j, p, q, y).

3. Now look at the word together and talk about what the word looks like; where the tall and short letters are, any patterns. This should give your child a more vivid mental image of the word and help him spell it in the future.

Variations:

- For an older student, choose a few of your child's trickiest spelling words or any words he usually has trouble with. Draw the shape of the word (with the boxes), and show it to your child. Have him search through his list (or Spelling Dictionary—see Idea #282) for a word that would fit into your puzzle.

- You could also give him a word shape and have him fill it in with letters to create any word he can from his ever-expanding bank of words in his head. For example, 1 short, 1 tall, 2 short, 1 tall could be "stand.")

- Encourage him to make some for you to try. He will have to look closely at the word, determining each letter's shape, and then review your choice to see if you were correct.

#300
Memory: Spelling Strategy

The soul never thinks without a picture.
~Aristotle

You may have a game like Memory or Concentration already at home. Young kids often play the game by matching pictures. Older kids like to play with a deck of cards to match numbers. You can quite easily make a Memory game with your child to help her practice her spelling words, too. Here's how to play:

1. Write each spelling word on two different index cards.

2. Make two piles of words, each pile containing one of each word so that you have two identical piles.

3. Spread out one pile on the floor. Leave a space, and then spread out the other pile on the floor. All words should be upside down.

4. You and your child can take turns flipping over a card from one side and then choosing a card from the other side to flip, hoping to get a match. If you do get a match, keep it.

5. If they do not match, flip them both back over. On future turns, try to remember where they are!

6. Those with the most matches when all cards are gone, wins.

Variations:

- Have your child write out the word cards if she is able.

- Depending on the words, could you write the first half of the word on one card and the second half on another? Those can be the two piles. Then, flip up a beginning on one side and an ending on the other, and see if you have made a word!

- Depending on the words, you could also do rhymes for each. One pile has the spelling words; the other has a rhyme for each word. Flip two cards. Do they rhyme? If so, keep them!

#301

Scrambled Words: Spelling Strategy

It's a (@#!) poor mind that can only think of one way to spell a word.*
~Andrew Johnson

Another fun way to turn practicing spelling words that are difficult into a game is to try some Scrambled Words, instead of scrambled eggs, at breakfast this morning! Of course, you can do this activity any time at all, but how fun to surprise your child at a time when he is not used to practicing spelling!

To do it:

1. Choose the words that your child is having the most difficulty with (either from his spelling list or from words you notice he needs to learn how to spell).

2. Scramble the letters, and write them down for your child in the wrong order.

3. Give them to your child with the challenge of trying to rearrange the letters to correctly form the word. He can either look at a list of words from which you have chosen the word or just use his ever-growing list of words he knows in his head. For younger kids, having some words to look at is definitely the way to go!

Variations:

- If your child needs practice with high-frequency words in general writing, try writing him a whole sentence (or even *message*) for him to unscramble! He will not only have to determine the correct spelling of each word, but will also have to figure out your message. For example: *oD uoy twna llejy no uyro ostta?* (*Do you want jelly on your toast?*)

- Have him write some scrambled words (or sentences or messages) for you. Although you will be doing the unscrambling, he will have to know how to spell the words in the first place in order to scramble them, check your work, and determine if your spelling is correct. (What fun for him when he finds one of your "mistakes!")

#302
Tongue Twisters: Spelling Strategy

If people never did silly things nothing intelligent would ever get done.
~Ludwig Wittgenstein

Depending on the group of words your child has for spelling words, here are some possibilities for making some fun out of practicing them.

1. Try making up some Tongue Twisters: If she has words with blends (such as *bl, br, cl, fl, sm, sp, sn,st, sw, tr*), she could pick out a few and find a few other like-words, and then make up something like "Six snakes snuck past six sharks snacking in a storm." Try it with words that have the same vowel sound such as *mane, sail, same, tame, tail.* They are fun for kids to make up and even funnier to hear their parents try to say!

2. Alliterations are a little more specific; all of the words begin with the same letter. If her spelling words do, try putting some together (along with some new words, if needed) to form a sentence. "Peter Piper picked a peck of pickled peppers" is an example of an alliteration and also a tongue twister! In all of her effort to put these words together into tongue-twisting sentences, she will also be getting good practice with their spelling!

See our workbook for some tricky tongue twisters to try!

#303
Rainbow Words: Spelling Strategy

And when it rains on your parade, look up rather than down.
Without the rain, there would be no rainbow.
~Gilbert K. Chesterton

You can probably remember having to write your spelling words 5-10 times each when you were a child. Well, there is something to be said about the *theory* behind that (repetition helps aid retention), although it is also a good way to bore children and could quite possibly make them dislike spelling. What if there were a way to get them to write their spelling words a few times each in a fun and interesting way?

If your child seems to benefit from repetition when it comes to learning his spelling words, then you may want to try Rainbow Words. To make Rainbow Words, have your child:

1. Choose 3-5 different colored pencils or crayons. (The number of colors corresponds to the number of times the word will be written and also spelled out loud, so it will depend on your child's skill level, need for repetition, and enthusiasm for the activity. Play around with it; see what works best.)

2. Have him write one of his spelling words on a piece of paper with one of the crayons, saying the letters aloud as he goes. Saying the letters in meaningful chunks can help. For example, instead of spelling America like a robot "A-m-e-r-i-c-a," it is more helpful to group the letters that go together, possibly syllables. "Am-er-i-ca.")

3. Now, he traces directly over the word with a different color, again saying the letters aloud. Look how pretty the word is now!

4. Now, pick another color to trace the word again until he has done this with each crayon chosen.

5. The result is a very colorful (rainbow) word that he has written several times, spelled aloud for added learning, and chances are, he hasn't been bored a bit!

6. Repeat with all words chosen for this activity. Some kids like to use the same colors in a different order to see the effect or choose entirely new colors. It's up to you!

You may not want to do this with all of his spelling words or even every week. You could choose just the words that he is having trouble with each week or offer it as one of the many choices that you've collected in this Part that he can pick from each week as a way to practice his words. Using colors in this activity helps visual learners and saying the letters aloud helps auditory learners.

See our website for a list of all of the strategies found in this Part. Perhaps hang it at the message center or at his work space so that every time he has to practice his spelling words he has options to choose from.

Part 11
Developing Critical Thinking Skills

INTRODUCTION: This Part will provide activities to get your child thinking critically with an overall general wrapping up of the many ideas you've learned. It will also tie things together. In many of the ideas, you will be reminded of other ideas from this book and new ways to incorporate them.

Bloom's Taxonomy is often used in the teaching profession to help teachers create lessons that focus on the different levels of thinking. There are six levels (Idea #304) that describe varying degrees of questioning and reasoning. Teachers strive to develop lessons and activities that focus on *all* six levels with an emphasis on the higher levels. *You* can, too. This will certainly help your child to become a critical thinker by encouraging her to use higher-level thinking skills, rather than simply recalling facts.

Good students not only know the facts but also know how to *apply* their new knowledge, understand how it relates to other areas, and make discriminating conclusions of their own about it. We have used these multiple levels throughout this Part.

In the beginning of this Part, we have written some general ideas and activities for you and your family to try. We hope that you will modify and extend them to meet your family's interests and work on them together to provide a role model for your child to follow.

For the last half of this Part, we have provided you with specific mind-benders and challenges for you to work on with your child. Again, we hope that you will extend those that your child especially enjoys, make up some of your own, and keep up a dialogue by discussing your thought processes.

Finally, children love creating puzzles that stump their parents, so be sure to give yours a chance to invent a few!

#304
Bloom's Taxonomy

We are what we repeatedly do. Excellence, then, is not an act, but a habit.
~Aristotle

Below is an explanation of Bloom's Taxonomy. The six levels are explained briefly and a few action-oriented words that are common to each are offered so that you can reference them when preparing an activity for your child.

Knowledge: Remembering previously learned material. (This is a basic recall level. We often think that this shows true learning. However, as you will see as you read on, there are many higher levels of learning!)
Terms: define, describe, identify, list, match, name, recall

Comprehension: Grasping the meaning of material.
Terms: defend, distinguish, estimate, explain, generalize, interpret, explain, summarize

Application: Using learned material in a new situation.
Terms: change, compute, demonstrate, apply, show, use, solve

Analysis: Breaking down material into parts.
Terms: distinguish, outline, relate, organize, discriminate, conclude

Synthesis: Putting parts together to form a new whole.
Terms: combine, compose, create, design, rearrange

Evaluation: Judging value for purpose based on criteria. (No guessing.)
Terms: criticize, compare, support, conclude, discriminate, contrast, summarize, explain

See our workbook for a list of these to print out.

#305
Something Old...Something New...

The most important thing is not the camera but the eye.
~Alfred Eisenstaedt

When you find something that is about to be thrown away, salvage it, and create something new and useful with it, you have brought recycling to its best. Brainstorm today with your family something that needs better organization (a junk drawer for example) or something your family would like to have (such as a bird feeder). Discuss household items that could be refurbished or reused (such as boxes, cans, jugs) and ways they could be combined cleverly, rearranged, or modified to be beneficial to your family.

Let your child decide a plan of action in order to turn these items into the new one your family desires. Keep this in mind all year long if you are about to throw something away that has potential for becoming something cool. Begin saving cardboard rolls, clean cans or cartons, ribbon, stickers, and anything that your child feels has potential. That way, when the time comes to create something new, you will have a stash of items she could use. (In the next idea, you will read about a neat recycling opportunity for your child to elaborate on and direct.)

#306
It's for the Birds...

Imagination is intelligence having fun.
~Anonymous

Here's a fun activity for the whole family. Decide how you could create a bird feeder by recycling items already in or around your home. It could be a simple construction and take very little time and effort, or it could be an elaborate feeder that requires detailed plans and manufacturing. Design and make it together, letting your child do as much as possible. Can you incorporate the use of simple machines in its construction (Idea #238)?

Now, predict which types of birds will visit your new feeder once you put it out. Fill it with seed, and watch it at various times of the day. Keep a running tally of the different types you see. (If you display the tally chart somewhere visible, such as the message center, everyone can add to it conveniently.) If you are not sure of a type of bird, look it up! You could try the Internet, the library, or a bird book.

Use the information you gather over a week or so, and then have your child create a graph to show the results (Idea #189). What could he use to decorate the graph to show his knowledge of birds? Where could it be displayed for a while for all to see?

Try these variations and see what happens:

- Save the graph until a different season, and then try this again. Do different birds visit? Compare and contrast them.

- Try a different feed. Do different birds come now?

- Change the feeder's location. Does this make a difference?

- Change your focus and actually try to attract different birds by altering feed, location, time of year, and other conditions.

#307
Part of the Crowd

Never let the fear of striking out get in your way.
~George Herman ("Babe") Ruth

Here's a fun game to play as a family. It gets kids thinking and is a great opportunity for you to help teach some ways to memorize things. You can try this activity with your child alone or with the entire family.

- Gather ten similar items and display them on a cookie sheet or (if they are larger) lay them out on the kitchen table or living room floor.

- Have the other players study the items carefully for a minute or so, then ask them to close their eyes.

- Take away one of the items, and ask them to open their eyes.

- The other players either take turns guessing which item is missing, or answers may just be given as players think of them.

- After the item is identified, let another player choose one to take away.

- Try adding more items each time you play to increase the difficulty level. Change the items often to increase difficulty.

- You could also try choosing one item in your head and having your child ask yes-or-no questions until she guesses your item. Now, let your child do the same for you!

You can help your child with this activity by offering her memory-aid strategies. Try:

- Creating a mnemonic device using the first letters of the objects, and then looking for the missing letter (object). (See Idea #334 for some examples.)

- Singing the objects in an order that, when re-sung, will help your child find the missing one.

- Categorizing (or otherwise connecting in some way) the items into groups (in her head) and trying to find the one missing from each group.

#308
Compare and Contrast

All measurement begins (and in the end, ends) with ourselves.
~ K. C. Cole

Have you ever read a book and just loved it? If you later saw the movie, were you a bit disappointed? Over the past few years, an increasing amount of children's books have been made into movies. If you are aware of a book that your child has read that is also a movie, you can turn the watching of it into a critical thinking activity by comparing and contrasting them.

A *Venn diagram* can be used to easily organize your ideas. To make one, have your child draw two circles overlapping enough to create three equal sections. (Try tracing the bottom of a large butter tub or lid to another round plastic container to create a neat diagram or try ours.) Now, label the section on the left "Book," the section on the right "Movie," and the middle section "Both."

In the "Book" section, brainstorm ways that the book was unique. Think of the story elements (Idea #84) at first. If the book and movie were very similar, you may need to be even more discriminating by going beyond the story elements and into more minor details. Do the same for the "Movie" section. List ways that the movie differed from the book. In the "Both" section, identify ways that the book and movie were the same.

You can experiment with different Venn diagrams or create your own way to compare and contrast. Design one that helps tell about the major themes of the story line. For an added challenge, try choosing two similar (or very dissimilar) items to compare and contrast. If your child has a favorite TV show, you could use two episodes of it to plug into the diagram. To get even more clever, try creating a diagram using more than two circles. Use three circles to compare three fairy tales, three favorite books, etc.

Disney stories work well for this activity. You could also try *The Polar Express* by Chris VanAllsburg; *Charlie and the Chocolate Factory, James and the Giant Peach* or *Matilda* by Roald Dahl; *Diary of a Wimpy Kid* by Jeff Kinney; *Coraline* by Neil Gaiman; and *Because of Winn Dixie* by Kate DiCamillo. The list goes on! All have been made into movies and work well for comparing and contrasting.

See our website for a blank Venn diagram (Idea #143).

#309
Family Challenge

If you aren't in over your head, how do you know how tall you are?
~T.S. Eliot

You can help your child become a more critical thinker through discussions. In this family or group activity, someone chooses an object. (Try a mirror, shoelace, paper plate, anything.) The group members all take turns identifying one possible use for that object. After a few of the obvious answers are given, players must suggest an alternative application. They will have to think not only critically but also creatively to come up with clever uses for the object.

For example, if the object is a mirror, the first few answers might be:

- to see your reflection;

- to use with another to see the back of your head; or

- to magnify your face.

Soon, as the common answers are given, players must be clever, such as:

- to start a fire; or

- to see if someone's breathing by putting it under his or her nose and watching for fog.

See how far your team can go. How many acceptable answers (as judged by your teammates) can you all list? If you have enough people, try breaking into teams and comparing answers. Even try it completely individually by having each person write his own individual list and then sharing. Can you actually try *doing* some of the ideas you've thought of during the game?

Hint: It is often helpful to have a physical example of the object for players to manipulate although any form of the object can be used when answers are given. For example, a hand mirror may be passed around, but answers may be given regarding anything from small dental mirrors to large whole-wall mirrors.

#310
Why Ask "Why"?

The important thing is not to stop questioning.
~Albert Einstein

Since your child was about two or three, you have probably heard, "Why?" close to a million times. Does it seem like every time you casually mention something (like needing gas), it escalates into an in-depth discussion on what gas is and where it comes from and how it gets here? It is perpetuated by a curious child asking, "Why" over and over, just trying to fill up his mind with information.

Today, think about all the times you can now begin to ask the same question of your child. You could pounce on opportunities when your child casually brings something up, and say something like, "Oh, really? Why?" The next time he asks you, "Why?" you could say, "How could you find that out on your own?", "I'm not sure. Why do you think?" or "Let's find out!" (See Idea #9 for more ideas.)

Every day offers many opportunities for this if we are ready to seize them. There are many opportunities for learning about research and resources. When your child explains something to you, he is helping himself to learn it more thoroughly and will be more likely to remember it for a long time to come.

#311
Point of View

There is nothing insignificant in the world. It all depends on the point of view.
~ Johann Wolfgang von Goethe

In Idea #130, the suggestion of thinking from someone else's point of view was offered as a writing activity. Now, you can take it one step further and try it again, concentrating on the various levels of thinking.

Have your child choose something, either living or not, and brainstorm a few ideas about it. What does it look like, do, eat? Where does it live? What's its size? Now, have your child close her eyes and pretend to actually *be* that thing for a few minutes. Encourage her to use her five senses to identify and record what she sees, hears, smells, tastes and feels. Now, have her either write or talk about it from the perspective of that object.

For example, she might say, "I am an object that gets dirty at times. Sometimes, I even smell. When I was first made, I looked great. I had hundreds of others all around who looked just like me, maybe a little bit bigger or smaller, though. Then, when I was taken from my first, nice home in a box and used, I was never the same again. I now have these rope-like things tangled up all over me. Some big smelly thing gets put inside of me and then the ropes tighten. From then on I can't relax. I'm being stomped around, trudged through the mud and dirt, and sometimes even stuck on some chewed up gum! I usually get kicked off around nighttime and actually get to rest until morning and then it all begins again."

Encourage her to be vague at first, slowly giving more detail, and then finally telling the answer at the end. ("I am a shoe!") You could play games with this idea, having those listening guess to see who can figure it out the quickest. She could also draw an actual possible view from the object's point of view and have others guess.

Shel Silverstein has a poem called "Point of View" in Where the Sidewalk Ends *that offers some different perspectives in a cute way.*

#312

Critical Thinking in the News

A challenge only becomes an obstacle when you bow to it.
~Ray Davis

Do you remember back in Part 1 when we discussed the value of having newspapers (and a wide variety of other reading material) around the house? Well, now you can find value (and fun!) in other ways using the newspaper. You could:

1. Try flipping to the classified section and taking turns reading a want ad out loud to other family members. See if they can guess what job is being discussed. Have each person defend his answer by explaining his reasons for his guess with supporting details.

2. Cut several headlines out separately, and the stories that go with them. Post them on separate sides of the message center or hand them all to your child. Have him match the headline with the correct article. Ask what words he used in the headline to help him find the right story.

3. Post another headline on the message center (without the accompanying story). Challenge your child to write a story to match the headline. When he's done, compare his story to the actual story. Have him notice the similarities and differences.

4. Take a comic strip and cut the scenes apart. Have your child arrange them in the proper order. He may even find a different order than the original. That's fine. Ask him to develop the dialogue for his newly arranged comic strip.

5. Use the map you have hanging in his study area to find the different countries mentioned in the news stories. Point out surrounding bodies of water, bordering states/countries, the capital and anything else of interest to help increase his global awareness.

6. Increase his vocabulary by asking him to find five words he doesn't know. Have him add the words and their definitions to his dictionary. Look for opportunities to use the new words in everyday conversation to help him remember them.

7. Use the classifieds to create real world math problems. For example, how much money would he make if he had a job from the paper that paid $10.40 an hour and worked 40 hours a week? Look at the apartments or houses for rent. Could he afford any of them on that amount of money a week? What if he wanted to buy a car? What is the *average* cost of a used car? Challenge him to find more real world math in the paper.

Can your child think of another activity to use with the classifieds?

If your family does not get the newspaper, these activities can be done with online newspapers. For some of the activities, you would print out the articles. Newspapers (printed or online) provide great opportunities to help your child connect with the world, encourage great discussions, and help build critical reading and thinking skills, all while making learning fun!

#313

Number Sentences

One who makes no mistakes never makes anything.
~ Source Unknown

Young children can be helped to develop critical thinking skills best by working through things aloud with others. It helps children to be able to discuss what they are doing and thinking. It is also beneficial to hear a role model talking through her own problem solving. Therefore, included in this Part are a variety of activities that center around working together as a family. Here is another critical thinking activity you can all work on together.

Hold a family contest. See who can create the most number sentences with the answer of 100. This can be done individually, of course, but working in teams or all together will help your child the most.

According to your child's ability level, decide on the operations that will be used (addition, subtraction, multiplication, division, decimals, or fractions.) For younger children, use a smaller number. For slightly older kids, you can set rules like everyone must use only addition to get to 100, such as 20+10+5+25+8+12+17+3=100 and so on. Older children can be challenged to combine many or all operations. Your family could begin a list today of some different ways and then post it at the message center. Then, each of you could add to it as you develop new ways.

You may wish to have a calculator handy both for the developing and checking of new number sentences since the goal here is not to actually learn how to add etc. but to use numbers in fun and challenging ways. Make up your own rules! Have fun!

#314
20 Questions

As long as you're going to be thinking anyway, THINK BIG.
~ Donald Trump

Children love to solve riddles. From now on, you can know that you are helping your child to become a more critical thinker when you give him a few to solve. Try playing 20 Questions as a great way to get started. To play:

1. Secretly choose something. (It could be a thing, animal, person or book character, place...*anything.*) You could set guidelines before playing, or play as anything goes!

2. The other players are allowed to ask you 20 yes-or-no questions, trying to determine what it is. Each new question will likely depend on the answer he just received.

3. Don't forget to allow your child to be the chooser also. He will enjoy trying to think of something that will really stump you!

Variations:

- You might decide to have your child *record* the information he hears in order to help organize his ideas.

- You may allow players to make guesses at any time during play if they have one or make them wait until all 20 questions are used up.

- You could require a player to make a guess after each and every question answered. At first, this will obviously be difficult since the clues will be quite broad, but soon the information will narrow and the guesses will be based on more information and turn into thoughtful predictions.

- You could play this game completely aloud with any aged child or even turn it into a *Hidden Treasure* game by writing the clues down onto note cards for children who also need to practice reading in fun ways!

- You could play strictly for fun or even as a way to practice a subject from school by choosing topics you know your child is studying. For example, with states, famous people, science terms, or other pertinent topics.

#315
The ABCs of Reading Fun

Success is that old ABC—ability, breaks, and courage.
~Charles Luckman

There's no reason you can't practice reading or writing at the same time as developing critical thinking skills. Children of all ages will like the following activity because you can tailor it to meet their needs and likes. The goal is to compose an ABC book about a topic your child enjoys. Here's how to do it:

1. Your child will need to choose a topic to categorize (such as sports, toys, places, animals).

2. Next, begin to think of something within that category that begins with each letter of the alphabet and jot it down as a rough draft. (Note: Here is a great opportunity to do a little research at the library, on the Internet, by asking others… to gather information for the particularly tricky letters.) For some of the tricky letters like Q, X, Z, talk about ways to get creative with answers.

3. When the rough draft is complete and all 26 letters have an idea next to them, your child can decide how he wants to "publish" it. She could turn it into a book (with one letter per page and room to illustrate), create a poster of all 26 ideas together, or just be fine with the list.

Variations:

- You could challenge older children to compose more than one word for each letter.

- She could create a rhyme using each letter: The *Ants* put on their *pants*.

- She could create an *alliteration*: Bob the Bear Brought Berries to the Barn.

- By choosing a topic that she is studying in school, she can practice and you can help her reinforce the concepts in a fun way.

- Turn this into a family game by selecting a category and then seeing how many letters of the alphabet each player can find an answer to quickly. Try it alone or in teams.

The Z was Zapped *by Chris VanAllsburg is a super book to get children enthusiastic about this idea.*

See our workbook for a sheet to organize this activity.

#316
Fractured Fairy Tales

Life itself is the most wonderful fairy tale.
~ Hans Christian Andersen

Whether your child loves fairy tales or not, he is sure to enjoy this challenge. Read a classic fairy tale to your child, buddy-read it, or allow him to read it on his own. Discuss and record the important story elements. Now, challenge him to compose a fractured fairy tale of his own.

A fractured fairy tale is one in which one or more of the most important story elements are altered in order to create a clever, unique, or silly twist. You and your child could discuss possible scenarios (changing different story elements) to determine which would work the best.

For instance, if you read the classic Disney fairy tale *Snow White*, you might try changing the setting and having Snow White and her seven dwarfs come to a big city (setting change). Or you might try having her Prince Charming wind up being afraid of everything, even dwarves (character change)! Or he might make a different fate for the Wicked Queen (plot change). There are many opportunities for your child to create a fractured fairy tale.

To get started, you might try reading one of the many published fractured fairy tales and similar stories at the library. Try *The Paperbag Princess* by Robert Munsch, in which the princess ditches the snooty prince at the end for being too picky. *The True Story of the Three Little Pigs* by Jon Scieszka tells the classic story from the viewpoint of the poor old wolf who claims he was framed and tells the story the way it all "really happened." *The Stinky Cheese Man and Other Fairly Stupid Tales* by Jon Scieszka and Lane Smith is full of familiar fairy tales with a twist.

See our website for a list of other fractured fairy tales.

#317
When They *Do* Watch TV...

Children are like wet cement. Whatever falls on them makes an impression.
~Haim Ginott

Obviously, it is a good idea to set limits on television and encourage your child to get involved in a variety of other activities during her free time, but when your child *does* watch TV, you could take some time to watch it with her. This not only allows you to know what she is watching and gives you an opportunity to discuss it with her, but it also opens up another chance to do some critical thinking together!

Instead of fast-forwarding through the commercials between shows, take a break and actually watch them together. You may think that commercials are tuned out by children, but unfortunately they probably have more impact on our kids than we think. By watching them together, we can discuss what our children might be thinking and clear up any misconceptions.

Select an ad and try:

1. determining an ad's target audience or age group;

2. listing ways that advertisers try to make the ad appealing to the target audience;

3. comparing and contrasting it to other ads aimed at this audience or to other similar products' ads;

4. finding any exaggerated claims and discussing what is really likely to occur;

5. discriminating whether the product would really be as fabulous to own as it claims to be; and

6. looking for disclaimers, usually printed very small at the bottom of the screen, and discussing their meaning.

TV is a part of our children's lives whether we like it or not. There are many good programs worth watching, too. (Though finding them may be tricky!) When you help your child become a critic not only of the television shows she watches but also of the commercials she will inevitably be bombarded with over the years, you are giving her critical thinking skills that will benefit her in many ways.

#318
Invent a New Product

Vision: the art of seeing things invisible.
~Jonathan Swift

Now that you have learned about advertisements and the methods used in them to persuade young people to buy the products, use the information to your advantage and put your child's critical thinking skills to use as well.

Many people, at one time or another, have thought about a new invention or a new product. Whether it is simple or complex, something brand new or an improvement on an existing product, we could all certainly brainstorm a neat idea. Try now to identify something your child would like to invent and make a pretend plan to market it. Items for children such as toys make great ideas.

When you watch TV commercials together, discuss again together and list the ways in which advertisers target certain age groups. Which age group would *his* new product be for? What would he want to put into a TV commercial to promote his new product? Now write one!

- Design the set.

- Compose the script.

- Explain why this product is so great.

- How would he make it appealing visually and orally?

- Who would he choose to have in the commercial?

- How would he compare it to other similar products?

- When would he put it on the air?

By watching ads together in this way you not only help him discern ideas for his own ad but also help him to become a more discriminating viewer of persuasive advertising. This is a great opportunity to point out the tricks ad makers use to get kids hooked. Instead of making it a boring lesson to learn, you can use this activity, have fun together and enjoy the creativity of inventing something new!

Now, can you and your child actually make a mock-up of the product using recycled items? Draw a magazine ad for it? Videotape the commercial for it? Have some fun! Get creative! Take it as far as he wants! Who knows, with all the effort he *could* put into this, maybe it will become a real product someday!

See our workbook available for purchase online for a sheet to organize this activity.

#319
What's the Password?

The journey is the reward.
~Tao Saying

Here's another activity that can involve the whole family. Similar to the old Password game, this game is played one clue at a time and can take minutes or last days, giving players more thinking time. To play:

1. Place a piece of paper on the table (or at the message center).

2. Have one player secretly choose a thing. (Be creative. It could be a person, place, thing, animal, book…anything.) She can write the word down on a piece of paper and hide it away for now.

3. That player writes a one-word clue word that describes the object on the paper. (This first clue should be very vague, such as "It's a person.")

4. Other players should all make a guess. (Of course, it will be a fairly wild guess at first without much to work with!) If playing a quick game, players can say their guesses aloud and new clues can be given until the secret word is guessed. If you want the game to last longer, post the paper with the question on the message board and players can think about it during the day and make guesses at any time of the day. If no one solves the puzzle and guesses the secret word, then another clue word is given or written, and the same sequence follows. Clues gradually become more descriptive, narrowing down possible choices.

5. Players continue to draw conclusions and make or write guesses based on the information given until someone guesses the secret word. (When someone does guess it, she can pull out her original word and prove that they got it!)

Don't forget to allow your child a chance to be the "Chooser". You might encourage her to write down her word clues and rearrange them in an order that lends itself to this game from most general to most specific. She will be using many critical thinking skills whether she is guessing or making up the clues herself!

See our workbook for a sheet to help organize this activity.

#320
Magic Squares

The harder you work, the harder it is to surrender.
~Vince Lombardi

This activity is the first of many ideas offering you quick and fun ways to work on critical thinking skills with your child. Try each idea, but don't stop there! Make up some of your own, and challenge your family. What a fantastic critical thinking activity in itself to have your child create some of his own activities by rearranging, changing, rewriting, or combining the examples here! Have fun!

Below is an example of a Magic Square. Magic Squares are unique because the numbers in each row, each column and each of the two diagonals add up to the same number.

Have your child analyze the square. Have him check each row to be sure it meets the criteria. (Each row adds up to 15 in this example.)

8	1	6
3	5	7
4	9	2

After he looks over the example above, have him explain it out loud. Now, show him this next one, and see if he can find the pattern (what each row/column/diagonal adds up to) and find the missing numbers in the grid to accurately complete the magic square:

2		6
9	5	
4	3	8

A magic square can be a 3 x 3 grid or larger. Perhaps your child would enjoy designing his own magic square to challenge family and friends. Older children can apply their knowledge of multiplication and even decimals or fractions to make a more difficult magic square. Get the whole family involved, and create another magic square that works. How big of a one can you create together? If adding is too easy, try one of the more difficult ways. If you create a particularly challenging one, consider leaving some blanks and sending it off to relatives or friends via the mail or Internet to solve!

See our workbook for a worksheet to practice these.

#321
Place Value Puzzle

You must do the thing you think you cannot do.
~Eleanor Roosevelt

Here's an activity that will allow your child to demonstrate what she's learned about place value by using clues to conclude which numbers can be eliminated and which numbers are possible answers in a puzzle. Have your child read through all the clues first. After she discovers how large the number will be (3 digit, 4 digit, other), encourage her to draw the appropriate amount of lines to work on (__ __ __ __). Then she can read the clues again to determine which number goes in the ones, tens, hundreds, and thousands place.

Example: I am a four-digit whole number.

I am greater than 5800.

I am less than 6200.

The sum of my ones digit and my hundreds digit is 9.

The sum of my tens digit and my thousands digit is also 9.

I am divisible by 5.

My hundreds digit is 9.

What number am I? (answer 5940)

Your child may find this puzzle fun to solve but it may be difficult to create one of her own. When designing this type of puzzle, children have to work backward. Have your child start with the answer. Then, she will have to compose clues to lead the puzzle solver to the answer. If she has practiced a few of yours, she will have some examples of clues she can write as well. It will take practice before she is able to truly challenge family and friends with her puzzles, but just think how excited she will be when she does!

#322
What's Your Sign?

If you don't make mistakes, you aren't really trying.
~Coleman Hawking

This activity allows your child to apply his knowledge of the different math operations to solve a challenging equation. Basically, you begin with a series of numbers that make an equation, but none of the operation signs are there!

Try this:

1. Begin by giving your child an equation without any signs except the equal sign.

2. For example: 3 4 1 2 = 6 (Hint: To make this easy, make up any series of numbers first, plug in the appropriate signs for your child's age, and *then* figure out the answer. Then, simply rewrite it without the signs and give it to him.)

3. For younger kids, you can tell them which signs and how many of them they will need to add. For example, "Place two addition signs and one subtraction sign between the following numbers to make the left side of the equation equal 6."

   For older kids, you can let them figure out which signs are needed on their own.
   (Answer: 3+4+1-2 = 6)

As always, also let your child create his own puzzles for family and friends to solve. He may not even realize how much math he is doing in order to get things to work out right.

Variations:

- Don't even put the equal sign in! Let your child figure out if perhaps it needs to go on the other end of the equation. For example, "6 3 4 2 1 is solved by adding these signs 6 = 3 + 4 + 1 − 2."

- Depending upon the age level of your child, you may want to design easier or more challenging problems, using multiplication, division, 2-digit numbers, etc. For example, "2 4 3 4 = 6 is solved by using these signs 2 x 4 x 3 ÷ 4 = 6."

#323
Plexers

The problems of puzzles are very near the problems of life.
~Erno Rubik

Looking for a sure-fire, fun puzzle? Plexers may be the answer! Plexers are visual word puzzles in which a word, name, familiar phrase, saying or cliche is presented in an unusual way. Plexers help children look at things from a different view. After all, everything in life is not always black and white. Plexers encourage children to think of a different way to look at a problem. They will be reading words backward, up and down, spaced apart—ways that are at first foreign to them. Here are a few examples:

1. LOOHCS = "Back to School" ("School" is written backward.)

2. LEM
   π = "Lemon Pie" ("Lem" is ON the symbol for pi).

3. TIOGME = "Go back in time" (The word "go" is backward inside the word "time.")

4.　　　R
　　K clock O =
　　　　C

"Rock around the clock" (The word "rock" is written around the word "clock.")

There are books full of plexers like the ones above. Try asking a librarian or bookstore clerk to search for the newest books available. Once your child becomes adept at solving these puzzles, she will probably enjoy *creating* plexers of her own.

See our website for more Plexers to solve.

#324
Find the Pattern

Nothing in the world can take the place of persistence.
~Calvin Coolidge

Here's an activity that focuses on finding the pattern in a group of numbers. Ask your child to look at the numbers below. Tell him that in some way they form a pattern. Challenge him to identify the pattern and find the next three numbers missing in the sequence.

Easy: 1, 4, 7, 10, 13, _____, _____, _____, (answer: +3)
　　　1, 2, 4, 7, 11, 16, _____, _____, _____ (answer; +1, +2, +3, +4...)

More difficult: 1, 2, 6, 24, 120, 720, _____, _____, _____ (answer: x2, x3, x4, x5...)

After your child feels competent in solving these number patterns, ask him to compose new patterns of his own. He will be excited to share his number patterns with family and friends and especially proud when it's a challenge for you to decipher!

#325
Palindromes

A winner never stops trying.
~Tom Landry

Palindromes are numbers that read the same forward and backward. Some examples are 45354, 353, and 77. Challenge your child to compile a list of palindromes she hears or sees during her day. There are more than you may think! Even if she glances at her clock when it reads 3:43, write it down. It's a palindrome!

Here are a few other ways to play with palindromes:

- Make a list of all the 3-digit palindromes that begin with 7. An example is 717.

- Make a list of all the 3-digit palindromes whose digit sum is 10. For example, 505. Its digits added together would be 5 + 0 + 5 = 10.

- What is the least 3-digit palindrome that is a square number?

- Words can also be palindromes, e.g., *Mom* and *Dad*. "Wow", you're getting it now! What others can she find?

As you discover palindromes, your child will probably find many other ways to play with them. Enjoy and play along!

#326
Palindrome Challenge

Whatever is worth doing at all is worth doing well.
~Lord Chesterfield

If your child enjoyed the palindrome activities (Idea #325), he might want to take the Palindrome Challenge. Some mathematicians claim that *every* number can be made into a palindrome. Interested in testing this theory? Here's how.

Have your child write down any number. Next, have him reverse the numbers and write that number below the first number. Add the numbers. Keep doing this process (reversing the *new* answer) until the sum you obtain is a palindrome. Some numbers will have to be reversed and added several times before it becomes a palindrome, but eventually, it will!

> **Example:**   17
> +71
> 88 - Palindrome!

> **Example:**   82
> +28
> 110
> +011
> 121 - Palindrome!

If your child is curious and really wants to test this theory but feels overwhelmed, suggest he recruit some help from friends or family and divide the numbers he wants to test among all the helpers. Encourage him to distinguish patterns. If he discovers patterns, he will have to do less work.

Also, consider your child's age and whether using a calculator will be helpful. Of course, we want kids to know how to do math on paper, but there are certainly times when using a calculator will help turn a huge task, such as this one, into a fun one! If the purpose of an activity is learning how to add, then, of course, no calculators should be allowed, but if that is not the main goal, as here it is not, let him use one. Good calculator skills are necessary, too!

#327
Analogies

I wasn't afraid to fail. Something good always comes out of failure.
~Anne Baxter

If you've ever taken a high school or college entrance exam or have had your IQ tested, you've been exposed to analogies. An analogy is a logical way of making a comparison. Here is an example of an analogy:

Hot is to *cold* as *near* is to ______ (*high, far, wide*)

(Note: Sometimes it is written as *Hot : Cold :: Near : ______*)

An analogy compares relationships between two different sets. In the above example, the two sets are *hot/cold* and *near/far*. The subjects of the sets can be different (*hot* and *cold* relate to temperature and *near* and *far* relate to distance), but the items in one set must be related to each other in the same way as the items in the other set. Since *hot* and *cold* are opposites, the opposite of *near* is *far*.

Try this one:

Happy is to *glad* as *angry* is to ________ (*smile, curious, mad, scared*)

Happy and *glad* are related because they mean the same thing, therefore *angry* is to *mad* because they also mean the same thing.

Elementary children are not too young to learn how to interpret analogies. Try checking out a book on analogies. Read them and become familiar with how they work. Then, try to create simpler ones for your child to practice. Don't forget to challenge her to compose a few herself!

#328
What's the Connection?

Eventually everything connects - people, ideas, objects.
The quality of the connections is the key to quality per se.
~ Charles Eames

Here's an activity that focuses on determining the relationship of a list of items. It doesn't require paper and pencil and can include any number of people. It is fun to do in the car, waiting in line, at the dinner table, at family gatherings, and elsewhere.

1. Before beginning the game, the "traveler" (the player going first) must decide on a theme (which he will keep secret); this will determine which items he will take on a trip. Every item must be related to each other somehow according to the theme. For example, items that begin with the letter *a*.

2. The game is started by the traveler saying, "I'm going on a trip, and I'm going to take ____." The traveler then tells one item he will take on his trip that fits into his secret category, such as an apple for the letter *a*.

3. It is up to the other people playing to discover his pattern by asking such questions as "Will you be taking an orange?" (The guesser thought maybe he was taking fruits.) To this, he would reply, "No. I won't be taking an orange" (because it does not start with *a*). If they ask, "Will you take asparagus?" he tells them, "Yes, I will take asparagus" (because it does start with *a*).

4. Play continues as the traveler relates one item he *will* take and the other players alternately make one guess at a time.

5. When a player thinks he has solved the pattern, he tells the traveler. If he is not right, he (and the others) will keep trying to decipher the pattern. If he is correct, he can begin a new game and become the new traveler.

Encourage your child to create patterns (things to take on his travels) of his own. If you need help with ideas, here are some examples of themes to try:

- words with two syllables;

- words that begin with a vowel; and

- words that begin with a consonant blend.

Ask your librain for interesting and challenging puzzles for the whole family.

#329

Stretching the Brain

The brain is like a muscle. When it is in use we feel very good.
Understanding is joyous.
~ Carl Sagan

Here is an activity that will surely challenge your child and perhaps even you, too! Try the puzzle below. If your child enjoys it, look for books with similar puzzles and brainteasers to help stimulate and motivate her.

Using a pencil, connect *all* nine dots using only four straight lines. You cannot lift your pencil, and you cannot retrace any lines. Your child will have to predict, plan ahead, and perhaps rearrange her plan if unsuccessful at first. Tip: you can go "off the grid" or extend a line past the box of dots. Good luck!

o   o   o

o   o   o

o   o   o

It may help to have your child draw her own set of nine dots on a separate piece of paper to try (there will be a lot of erasing)!

See our workbook for the solution.

Ask your librarian for books full of puzzles like the one above to help develop critical thinking skills.

#330
Probability

Cultivation to the mind is as necessary as food to the body.
~ Marcus Tullius Cicero

Your child can discover the basic principles of probability by playing this game with dice. First, explain the basics of probability. For example, on a coin, there are only two possible results when you toss it: heads and tails. So, the probability for getting either side is 1 out of 2 or ½. If she has three cars in a box (two red and one green) and wants to pull one out, the probability of blindly pulling out a red car is ⅔ (two out of three cars are red), and the probability of pulling out a green car is ⅓ (one out of the three cars is green). You can continue to give her examples until it seems like she understands. Then, ask her if she were to roll a single die, what would the probability be of any number being rolled (answer: 1/6). What about if she rolled two dice? Let's find out.

- Have her create a probability chart. She would label the bottom of a piece of graph paper 2-12, the sums possible when rolling two dice. Draw vertical lines to separate the columns.

- After every roll, have her add the dice together and record the sum on her chart (if she rolled a 1 and a 2, she would color in one square [or mark an X if she does not have graph paper] above the number 3). The chart is a great visual representation of the probability of rolling the different sums 2-12.

- Continue rolling the dice and filling in the chart for 30 rolls (or more if she's enjoying it).

- See if she can explain why one number seems to show up more than others.

- Depending on her age, have her write the fractions for the probability results. For example, if the sum of 2 was only rolled one time in 30 attempts, there was a 1/30 probability of it being rolled.

She will see how the study of probability allows her to make sense of experiences involving chance and she will have a great time while doing it!

#331
Syllogisms

Life is a continuous exercise in creative problem solving.
~Michael J. Gelb

In ancient Greece, the philosopher Aristotle challenged students with logic problems called syllogisms. A syllogism has three parts and must be worded in a specific way. Example:

All dogs are barking animals.

All Dalmatians are dogs.

Therefore, all Dalmatians are barking animals.

The first and second lines give you two pieces of information called *premises*. The information from the two premises is combined to form a *conclusion*. The conclusion is the third statement in a syllogism. If the conclusion is supported or proved by the information in the premises, the syllogism is *valid*. If the conclusion is not supported or proved by the information in the premises, the conclusion is *invalid*.

Syllogisms can be very complex. You may consider looking for books to give you examples, and then try to create some of your own. When creating your own syllogisms, try to use words and situations your child can visualize and understand. Here's another example:

All flowers are pretty.

All roses are flowers.

Therefore, all roses are pretty.

The above syllogism is valid. Remember that the point of a syllogism is not to argue whether roses are actually pretty but to decide if the first and second statement can support or prove the third statement.

Think about this one:

All dogs are fluffy.

All cats are fluffy.

Therefore, all dogs are cats.

The above syllogism is invalid. Can you see why?

When you first begin using syllogisms with your child (or if your child is in lower elementary), you may want to begin with an example she can easily relate to, such as:

I love my children.

You are my child.

Therefore, I love you!

Drawing pictures can help children of all ages to visualize the syllogism and help them to conclude whether it is valid. Try illustrating this one:

All flowers are pretty. (She can draw some pretty flowers)

All dogs are pretty. (She can draw some pretty dogs)

Therefore, all flowers are dogs. (She will quickly see that this is not valid!)

Work together, and try composing a syllogism to stump another family member!

#332
Matrix Logic

Failing doesn't make you a failure.
Giving up, accepting your failure,
and refusing to try again does!
~Richard Exely

Some difficult problems are best solved by creating charts to organize the information. Matrix logic problems are examples of puzzles that are easiest to solve when organized into a chart. To solve a matrix logic problem, start by gathering information from the clues. These clues may be tricky. One clue may give you only a little information by itself, but it may give more information when you combine it with another clue. Here is an example:

Find out which kind of candy Mary, Susan and Jill like. Each child only likes only one kind and no two children like the same kind.

1. Mary hates chocolate bars.

2. Susan eats taffy.

3. Jill dislikes lollipops.

Steps:

1. To help *organize* the clues above, a matrix chart can be drawn :

	Chocolate	Taffy	Lollipops

Mary			
Susan			
Jill			

2. Use X to eliminate what you know is not true: Jill dislikes lollipops, so put an X in that column. Mary hates chocolate, so mark an X in the chocolate column for Mary.

3. Star what you do know to be true. Since Susan likes taffy, no one else can like taffy. Put a star for Susan and taffy and then, because we know that each child only likes one kind of candy, X out chocolate and lollipops for Susan.

	Chocolate	Taffy	Lollipops
Mary	x	x	★
Susan	x	★	x
Jill	★	x	x

4. Now the chart shows that Jill likes chocolate, and Mary likes lollipops and Susan likes taffy. Fill in any of the other boxes with Xs or stars according to what must therefore be true or not true.

When you begin making some of these for your child, you may want to use situations and names familiar to him to make it more meaningful. Older kids can then make one up for you to solve! (Encourage him to do his himself first to be sure it works out right before he gives it to you!)

#333
Circle Logic

Success is just a matter of attitude.
~Darcy E. Gibbons

This activity builds on the Matrix Logic activity. Circle Logic problems use circles just like a Venn diagram (Idea #143) to compare and contrast bits of information. Have your child create a 3-circle Venn diagram, and challenge her to use the clues below to determine where each item (in this case: child) should be placed in the circles.

Cola, orange juice and milk are popular drinks liked by many children.

In which area of the circles would each child stand?

1. Laura drinks only cola and milk.

2. Karen will drink any kind of beverage.

3. John drinks only milk.

4. Tim likes orange juice and milk but does not care for colas.

5. Bill says, "Orange drinks are the only thing for me."

Challenge your child to design one of her own, using familiar names and items, and ask you to fill it in. She will have to check it after you are done to see if you were right!

#334
Memory-Aid Strategies

No memory of having starred atones for later disregard,
or keeps the end from being hard.
~Robert Frost

Very often, we are required to remember a series of things in our lives. If we are lucky, we completely understand the information and need no help retelling or remembering it when needed. Often, however, we are not so lucky. Occasionally, we may need some help in remembering a long list, the specific order, or the especially difficult sequence of something. (See Idea #228 for an activity in which this may be needed.)

Showing a variety of memory-aid strategies to your child can provide him with alternative methods with which to solve problems. The critical thinking skills you've been working on in this Part will no doubt be helpful in the future. Here are a few strategies for the times when our memories tend to fail us:

Mnemonic devices: words or sentences that are intended to be easier to remember than what they stand for. An example of using a mnemonic device would be to help you remember the colors of the rainbow in order: "Roy G. Biv" uses the same letters as the colors of the rainbow in order: Red, Orange, Yellow, Green, Blue, Indigo, Violet.

Tunes from songs: Your child could borrow the tune from "Row, Row, Row Your Boat" or another well-known song to remember, for example, the items he needs to bring back to school for tomorrow's project:

> Cardboard box and paint
>
> Colored pencils, glue
>
> Glitter and some cotton balls
>
> Yellow paper, too!

Categorizing: When trying to recall a group of things (such as the items in the "Part of the Crowd" activity, Idea #307), you could help your child to categorize them into groups of similar things. They could be sorted by colors (red things, yellow items), shapes (round things, square-ish objects), size (small, medium, or large), use (toys, tools), and so on.

Rhyme, Chant, Repeat: When memorizing a group of things, it may be helpful to chant them and put any together that rhyme. Repeating this a few times helps you retain the information even longer.

Of course, nothing is more important than truly *understanding* the information at hand, but there are times when these memory-aid strategies can prove very helpful. Together with a variety of higher level thinking skills, your child can become quite a critical thinker with time, patience, and a lot of practice with you.

Don't forget to share your favorite ideas with family, friends, babysitters, and anyone else your child spends time with. They might enjoy working on some of these activities with your child!

Part 12
Building Self-Esteem and Self-Reliance

INTRODUCTION: In this last Part, we write about self-esteem and self-reliance, two things most parents want for their children. There is a difference between the two and some great and not-so-great ways to encourage both. We offer ideas that help nurture self-reliance and self-esteem in your child in healthy, natural ways. The trick is this: How can we show our kids how terrific we think they are but help them build up their own self-confidence and esteem, all while becoming more self-reliant?

To find out, read on!

#335
The Truth

In recent years, there has been a trend for parents, coaches, teachers, and other adult leaders to focus on fostering self-esteem in kids. We all want our kids to be happy; of course we do! Sometimes, though, we want their happiness even if it means trading a little of our own sanity for it. It sometimes means giving when it hasn't been earned. It often means sacrificing our own time, energy, and money to give our kids what they want. Of course, we want our kids to be happy, but lost in the shuffle seems to be making sure that they *earn* the things they are given and are *responsible* kids who can increasingly care for and do for themselves.

Ponder the following questions. Is there a way to have both? Is there a way to make our kids do important things, sometimes even tough things, even if they don't like them, and at the same time help create responsible kids who feel good about themselves? Is doing work the opposite of being happy, or can these be synonymous? If self-esteem is defined as pride in oneself and self-respect, can you ever *give* that to someone else? If self-reliance is defined as relying on one's own capabilities, judgment, and resources, can we just *tell* kids they have those qualities and therefore make it so? Can we help kids become independent in ways other than just telling them they are and offering up trophy after trophy to try to "prove it."

Though the answers to the above questions may not be easy to answer, one thing is true: you cannot *give* someone self-esteem. It has to be *earned*—through hard work and dedication. We can offer opportunities to help foster it. We can give kids opportunities to shine. We can tell them that we are proud of them and praise them, but a child knows the difference between the trophy she got because everyone got one and the unique trophy only she earned for a very specific reason. When she hears that everything she does is great, eventually she may not believe any *one* thing she does is actually great, or she may expect that same kind of praise for everything she does from teachers and coaches and feel inadequate and confused when she doesn't receive it. When we tell every little child they are the prettiest princess there ever was or the toughest kid ever, are we really setting them up to believe in themselves, or will they soon see through it and wonder if anything they have been told about themselves is true?

So, maybe the bad news is we cannot just *give* our kids self-esteem or self-reliance like we have been trying to do. Soon enough, they will see through that. However, there is also good news. You can, in so many terrific ways, provide your child with opportunities to develop her own self-esteem and self-reliance. We can't give it to them, but we can help them earn it for themselves. And wow! What a wonderful thing that is!

#336
Appropriate Praising

I do believe in praising that which deserves to be praised.
~Dean Smith

Overpraising does not create kids with a healthy self-esteem. Instead, it creates kids with an unrealistic view of how the rest of the world should be treating them. Instead, it can create entitled, self-important children. It's creating the opposite of what we set out to do. The truth is that the rest of the world won't always say those praising words to your child. The rest of the world will expect him to do something really good before he gets praised and feels great about himself. Teachers, coaches, and other leaders in your child's life will expect him to earn his praise. You can help prepare your child for that now.

As parents, we need to provide a balance for our children. Of course, we need to praise them and encourage them and tell them we think they are great, but there is a difference between "That was a great goal you scored" and "That was the most amazing goal scored ever!" We have to watch for opportunities to tell our kids that they are doing well at something specific, not for *everything* they do. *Then* they will feel proud! Too much praise of any sort can be unhealthy, and several recent studies have shown that the wrong kind of praise can backfire and even slow down their progress.

So, when your child actually earns praise, how should you praise him? Here are a few things to keep in mind:

- First, be specific. Don't just say, "Good job!" Tell him specifically what he did well. If you can't verbalize it, then that's a sign you probably shouldn't be giving it.

- Second, give praise concisely. Don't go into so much detail that the message becomes lost in the lecture. One sincere sentence right away is a great motivator.

- Third, praise *effort* as much as achievement. An improved score in math (even if it is not an A) is a success. Let him know it.

- Last, don't say it unless you mean it. Kids can tell when praise is given falsely. We do our kids more of a favor by being honest and supportive than by giving false praise.

Of course, it is good to praise your child. We all like to be told we've done a great job. Just start today to think about how and how often you praise your child. Find a good balance. Make it count!

#337
Constructive Criticism

Every human being is entitled to courtesy and consideration.
Constructive criticism is not only to be expected but sought.
~Margaret Chase Smith

In Idea #336, we wrote about overpraising a child. Today, let's take a few moments to think about the opposite: offering *constructive* criticism to her. The word *criticizing* has a negative connotation, but constructive criticism is meant to be helpful. Parents, teachers, coaches, and other adult leaders sometimes shy away from constructive criticism. We are afraid to offend kids or point out their weaknesses, often because we are afraid to hurt their self-esteem. True, there are sometimes ways to point out what needs improvement by only saying something positive ("*This* math problem is right because you remembered to start in the ones place first" implies that perhaps another is wrong because she did not start in the correct place.), but inevitably, we will have to give our kids some constructive criticism. Here are a few things to keep in mind when you do:

1. First, constructive criticism is necessary in order to grow. How the words come out of your mouth, though, can make all the difference. We all remember "The Golden Rule": treat others how you want to be treated. That's good to remember here. Think of how you would like to be told you did something wrong. For example, if you point to a specific math problem and say, "Don't forget to start in the ones column when you are adding", your child will look at what she did, see that she began incorrectly, and fix her mistake. "That one is wrong because you started in the wrong place again", will also see to it that she fixes that problem, but it may also make her feel insecure about trying more. Your goal is to help her see and correct the problem while encouraging her to try more. Besides, kids learn by example. If they have been talked to in positive, kind ways, they are much more likely to talk to others the same way.

2. Because we know constructive criticism is necessary, we also have to make sure that we *do* give it. Here's an example: years ago there was a movement away from teachers using red pens to correct mistakes on a child's paper. We were afraid it would scare them and make them feel bad to see all that red. However, if a child did make a mistake that is the very thing we *do* want to call attention to. We *do* want them to see their mistakes. That's the point of the red—not to make them feel bad but to help them learn from their errors and grow! Purple pen all over their paper might seem nicer at first, but eventually, won't kids grow to dread the *purple*? Kids will hear constructive criticism from others: teachers, coaches, and bosses. Better they hear it from their parents first so when they hear it out in the world, they can take it in stride and not fall apart.

3. While self-esteem is important, there are other things even more important. Like *skills*! Let's take swimming for example. Let's say you enrolled your child in a swimming class because she did not know how to swim. Would you like for the coach to promote her through the classes, telling her how great she is doing, if she actually is not? Would you feel good letting her then go off to a lake with friends, feeling so confident about her swimming skills as a result of her coach's praise? Is it more important that she *feels good* about her swimming ability or that she actually *knows how to swim*? Of course, that could be a life-or-death example, but it illustrates an important question. At what point do we care more about their actual *abilities* than how children *feel* about them? Sure, you want your child to feel good about his reading abilities, but more important, you want him to learn how to read.

The bottom line: constructive criticism is a part of all of our lives. None of us is perfect. We all need to be told at times that we need to do something differently. We are not protecting our kids by never offering them constructive criticism; in fact, we are putting them at a disadvantage if we shelter them like that. So, if necessary, give it. Give it nicely, but do give it.

#338
Crystal Ball

Happiness is the sense that one matters.
~Sarah Trimmer

Very often we, as parents, get caught up in our day-to-day problems, activities, and schedules, and we tend to live in the "right now." There's nothing wrong with being in the moment, but have you stopped to consider your child as an adult? What do you want for him overall? We are not talking about the job you want him to have, but what kind of *person* do you want him to be? Chances are you want him to be a happy, well-adjusted, productive member of society, someone who is happy with the choices he's made and is contributing to his life and society in a positive way.

When he turns 18, he will not suddenly become this person. If this is what you want for your child, it begins now, in elementary school. When your child is an adult and forgets his lunch at home, he will not need you to run it to him so he can eat. He will figure it out because when he was in elementary school and he forgot something, you did not drop all you were doing and bring it to him. He learned. He learned to check his bag and make sure he had his homework, snack, lunch and books so next time he wouldn't be hungry or receive consequences from the teacher. Avoid running to the aid of your child when it's not an emergency. Let him problem solve and learn from his mistakes.

As an adult, he will not get every job he applies for and he will not be devastated by that because he has failed before. You've let him grow and try to do things for himself, like study for a test. Perhaps he failed. If he did, he learned something. He learned he has to try something different to pass the next time. The world didn't end. He learned, and he will use that information to survive and thrive as an adult.

So, take some time now to consider your child as an adult, and ask yourself what you can do (or *not* do) now, in these early years, to help him work toward being the best adult he can be.

#339
Take 5 and Decide

Your mind is a garden, your thoughts are the seeds,
you can grow flowers or you can grow weeds.
Make your decision wisely.
~Ritu Ghatourey

"Take 5 and Decide" is a technique used to help you be more consistent in your parenting. More consistent parenting equals a more self-reliant child. Picture this scene: a mom and daughter are walking through the grocery store. The daughter asks, "Can I have these cookies?" Mom, distracted, answers right away, "No! Put those down!" The daughter doesn't put them down. She continues to walk with her mom and continues to ask, "Can we have these cookies, please?" Again, Mom says, "No." The daughter asks several more times until finally Mom says in exasperation, "Fine! Yes, get the cookies!" What has the daughter learned? She has learned that if she keeps repeating herself, she may get the answer she wants.

Now instead, imagine Mom using the "Take 5 and Decide Method." The key to this method is to not answer right away. Stop for five seconds and ask yourself as the parent if you really want her to have those cookies. If you really don't care if she gets the cookies, avoid saying "no" out of habit or distraction. Instead, take five seconds to think about it, make sure it's okay with you, and tell her, "Yes, you may have the cookies."

However, if you take five seconds and decide you do *not* want her to have those cookies, then say "no" and stick to it! Put the cookies back, look into her eyes and tell her she is not getting the cookies today. Will she stop asking? Probably not, especially if you are just starting to try this method, but if you do not give in this time or the next time or the next time, she will eventually stop asking again and again. She will have learned that when you give an answer, it's a thoughtful response and you will stick to it.

The cookie scenario is a very simplistic example, but it gives you an idea of how it works. Take 5 and Decide can be used for all aspects of your child's life. *Do I have to do my homework now? Can I sleep over so-and-so's house? Will you help me with my project? Can I ride my bike around the block?* Whatever the questions, train yourself to stop and think about the question for five seconds, make a decision, and stick to it! It takes a little effort from you now, but you will reap the rewards forever by not being begged endlessly! Your child will learn the limits of what she can expect from you, and she will start to take care of more and more things herself, becoming more self-reliant every day.

#340
Spend Quality Time Together

We need 4 hugs a day for survival.
We need 8 hugs a day for maintenance.
We need 12 hugs a day for growth.
~Virginia Satir

We are all so busy these days. All of the technology that is supposed to make our lives easier just seems to take up our time: checking emails, returning texts, blogging, catching up on Facebook... We often take our jobs home with us, too. Our kids also are busy with homework, sports, and after-school activities. How many times have you said goodnight to your child only to think that is practically the only thing you've said that day that wasn't a command: *Get dressed! Find your backpack! Brush your teeth! Get in the shower!* Today's quote says we need many hugs every day. *We* say hugs can also come in other forms: a smile, a fist-bump, kind words and more. The important thing is that it is directed right at your child.

As we get ever busier, it is easy to lose track of the quality time we spend with our kids. Of course, any time is better than no time, but good ole' quality time is best. Kids really do need it. While you may have lots of face-time in front of your kids driving them to and fro, cleaning up as they do homework in a nearby room, working on a report while they play video games next to you on the couch, ask yourself how much *really good* time do you get with your child? There is no best answer, no magic number. Instead, decide if it just feels like enough or not. If not, squeeze some in!

Working together on the ideas in this book is one good way to spend quality time together. (In addition, you are multi-tasking by also working on improving school performance!) What are other ways you and your child can really connect? Again, that is up to you. Here are a few basic ways to get you started thinking:

- find something he loves to do and suggest you do it together;
- choose something you love, too, and ask him to spend time with you on it;
- read to him, no matter how old he is;
- ask about his day and talk about yours;
- sit outside and literally stop and smell the roses;
- put on a favorite song and just dance;
- play a board game; and/or
- get out a deck of cards, and let him make up a game.

The ideas are endless, but the end result is the same: put down the video games and the Smartphones, step away from the homework and chores, and just enjoy each other's company for at least a little bit each day. Make it a habit. Your child will probably never remember the hours he worked on school projects or played computer games, but he will remember that you took time out just for him every day.

And, of course, don't forget the hugs!

#341
Life Skills

Make the most of yourself, for that is all there is of you.
~Ralph Waldo Emerson

You may have heard the saying "Do as I say, not as I do." The problem with saying that to a child is that she *will* do as she sees done, regardless of whether or not you say not to. Children learn by example. For many kids, her parents are her most important (and sometimes only) examples she has for how adults (and people in general) should act. Though it may be hard at times, one of the best things you can do for your child is to be a good example. Some skills are very difficult to teach young kids; they are more likely just picked up through observation. You know you are always being watched!

How you ask? Well, that part is up to you. Find ways in your everyday life to point things out to your child. Show her how you did something, why you did it, what you did *not* do. Be aware of your actions and your words. Here are some life-skills that, while difficult to teach, you can show your child just by providing her with a good example:

* caring	* integrity	* motivation
* respect	* initiative	* responsibility
* compromise	* flexibility	* patience
* manners	* perseverance	* friendship
* common sense	* organization	* curiosity
* assertiveness	* sense of humor	* kindness
* problem-solving	* cooperation	* forgiveness
* self-awareness	* curiosity	

Some will come naturally as you go about your daily life, and some you may have to look for opportunities to showcase. Either way, be aware that you are your child's first and most important teacher and most definitely a role-model.

See our workbook for a sheet to help organize this activity.

#342
The Sandwich Method

Little things affect little minds.
~Benjamin Disraeli

If you have ever been to one of your child's conferences, you have likely heard both good and not-so-good things about your child and his performance in the classroom. That is the teacher's job at a conference: to let you know both his strengths and his weaknesses. Of course, we love to hear all the good things people have to say about our kids, but we often don't like to hear what they need to work on. (Truthfully, teachers feel the same way about delivering the news; they love to share the good things and often dread telling parents the bad.) That is natural; no one really likes to say or hear the bad stuff. Kids are no exception.

Many teachers know that delivering not-so-good news is easier with something called "The Sandwich Method." To understand this concept, picture a sandwich: soft bread on top, the meat inside, with another layer of soft bread on the bottom. Now, think of delivering tough news. Is it better to just blurt it right out or to soften things first? Many teachers find that parents can hear the bad news (the "meat") better if they have heard some good news first. Kids are the same way.

So, if you have to deliver some tough news to your child or even just need to tell him to do something he may not like, you can use the Sandwich Method, too. Let's say you have to tell your child that, starting tomorrow, he has to do 30 minutes of homework at the kitchen table every day because his math grade is slipping. Don't just say, "Your teacher said you are not doing very well in math, so now you have to start doing homework where I can keep an eye on you every single day." Try the Sandwich Method instead:

1. First, the soft bread: say something positive such as, "Your teacher said you are really improving on your spelling tests and that you are trying harder to produce quality work."

2. Now, the meat: say what you need to get across such as, "However, she also said your math grades seem to be slipping; I was thinking that it might be better for you to do your math down here at the kitchen table instead of where you usually do it, so that I am close by and can check to see how you are doing and be nearby in case you have a question."

3. Don't just end with the bad news. Offer more soft bread: think of something else positive to say such as, "I am proud of all of the nice things your teacher said about you; if this new idea works, and your grades improve, you can start to choose where you do your homework again."

Sandwiching the bad news in between good news softens it for your child and makes sure that you are not speaking only out of anger. Better results will likely come of this, too! Knowing you want to say some good stuff both before and after makes you have to *find* some good stuff to say as well—and we *all* probably hear bad news better along with a little dose of good.

#343
Setting Goals

If you can DREAM it, you can DO it.
~Walt Disney

A great way to help your child learn to be self-reliant is to teach her to set goals. In Part 1 perhaps your child wrote down some of her goals (Idea #4). When kids start early not only thinking about goals but also writing them down, they do this on their own later in life. It becomes part of what they do. Set a goal, work toward it, accomplish it, and set a new goal.

If your child did set a goal when you first began this book, chances are lots of time has passed by, perhaps nearly a whole year! Take some time now to revisit those goals. Has she accomplished some or all of them? If so, help her to write some new ones. If not, maybe the original goals could be adjusted a little to be more reasonable or attainable. Perhaps, she has just not been working toward them like she should. If she wants to keep them, help her make a plan for how to reach them. You may need to gently guide her in the right direction not only with the setting of the goals but also on the path to attaining them.

Young or old, it feels good to accomplish a goal, but if you never set them, you never have the chance to attain them! Help your child learn, at a young age, how to set them, why we set them, and how to help herself achieve them. It is a skill that will last a lifetime.

#344
Be Consistent with Rules

Life is a big canvas, throw all the paint on it you can.
~Danny Kaye

Can you remember back to your childhood when you were mad at your parents for a rule they had that you did not think was fair? Are there any of those rules you look back at now with grown-up vision and see that they were for the best? Though they would certainly disagree, kids do want rules. They want parameters. They want certain expectations. Like everything, there has to be a balance. Not too many rules, but enough. Not too harsh, but stiff enough.

One of the best things you can do to help your child be self-reliant and have good self-esteem is to give him rules. Sometimes, creating rules together with input from all sides works well. With other kids, you just have to lay down the law. Many parents these days just want their kids to be happy, and they think that means they should ease up on rules so that their child isn't upset. However, kids do better *with* rules. While it is in their nature perhaps to test those rules (sometimes until we think we might go crazy), it is also in their nature to need them.

As we said, finding a balance is the key. You don't want to have a rule for every single thing in your child's life. Too many makes a child want to tune right out of all of them, and rules you may have for one child just may not be necessary or may be different for another child. Another household's rules may be nothing like yours. What matters most is that you:

- are aware of what needs to be a rule in your house;

- make a rule to address the need. (Sometimes it is best, depending on the child, to do this Part with your child. Come to a consensus as to what is a fair rule. For some kids, that might not work and you will just need to make it up yourself.);

- create consequences if the rule is not followed; and

- are consistent in following through with the consequences every time. *Every* time!

Let's face it, kids will have rules all of their lives at home, in school, at their jobs, driving a car, and in their own families one day. They simply must learn at a young age how to follow rules gracefully, without falling apart when being told what to do. They need to know how to get through something even if they don't like it. They have to learn to do things sometimes even if it doesn't seem fair. There will always be rules they don't like! You have them, too. We all do. It is just part of life, and it is part of your job to help your child prepare for life. Even this kind of tough stuff.

Kids like to have expectations that they are fully aware of. They like to know someone is watching out for them. Even if they cannot verbalize it now, that is how rules make them feel: safe. Their confidence builds as they adjust to expectations and follow rules. You and your child will both like the less-frequent arguing and pleading that rules might extinguish. They may not thank you for rules now (or ever) but they will reap the benefits of them when they are leading productive, responsible lives.

#345
Praise, Prompt, and Leave

If children live with ENCOURAGEMENT,
they learn to be CONFIDENT.
If children live with APPROVAL,
they learn to BE THEMSELVES.
~Dorothy L. Nolte

In the introduction to this section, we discussed how children become self-confident. It is *not* because they are told over and over that every single thing they do is totally terrific. We may be tempted to think that gives them self-esteem, but in reality, self-esteem must be earned and cannot just be given to a child.

To illustrate this point, imagine you are playing a new game on your computer. Imagine playing for the first time and winning. *WOW*, you think. *Am I good at this!* But then, say you play a few more times and win every single game. Now, do you feel so talented, or do you feel that there is something wrong with the game? Maybe it is set up to let you win every time? Well, that's no fun. Now, imagine you play this new game and lose (spectacularly!) at first. Then, you play again and get close but do not win. So, you play again and do better. You are encouraged to keep playing, aren't you? You are getting the hang of this. You are determined to work harder to beat it. When you finally do win, how do you feel? Probably, like you have *accomplished* something. Like you *earned* it. *This* gives you a dose of self-esteem. Winning every time did not.

Think of that example when you are praising your child. Try not to tell her that everything she is doing is wonderful. Instead, look for genuine opportunities to tell her that something she is doing, or has done, is really good. Be specific, too. Instead of just saying, "Your story was really good," try to find something in particular and emphasize that, like, "Your story was really good. I especially liked the part at the end when you had the main character figure out the plan like that."

If she is in the middle of something, a nice strategy that teachers use is called "Praise, Prompt, and Leave." What this means is to walk by, notice something she is doing well and tell her (and possibly encourage her, or guide her a bit if needed), then move on and let her get back to accomplishing it on her own. Leaving her to continue on her own shows her that you have confidence in her ability to finish on her own. This boosts her self-confidence.

Also, be aware that sometimes simple words can be more powerful than big ones when praising. "Your painting turned out lovely. That bird is really very lifelike!" can mean more to a child than, "What an amazingly fabulous painting! That bird is really epic!" Popular words sound cool and are fun for kids to say, but when they are hearing about their own work from grown-ups, the good old regular words carry more meaning.

#346
Finding a Niche

Use what talents you possess;
The woods would be very silent if no birds sang
there except those that sang best.
~Henry Van Dyke

Every child is good at something. Help your child discover his natural talent, his niche. It's tempting to put him in sports, let's say, when all his friends are playing, but is he really enjoying it? Does he complain about going? Perhaps he might enjoy something else like music lessons, acting, building things, or drawing. When your child is truly good at something, it builds his self-esteem. If you can find what he's good at and enjoys, you are helping him develop his self-worth. Listed below are a few things to try.

- Talk to your child about what makes him unique.

- Give him opportunities to explore what he may be interested in. Something that sounds like a good idea at first might not be when he's actually doing it. He won't know unless he tries.

- Give him specific, positive feedback on his talent (making sure it's real, earned praise).

- Don't assume he will find his strengths through school or friends - get involved and take on the responsibility of helping him find his natural talents.

- Be supportive. Cheer him on. He's bound to stumble and fall as he makes this journey. Let him know you are there for him and proud of what he's doing.

- Be a role model. Let him see you doing things that you are naturally good at and enjoy doing.

There is something for everyone. Take time to find out what that is for your child. You will increase his self-esteem, help him gain confidence, and may even provide him with opportunities for social interaction with other children who enjoy the same thing.

#347
Self-Fulfilling Prophecy

Be what you are. This is the first step toward becoming better than you are.
~Julius Charles Hare and Augustus William Hare

What you think of your child is reflected in the things you say and do. Your child picks up on those feelings and is affected by those words. If you tell a child "you're lazy" too often, she begins to see herself that way. That's self-fulfilling prophecy. If your child struggles with math, for instance, and she hears you telling someone on the phone that "math isn't her strength; I don't think she'll ever get it," you are unknowingly telling her that she shouldn't even try because she is bad at it. That is not the message you want to send! While you want to be mindful of unearned praise, you also want to be wary of negative messages you may be accidentally sending to your child.

On the other hand, if you praise your child for being responsible when she's actually being responsible or tell a family member about her responsible behavior when she's listening, she will believe she is responsible and will be more likely to continue that behavior as a child and also into adulthood. If we have a positive view of our children, they are likely to feel the same about themselves.

Teachers have an acronym for this: TESA, which stands for Teacher Expectation, Student Achievement. Teachers are taught if they expect their students to achieve a certain task or behavior, they will. You can use this same idea. Maybe you can call it PESA - Parent Expectation Student Achievement! You'll be amazed at what your child can accomplish if she knows you truly believe she can.

#348
Show Your Pride

Each day of our lives we make deposits
in the memory banks of our children.
~Charles R. Swindoll

A very simple way to help increase your child's self-esteem is to show him how proud you are of him. *Telling* him is certainly important, but *showing* is even more important. Remember that saying, "Actions speak louder than words?" Well, they do! Below are a few easy ways to let your actions speak for you.

- Take a particularly good art project to work to hang in your office. Tell him exactly why you like it, and ask if you can take it to work so you can look at it often and show others.

- Display some of his work around the house. Don't do this with all of his work. That will eventually not have an impact. Be choosy, and tell him exactly why you would like to hang something up. Look for an interesting poem or a great spelling test or a math test that shows much improvement and hang it on the fridge.

- Buy an inexpensive frame to display an award given.

- Take a photo of him doing something he does particularly well. Most kids love to have their picture taken. When you do, it shows them you care and think that what they are doing is important.

- Videotape him doing or reciting something he has mastered like his multiplication facts or the ABCs or the Preamble to the Constitution.

When you show as well as tell him how proud you are of him (and are specific, not overly gushing about everything), you are reinforcing that you think he is good and that what he does is good. Feelings like that build on each other. Who knows, it may also encourage your child to show others how much he is proud of them!

#349
Accountability

There are two lasting bequests we can give our children:
One is roots. The other is wings.
~Hodding Carter, Jr.

Another fantastic way to nurture self-reliance in your child is to hold her accountable for what you know she has learned. There is a tendency to study hard for a test or work hard on an assignment and then just forget about that stuff. However, if you keep up to date on what your child is learning, you can watch for those skills to come up later and make sure she is still using them.

Let's take spelling, for example. Say she studies for a spelling test on homophones (sound-alike words). She studies a lot and gets an A. You are proud of her and tell her so, but don't let it stop there. From now on, she should be spelling those words correctly in her own writing. If you see her use the wrong *there* in a sentence, remind her that she learned the three ways to spell *there* and have her fix it. If you have seen worksheets come home teaching proper punctuation for quotations, then after that, make sure she is using it correctly in her writing. Sure, tests are important, but the main goal is to check for understanding. An A (or, really, even an E) on a spelling test is not nearly as important as whether she spells those words in her own writing correctly later on.

Many schools have grade-level lists of words that kids are expected to "never again" misspell. You could hang it on the fridge, at the message center, or at her homework spot so that it is easily available should she need it. To keep up with what your child is learning in school, check folders and back packs. Ask her teacher for a general list of concepts for the week or month if one is not sent home. The more you know about what she is learning, the more you can encourage carry-over at home.

Sure, we all forget stuff, but a lot of times with kids, it is just laziness or lack of attention to details that make them not fix up their work. Many kids don't like to edit their writing, but if a child spells a word wrong too many times and isn't asked to correct it, it can become a habit to spell it that wrong way—and we all know how hard it is to break a bad habit. Editing your own work, whether it be for spelling, punctuation, math accuracy or whatever, is a life skill, so now is the perfect time to start.

#350
Conflict Resolution

The truth of the matter is that
you always know the right thing to do.
The hard part is doing it.
~General H. Norman Schwarzkopf

You are so many things to you child: mentor, teacher, leader, nurse, counselor, and more. Have you ever felt like a referee? If you have more than one child, you most likely have been called on to solve many conflicts. Use these conflicts as an opportunity to teach Conflict Resolution. Conflict Resolution gives your child the skills he needs to solve problems without relying on adult supervision. You will, of course, have to model the procedure first and monitor it until it seems like he understands it. Here's how it works.

- When a conflict happens, separate the children involved for a few minutes so they are not reacting on emotions.

- Teach them the "I" message. When someone starts a sentence with "YOU never" or "YOU always," it puts the other person on the defense right away. Instead, teach him to start his sentences with "I," such as "I was angry when you took my ball at recess."

- Follow it with an "I wish" message. Using the example above, you might say, "I was angry when you took my ball at recess; I wish you would ask first and wait your turn."

- Let each child have his say—no interrupting each other. Based on the above scenario, you might think the second boy is mean by taking the ball. What you might find out when the second boy has his turn to speak is, "I was mad because you never let me play on the team at recess; I wish you would include me and let me play, too."

- Be there for them if they need you, but let them know they are in charge of solving their own conflicts. Have them come to you with the solution to the conflict, and praise them for figuring it out.

This skill will help your child throughout his school days and into adulthood, too. Imagine him using this technique as an adult at work, in relationships, and with his own kids. What great relationships he will have when he realizes the power of conflict resolution.

#351
It is Better to Have Tried and Failed....

He who laughs, lasts.
~Mary Poole

Have you ever watched someone do something and thought to yourself, "Boy, I would love to be able to do that"? Then, the next thought pops into your head, "But there's no way I could!" If so, then chances are your child has felt that way, too. Another thing you can do for your child is to encourage her to try for what she wants.

We often say to our kids, "You can be anything you want to be." Though that is not always 100% true (because, honestly, not everyone is cut out for every possible thing in the world), to a large extent, it is. What is also true is that many of the goals we may dream up for ourselves will take a lot of work to get there. That, more than anything else, is generally the thing that stops most of us. Not everyone is born with the natural ability to sing like Andrea Bocelli, play hockey like Wayne Gretzky, dance like Mikhail Baryshnikov, or think like Albert Einstein. That doesn't mean, though, you still can't become a *really good* singer, dancer, hockey player, or mathematician or even just have some fun trying it out.

Most of us are not born with a terrific ability, so we will just have to work for it. That is usually the deal-breaker for most kids (and adults, too). We want stuff, but working for it is hard! Here is where helping your child to set some reasonable goals comes in handy again. She wants to paint like Picasso? Well, what are the steps to get there? Kids often need your help figuring out where to start. They want to jump right in and get discouraged when they aren't very good. That's when they quit. However, if they had started at the beginning by taking some lessons and slowly worked their way up by practicing every single day, they would have probably had much greater results.

So, what if you help your child to dream a dream and make a plan to get there, and she is brave enough to try, works really hard, and still doesn't get what she wants? That certainly does not feel good and may discourage her from ever trying things like that again. Again, you can play a big role here. Remind her how much she did learn, laugh together at the mistakes and bumps along the road and, most important, be a role model by trying things yourself. You can teach invaluable lessons without ever saying a word by taking piano lessons and letting her hear your not-so-terrific scales at first, watch you laugh at your mistakes, and see how you work at it a little every day. Of course, that is just one example of a million.

Encourage her to try. Let her see you try new things. Try some new things together. Practice. Laugh at mistakes. Remind her that, even though it may seem so at times, no one is perfect. Praise *progress* not perfection. Remind her that she is not failing as long as she is trying. Sitting back and watching your dreams fly away without you is the only real failure.

#352
Don't Give Up

Our greatest glory is not in never failing, but in rising up every time we fail.
~Ralph Waldo Emerson

In the previous idea, we discussed the importance of trying new things you might be interested in, but no matter who you are, you will make mistakes. Sometimes young kids have a very hard time coping with making mistakes. Getting back up (sometimes literally!) and trying again may not be the easiest thing to help your child learn to do. Sitting him down and talking about it will not have near the impact that a spontaneous lesson right there at the scene of the error may have.

If you are lucky enough to be with your child when he fails, use that as a teachable moment. Look for those moments in your child's life. They are likely to show up during sports (particularly if the coach seems "tough" or the other players seem better than he is), during a difficult homework assignment, while learning a new skill like bike riding, or in learning to play a new game. Remind him that even the people who are the very best in their field, failed many times first. The best hockey player most definitely fell many times while learning to skate. Einstein didn't talk until he was four and didn't learn to read until he was seven. Thomas Edison had about 1,000 failures at making the light bulb before he succeeded. They didn't give up. They kept trying, learned from their mistakes, and eventually they achieved their goals.

You've heard the old saying, "If you fall off the horse, you need to get right back on." It means that the longer you wait to try again, the less likely you are to try again. A great thing you can do for your child is to encourage him to get right back to it and try again. You can also let your child see you make mistakes or fail at something and then get right back at it again. When he sees you do it, he begins to assume that is how tough things are handled. No need to scream and cry and pout and run away. Just try it again! True self-esteem comes from trying hard and finally accomplishing something.

#353
Responsibility

Should you yield the canyons from the windstorms,
you would not see the beauty of their carvings.
~Elizabeth Kubler-Ross

What is character? How is it built in a person? What do you want your child to grow up to be like? These are questions that you and your family have to answer for yourselves, but there are some characteristics that probably top many lists like being kind, responsible, persevering, and well-rounded. As you have read, one of the most important things you can do to build good character in your child is to be a good role-model. Another is to give her lots of opportunities to display the kinds of characteristics you want to see.

A very simple and yet highly effective way to incorporate many character-building qualities into one thing is to give your child chores to do. In Idea #22, we discussed giving your child chores. Revisit her list. Does it need to be revised? Start out small so she can feel successful and not overwhelmed. Show her clearly how to accomplish the task, and then let her try while you are there to guide her and answer questions. If that goes well, add a little more responsibility. Self-esteem comes from working hard, accomplishing something, and doing well. Chores are a perfect vehicle for that.

Chores make a child feel useful, responsible, and valued. True, kids often complain about them, but you know, as her parent, that sometimes you have to do some un-fun stuff for her own good down the road. By providing them with opportunities to shine, we let our kids spread their wings and soar. After all, how will we ever know if they will become responsible adults if we never give them opportunities to be responsible kids?

#354
Being "Grown Up"

Age is of no importance unless you are a cheese.
~Billie Burke

Another way to help foster self-esteem in your child is to find ways to help him feel grown-up. Only you know when your child is ready for something, but here are a few things to let him try when you feel he's ready to and, of course, with your guidance:

- answer the phone (practice what to say if no one is home and how to take a message);

- order for himself at a restaurant;

- pay the bill at a restaurant: figure out the tip, go to the register, estimate change back;

- go to the corner store;

- get the mail;

- ask a salesperson a question;

- help make dinner;

- set and clear the table;

- run a load of his own laundry; and

- clean the bathroom sink.

If your child does not like to talk to other people or do things like order for himself, tending to whisper things in your ear so you will ask for something for him, avoid supporting that behavior by saying, "He's just shy." He may be shy, but in order to outgrow it, he must be encouraged to speak for himself. Try not to talk for your child. Let him develop his voice. You cannot be there for him to do his talking in school and with friends, and you don't want him to be taken advantage of or miss out on something because he was afraid to speak up. Starting now in small ways, while he's young, will help him outgrow this habit quicker than if you wait until it really becomes a problem.

Kids' self-esteem increases naturally when they accomplish things for themselves. As they get older, naturally give them more responsibilities so that one day they can move out of your house and maintain one themselves. Sometimes, though, we hesitate to give them a new responsibility because it may be messy or not turn out as well as if we just did it ourselves. Today, though, think about what really matters. What will really happen if he dresses himself for school and doesn't quite match? Will anyone really care if he wears last year's Halloween costume to the grocery store? When kids feel that they have learned something new, learned to speak up, and take on a challenge, they feel important, and it builds their character and their self-esteem naturally.

#355
Revisit Your Homework Policy

There is overwhelming evidence that the higher the level of self-esteem,
the more likely one will be to treat others with respect, kindness, and generosity.
~Nathaniel Branden, via Positive Press

Working hard and doing well makes us feel good and naturally raises our self-esteem. For young kids, school is a perfect place to try hard, study, and accomplish things. To help kids do well in school, teachers often assign homework. Homework gives kids extra practice with concepts. It also lets parents know what is going on in the classroom and allows them to see how their child is doing. In Idea #17, you read about creating a homework policy. Perhaps now is a good time to revisit it. Below are some things to consider.

- Sit down with your child, and ask how it is going with homework. If homework is consistently getting done and done well, keep up what you've been doing; if not, try to figure out what is getting in the way. There could be many things interfering like playing video games, too many after-school activities, or simple procrastination.

- Though every family is different and every situation is not the same, it is generally a good idea to require homework to be completed before anything else. If there is a lot of homework, you and your child might feel good about building in some breaks where she can step away from the homework and do something she enjoys for a few minutes before coming back to it. The important thing is to make the homework a priority.

- Setting rules in writing, and posting them somewhere where she can see is also helpful. It saves you from constantly having to be the bad guy, telling her you think she should get back to work. You can just refer to the posted "Homework Policy" when she needs a reminder. For instance, if she whines, "Please can I go to Emily's house before I do my homework," you can say, "Check the Homework Policy," instead of having to make the choice yourself.

- If you find that your child is rushing through her homework just so she can go do other things that she really wants to do, you can modify the "Homework First" rule and change it to something like no TV, computer, or video games until 8pm. That way, hurrying through the homework doesn't matter anymore since she can't just go right to the fun stuff anyway. She might as well take her time now.

- If after-school sports or other activities are taking up too much time in the evenings or occur on too many days of the week, you might want to rethink that area, too. While it is great to have your child in sports or hobbies that she likes, if it is interfering with school (taking away studying time), then you must ask yourself if it is worth it.

As her parent, it is up to you to ensure homework gets done and that she completes it to the best of her ability. The odds of her using her sports (or video game!) skills in her future career are pretty slim; however, using what she's learned in school is quite probable. Find ways to calm her life down so there is always time for homework first.

#356
Encourage Free Time

Don't go through life, grow through life.
~Eric Butterworth

Today, take a few minutes to look, really look, at your child's life. Is he bored with not much to do? Is he so overbooked he doesn't have time for homework or for just hanging out? Or does he have a nice balance of both work and play? Of course, there are no right or wrong answers to any of these questions. The real answers come from your family values. However, there is something you may want to consider: Kids need "down time." (See Idea #28.)

Children need some time where they are not scheduled to be somewhere doing something. The hours at school and doing homework after school take up about 40 hours of your child's life. That is a full time job! Then, we pile on Boy Scouts, drum lessons, soccer practice, and so many other things that sometimes what our kids lose is free time. In preschool and even kindergarten, teachers build in play time, knowing how much kids can learn through play. Then, when first grade comes, that play time is usually gone, replaced by more structured ways of learning. That is why it is even more important that you offer that time at home. When your child has time to just sit, to just be, he gains some beneficial skills:

- learning to occupy himself, which sparks creativity and imagination;

- learning to quiet himself and observe things, which are important skills in both school and in life;

- learning to do what interests him the most;

- learning to become more self-sufficient;

- learning to relax, which allows his stress levels to fall; and

- learning to be comfortable with himself, which raises self-esteem.

An important thing to remember about free time is to make sure that part of it (a huge chunk of it, we say) is not in front of technology (Idea #25). While free time of any kind is important, part of the benefits of your child being alone or choosing his own activities means that it gets him thinking, creating, going outside, finding things to do. Learning to occupy himself, slowing down enough to regroup, and taking time to observe his surroundings, helps not only his mind and spirit but also with other, academic, areas as well.

So, the next time you hear the whine, "I'm bored," smile to yourself. It's a good thing!

#357
Children Can Be Teachers, Too!

I believe... that every human mind
feels pleasure in doing good to another.
~Thomas Jefferson

If you are looking for good, authentic ways to help your child feel good about herself, think again about letting her teach someone something she knows how to do. In Part 1, we wrote about how valuable it is to let her do this (Idea #23). Teaching something to someone else is one of the highest forms of learning. If you can explain it to someone else, you must truly understand it. Today, though, let's also consider its potential as a great confidence-booster. Below are some things to think about.

- Think about something your child does well. Is there someone who could benefit from her knowledge? If so, suggest it to her and help arrange it.

- Ask her to show you how her teacher has shown her to do something. Math is a good area. Lots of methods we were taught are now outdated. Have your child show you the "new way." Better yet, know what is coming up in school by keeping up with classroom newsletters or asking her teacher. Then, when you know she is going to be learning about the start of the Civil War, tell her, "When you get home from school today, I hope you can refresh my memory of how exactly the Civil War began; it's been so long since I've learned about it." She now has yet another reason to pay close attention to the lesson; she knows she will be explaining it to you!

- If she learns a new skill in a sport or hobby, have her show you (or Grandma, the nice neighbor, or even her cat!) how it's done. If she is interested in something, have her research it and share what she's learned. Even teaching Uncle Ben how to do a card trick can be a big self-esteem boost.

Think of ways for her to show off what she knows. It is a good way for her to be more self-confident in the best way possible—by earning it.

#358
Healthy Arguing

Challenge of the day: Find something good in everyone.
~Unknown

Is it ever okay to encourage your child to argue? Before you answer no, you first must understand what an argument is. When asked, most people think of an argument as a fight, but the two are quite different. An argument is good; a fight is not. The goal of a fight is to dominate your opponent, but in an argument you are trying to get the other person to agree with your side. You do this by using logic and reasoning, very useful skills to have. If children aren't taught how to argue appropriately, they will turn to fighting.

Consider two kids who both want the front seat of the car. If they have never been taught to argue persuasively and intelligently, it will automatically escalate to a fight with loud words, angry voices, and maybe even name calling. It may even turn physical, something you definitely want to avoid. The fighting is the result of frustration because children don't know how else to handle the situation. You can help your child learn arguing skills so that she can handle any problem that comes her way in a healthy way.

When your child wants something, let's say a later bedtime, she's likely just to whine and beg. Before she gets to that stage, sit down with her, and tell her you want to talk about her bedtime. Tell her you're going to talk first, and then she will get a chance when you're done. Give her the reasons why you think she needs to go to bed at the designated time. Then, when you're done, tell her you will give her a few minutes to gather the reasons why she thinks she should stay up later. It's okay to tell her that some arguments are just not up for discussion like *My older sister doesn't go to bed this early* or *It's not fair*. Explain to her you need to know *why* it's not fair in her eyes. You need specific reasons.

Listen to her reasoning. It's very common at this point for her to have a hard time coming up with reasonable arguments like you did. Explain to her that if she can think of real reasons, you can talk again about bedtime. If she does come up with a reasonable argument such as, *"I'm not tired this early. Can I stay up an extra half hour and if I don't get up easily in the morning without complaints, we can go back to my old bedtime?"* you may find that you are willing to give it a try.

By listening to her arguments, you are showing her that her point of view and ideas are important and valid. She will know you take her seriously, and you will honestly consider what she has to say. You will be creating a person who is not afraid to stand up for what she believes in by presenting an intelligent argument that's hard to say *no* to. If she can calmly and effectively stand up for herself now, imagine all the different ways she can use it in the future to resist peer pressure, to get a job, and to be a leader at work—and a very confident and self-reliant person!

#359
Pulling it all Together

Recipe for a Healthy Attitude
1. Learn to face realities;
2. Learn to make decisions;
3. Develop self-discipline;
4. Be interested in other people;
5. Avoid hurry and worry;
6. Work, rest, and play in proper balance;
7. Accept disappointment;
8. Develop a sense of humor.
~Dr. Strodes

The quote above speaks volumes. It is a terrific recipe not only for a healthy attitude but also for a healthy *kid*! Many of the points made in the above quote we have covered in this book. As this year of activities and ideas comes to a close, be on the lookout for opportunities to use the ideas in this book in everyday experiences like cooking. For example, since we were talking about recipes, let's say you decided to ask your child to help make a special meal with you. This one activity (cooking) will incorporate many ideas from the math, self-esteem, and critical thinking Parts. Below are just a few of the ways you might pull in ideas.

- Ask him to help you plan the menu. By letting him help choose what to serve, you are helping him become more self-reliant and likely increasing his self-esteem by showing him that you want and trust his judgment.

- Bring your child along to shop for the ingredients. Have him compare prices of similar items. Which is the best deal? Ask him to estimate the cost of everything. Have him count out the money.

- Let him help you prepare the meal. Put him in charge of a few things that he and only he will do. Discuss fractions in measuring, how to halve or double recipes, cooking times, and temperatures.

- Ask him to set the table.

- Tell the other diners which items he was solely responsible for so they can compliment him if they'd like.

- Ask him to help clear the table, too.

All of these help to teach him responsibility and to become more self-reliant while incorporating other skills, such as math and critical thinking, in a fun way. He also feels good about helping you and about serving things he prepared. You do not need to make lessons out of these things. You want it to be fun, but there are teachable moments everywhere if you look. While it would be cumbersome and boring to turn *everything* into a lesson of some sort, there are many opportunities to approach teachable moments in a natural way, to help your child with some life skills while simply going about your day.

Cooking a special meal together is just one way of tying it all together. How many others can you think of?

#360
Staying Organized

A large part of getting organized is learning to act from a place of self-esteem:
knowing what we want and don't want to do,
knowing what we can and can't do,
and taking good care of ourselves.
~Marilyn Paul, Ph.D

Part of becoming a self-reliant person is learning to be organized. For some people, this comes easily and for others it is a never-ending battle. Helping your child to become organized at a young age will help her be more successful not only today but also in the years to come.

In Part 1, we covered a few ideas to help your child and family get ready to make some changes and become more organized. In Idea #13, we gave you a few ways to keep organized for school. Idea #18 explained the importance of having a good place to work on homework. Take some time to reflect on your child's home/school routine, and ask yourself how organized it is. Below are some things to think about.

- If your child's teacher has given her a planner or homework folder, make sure it is being utilized. Having a planner is an extremely beneficial way to begin a path to organization. Many adults use an actual or virtual planner daily. Of course, your child is not likely to be as busy as you, but she still has short-term and possibly some long-term homework that may need to be planned out. Check to see that she is filling in her planner at school and go over it with her daily. Make it part of your homework policy (Idea #17). Help her to plan what needs to be done first, what is due the next day, and what can wait until later. (Checking her planner also keeps you up to date on what is going on in her classroom and lets you be more involved at home.)

- Utilize the message center (Idea #6). Posting important notices there regularly helps show your child that there is a right and a wrong place to put important information. Having one specific place helps both of you stay organized.

- In elementary school, having one teacher helps avoid information overload. In middle and high school, however, she will likely have many teachers who will all do things differently. She will need ways to be organized. Later, you can show her fun tricks like color-coding classes. For example, maybe she'll choose blue for science so help her pick out a blue folder and a blue binder for that. For now, she can still get different folders for the various subjects taught in her classroom. Label them clearly. Perhaps get a special folder for homework. Whatever she needs to bring home to work on can go in there. Remind her to check it right when she gets home from school. Help her make a plan for when it will get done (Idea #17).

- Go through her backpack together once in a while. Backpacks are notorious for collecting junk. Show her the value in taking everything out (every single thing) once in a while and only putting back what is necessary. (This is a good skill to try out on other things of hers, too, like drawers and closets and her desk at school.) Sometimes, enlisting the help, or at least company, of someone else can make cleaning out stuff more fun. Another way to make it fun is to race her. You pick perhaps a kitchen drawer, and tell her to do her backpack. Race to see who can clean it out first!

Being an organized adult doesn't just happen magically in high school or when she moves out on her own. It comes from practicing in many ways, starting at a young age, and from watching what others do. Don't forget to be a good role model, and show her how you stay organized. Chances are whatever you do at home now that works, she will copy herself when she is on her own.

#361
Memorize Stuff!

Character is higher than intellect.
~ Ralph Waldo Emerson

It may not be the most fun thing in the world to do, but at times, we all just have to memorize things. In elementary school, some of the most common things to memorize are spelling words and the basic math facts for addition, subtraction, multiplication, and division. Yes, your child can get along without memorizing these things. He can still do math even if he has to count things out every time. He can use a dictionary for tough spelling words. However, math will be so much easier (and faster!) if he has his facts memorized; reading, writing, and spelling will be so much more fun if he knows how to spell.

For some kids, memorizing things like math facts, spelling words, state capitals, names, and dates comes easily. For others, it is such a chore that we sometimes think it is not worth it, but it *is* worth it. Below are some tips for making memorization more fun.

- Practice is always more fun if it doesn't feel like drilling. Try to make a game of it. In Part 7, for instance, we offered you several open-ended math games that you could use to practice math facts. Try some of those at first. Weed out what is already memorized, and then only focus on what is not. Part 10 is full of fun ways to memorize spelling words. Be sure to ask his teacher if you are not sure of grade-level math standards or need a list of grade-level reading or spelling words. In Part 11, Idea #334 has ideas for memory-aid strategies that will help tricky things be more easily memorized.

- Summer vacation is a good time to catch up on memorizing things that didn't quite stick during the busy school year. Sit down with your child at the beginning of summer (perhaps after that last report card so you can see exactly what still needs work). Choose an amount of time per day or week that he will practice memorizing what is needed. He will be so happy in the fall when he feels more confident.

- Summer vacation is also a good time to get a *head start* on memorizing something for the next school year if you know it is coming up. (Ask his teacher for suggestions.) How great he will feel when he has a jump on everyone else in the fall!

- Some other good times for throwing in some practicing of memorization include in the car, standing in line, during commercials, sitting at the breakfast table, while brushing his teeth before bed, and before any technology time!

- Keep in mind that, once a skill is taught, the teacher will expect it to carry through in all future lessons and grades. Those memorized facts, words, and information will be used in other, new ways, too. For instance, in math, knowing the basic multiplication facts will be necessary for learning about fractions, decimals, percentages, area, perimeter, long division, multiplication and... well, you get the picture.

Kids who did not memorize the basic math facts find most future math more difficult. Young kids who don't have grade-level reading words memorized struggle more with reading. Older kids who don't have grade-level spelling words memorized struggle more with writing. Help your child now by knowing what does need to be (and doesn't need to be) memorized. Find time—and fun ways—to work on memorization. The dedication teaches him self-reliance, and the results (better grades, an easier time with homework, etc.) increase his self-esteem. He may not love doing it now, but he will be forever grateful he did.

#362
Build Vocabulary

The most important thing is to read as much as you can, like I did. It will give you an understanding of what makes good writing and it will enlarge your vocabulary.
~J. K. Rowling

Parents are their children's first role model for vocabulary. So, it is important for you to create an environment that enriches your child's vocabulary. Below are some ways to help increase vocabulary at home.

- Post your child's spelling words at the message center, and challenge the family to try to use as many of them as possible during the week.

- Start a Word of the Week activity. Each family member can take a turn choosing a word for the week. Try to make it one you may actually use in conversation. Think of a common word like *talkative* and find a more interesting word for it like *loquacious.* Put the word and its meaning on the message center. Look for opportunities to use it during the week. "You're being awfully loquacious today. Why don't you let your sister have a turn to share about her day?" The next week another family member can decide the Word of the Week.

- Start a hunt for homonyms. Start the list with your own homonyms like *aunt* and *ant* or *ate* and *eight.* Encourage others to add to the list when they think of other homonyms.

- Play the blending game. One person starts by picking a blend such as *br.* Each person takes a turn, saying a word beginning with the blend (e.g., *brush*), until all the words are exhausted. When everyone is out of words with that blend, the next person chooses another blend, and the play continues.

- Play Choose a Category. One person chooses a category such as "fruit," and every player says a word that fits into that category (strawberry, grapes, apple, etc.). Players take turns, choosing categories. If you want to make it more challenging, choose a letter of the alphabet that each word in the category must start with.

- Create new analogies together (Activity #327).

- Have fun with words. Create your own onomatopoeias or oxymorons.

- Play a game of Scrabble. Keep a dictionary close by!

- Listen to books on tape while in the car or at home. This is especially beneficial if the book is at a higher reading level. Your child will pick up new words and their meanings just by listening.

- When teachers teach content areas like science or social studies, inevitably new words come up. Kids are then expected to be able to understand, and more importantly *use*, these new words. So, watch for newsletters and/or worksheets that explain what is going on in the classroom and see if you can support it by using those words at home, too.

- The most important way to increase vocabulary? *Read!*

Everyone will enjoy these activities, and, you never know, you may even learn a new word or two yourself!

#363
READ!!!!!

We worry about what a child will be tomorrow,
yet we forget that he is someone today.
~Stacia Tauscher

What kind of a book would this be if we did not, right before ending, remind you again how very important reading is for your child? In fact, the very first idea in this book was to make some time every day to "Drop Everything and Read (DEAR)." Are you and your family doing this together? Are you having your child do a little reading every day? Today, we want to remind you of its importance and also that so many things can count as reading.

Reading a little every day is so important that many teachers count it as part of homework and require it. If this is the case, it ends up being a little easier on you; instead of having to tell your child every day that *you* want him to read, you can simply remind him that his teacher requires it. If, however, it is not mandatory, you can still make it a little easier by simply *requiring* it yourself. If it is a struggle to get him to read, put it on his list of things to do each day. It can also be a separate "rule" posted at his homework spot or at the Message Center or anywhere, reminding him that reading is required. It's always easier to say "read the reminder," and let it tell your child, instead of you. Moreover, it encourages responsibility, which promotes both self-esteem and self-reliance.

Play around with a good amount of time for your child's age. Start out small, and increase gradually. Try not to get picky about what your child chooses to read. Reading is reading. Young kids like to read the same books over and over because they feel confident and can sound like a "good reader." Don't worry. They won't choose those books forever. They will naturally want to progress to something tougher. Make available magazines (maybe subscribe to one just for him), have the newspaper lying about, and allow comics if they interest him. Even exploring charts and graphs in the news is helpful.

Don't forget that even upper elementary kids may still enjoy being read to. Reading to your child lets you pick a book above his reading level (something he might not be able to read on his own) and try something a little tougher, deeper, with lots of opportunity for discussion.

Either way, have a bunch of books to choose from. See if your local library has used books for cheap prices. Find a used book store, or go to garage sales. Some social media websites also have programs where things can be traded and shared, like books. See if friends with older kids have books for younger kids they would like to get rid of. Try also to find a variety of genres so that your child can try out a few different kinds to see what really catches his attention.

The more a child reads, the better reader he becomes. He also becomes a better writer, develops a richer vocabulary, learns to spell better, gets interested in new things, and gets to relax. It truly is one of the best things you can do to help your child improve in school.

#364
The Most Important Lessons

The key is taking responsibility and initiative,
deciding what your life is about and
prioritizing your life around the most important things.
~Stephen Covey

In this book, we have written about 363 ways you can help enhance what your child learns in the classroom, but we also hope you have learned that inside the school walls is definitely not the only place where learning takes place. Here are a few things we hope you see a little differently now:

- there are teachable moments everywhere when you know what to look for;

- often it is the questions that matter more than the answers;

- practicing can be fun;

- setting a good example is an easy (and possibly the most effective way) to get your points across;

- having a plan and being organized can solve so many problems and completely avoid many others;

- not everything works with every kid, but there will be *something* that works for yours;

- making what she learns relevant to her own life greatly increases the chances that she will understand and remember it;

- teaching something to someone else is the highest form of learning;

- good communication with your child's teacher is not only helpful, but necessary;

- tests and grades are not the only measure of what your child knows;

- growth toward a goal is just as important as accomplishing a goal;

- praise (like true success) must be earned;

- your child needs you to guide her and set rules and follow through. Even when it is tough. Even when it is *very* tough;

- only you and your family can figure out what is best for your child (Don't worry about other families and other kids; just figure out what matters most to you and stick to it);

- giving your child more responsibilities feels better to them deep down than giving them more video game time;

- trying new things is worth the risk;

- kids need free time, down time—avoid overscheduling their lives;

- helping your child to become a good reader (not someone who sounds good reading out loud, but someone who understands and connects with what she reads) is probably the most important skill you can help your child develop; and

- spending time with your child is invaluable. Play. Sit. Cook. Clean. Read. Laugh. Walk. Drive. Explore. Invent. Just do it together!

#365
Congratulations! Take a Look Back...

There is no point at which you can say,
'Well, I'm successful now.
I might as well take a nap.'
~Carrie Fisher

If you have been following the ideas in this book one per day, you began just about a year ago! Congratulations! You and your family have undoubtedly put a lot of time and effort into helping your child become more successful in school. Hopefully, you have had fun along the way and built some lasting habits.

Ideally, you will not just throw this book aside now and think, *"We did it! We're done! My kid is as smart as he can be!"* You have a lot of good choices as to what to do now. Below are some options.

1. Go back through the book again, one activity at a time, reminding yourself of each idea. Maybe you skipped one because it didn't seem to fit where your child was at the time. Does it now? Bookmark ideas you loved for future reference. Try some again when they come up if you loved them the first time.

2. With the bigger ideas like setting goals (Idea #4) and defining success (Idea #3), sit down with your child, and determine if they need to be revised at all. Another year older, another grade further, perhaps things have changed.

3. Look back through any journals your child kept. Did he keep a personal journal (Idea #5)? A science log (Idea #224)? Decide whether he will continue with them, begin new ones, or ditch them.

4.   Do you have everything in place for homework success? Look back through many of the ideas in Part 1 (Ideas #17 & 18 especially) that helped you set up a good study area and establish routines.

5.   If you don't want to go through the book one activity per day again, keep it handy anyway. When an issue comes up and you recall that it was covered in here, look it up!

6.   Keep checking in with us at our website (*www.365TeacherSecrets.com*) for any new ideas!

7.   And last, be sure to congratulate yourself for taking the time to want to help your child, for getting this book, for reading each of these ideas, for doing so many of them with your child, and for finding more ways to help your child be successful.

Kids don't need more toys or more cool shoes or more video games or more unearned praise. They need grown-ups who care about them. They need you.

Your child is very lucky to have you!

Appendix

Idea #214.
Examples of how to teach the new math methods:

#214 **Steps for Partial Sums** 

Partial Sums is a method some elementary teachers use to introduce adding multi-digit numbers to young children. Here is how you do it!

Take, for example: 68 (think: 60+8)
    + <u>47</u> (think: 40+7)

1. First, think about what each digit is worth. (ie: the 6 in 68 is actually worth 60, not 6; and the 4 in 47 is worth 40, not just 4.)

2. Add the tens column up first.

$$
\begin{array}{r}
68 \\
+ \quad 47 \\
\hline
60 + 40 = \quad 100
\end{array}
$$

3. Then add the ones column.

$$
\begin{array}{r}
68 \\
+ \quad 47 \\
\hline
60 + 40 = \quad 100 \\
8 + 7 = \quad 15
\end{array}
$$

4. Now add up the two answers. This is your sum!

$$
\begin{array}{r}
68 \\
+ \quad 47 \\
\hline
60 + 40 = \quad 100 \\
8 + 7 = \quad 15 \\
\hline
115
\end{array}
$$

#214 Steps for Partial Differences

Partial Differences is a method some elementary teachers use to introduce subtracting multi-digit numbers to young children. Here is how you do it!

Take, for example: 746 (think: 700+40+6)
           - 251 (think: 200+50+1)

1. First, think about what each digit is worth. (ie: the 7 in 746 is actually worth 700, not 7; the 4 in 746 is worth 40, not just 4.)

2. Subtract the hundreds column first.

                           746
                      - 251
700-200 =   500

3. Then subtract the tens column.

                           746
                      - 251
700-200 =   500
40-50 =   -   10

*NOTE: If the first number is smaller than the second, be sure to put a minus sign in front of it!

4. Lastly, subtract the ones column.

                           746
                      - 251
700-200 =   500
40-50 =   -   10
6-1 =   5

5. Now combine all of your partial differences. (Add them all up, subtracting any with a negative sign in front.) This is your answer!

$$
\begin{array}{rr}
 & 746 \\
- & \underline{251} \\
700\text{-}200 = & 500 \\
40\text{-}50 = \quad - & 10 \\
6\text{-}1 = \quad + & \underline{\ 5} \\
500\ \text{-}10\ \text{+}5 & 495 \\
\end{array}
$$

#214 **Steps for Partial Products**

Partial Products is a method some elementary teachers use to introduce multiplying multi-digit numbers to young children. Here is how you do it!

Take, for example: 38
x <u>45</u>

1. First, think about what each digit is worth. (ie: the 3 in 38 is actually worth 30, not 3; the 4 in 45 is worth 40, not just 4.)

38 (think: 30+ 8)
x <u>45</u> (think: 40+5)

2. In the next steps, you will multiply every part of 38 by every part of 45. Let's begin in the tens column, multiplying the 30 times the other tens digit.

38
x   <u>45</u>
30x40=   1200

3. Next, multiply the same 30 by the other digit in 45, the 5.

38
x   <u>45</u>
30x40=   1200
30x5 =   150

4. Now that we've multiplied the 3 (in 38) by both digits of the 45, let's move on to the 8. Multiply it by the 40 and then the 5.

38
x   <u>45</u>
30x40=   1200
30x5=   150
8x40=   320
8x5=   40

5. Now add all of your partial products. This is your answer!

```
                       38
                 x     45
    30x40=            1200
    30x5=              150
    8x40=              320
    8x5=          +     40
                      1710
```

#214 **Steps for Lattice Multiplication**

Lattice multiplication is another method some teachers use to introduce multiplying larger numbers to kids. It looks a little confusing, but the multiplication is simpler. The answers go in special boxes divided like this:

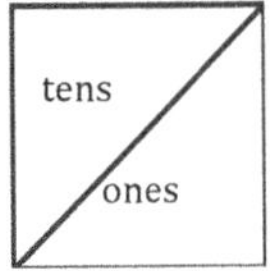

So for 3x5 we would set it up like this: (The answer goes inside.)

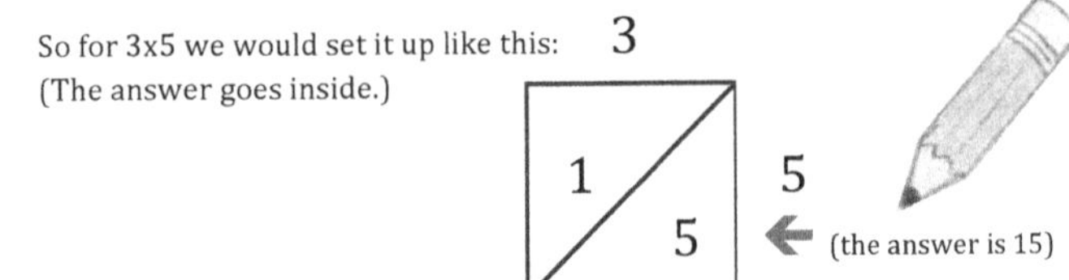

2-digit numbers need more boxes.

Let's use 34x 25. There are 2 digits in 34, so there needs to be 2 of the divided boxes *across*. Because 25 also has 2 digits, it would also need 2 boxes *down*. It would look like this:

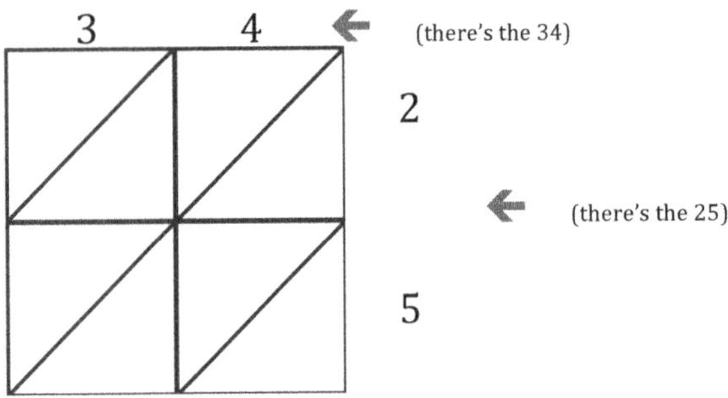

The next step is to begin multiplying a top number by a side number and putting the answer into the box where they meet. We'll start with 3x2=6. (Note: if the answer is only 1 digit, it still must take up 2 triangles, so we'll write it as 06.)

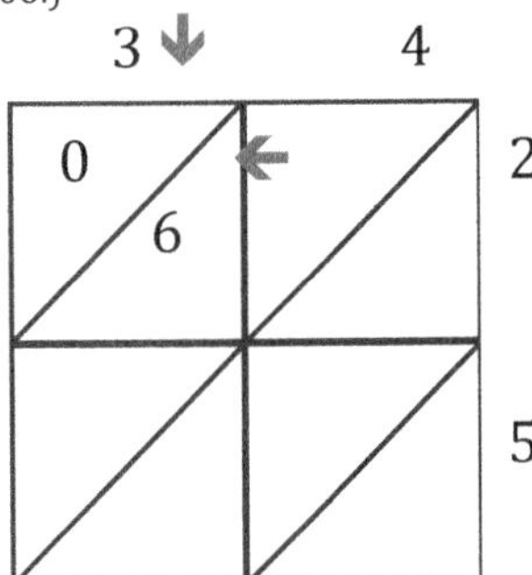

Now continue on, multiplying one top number by one side number and putting the answer in the box where they meet.

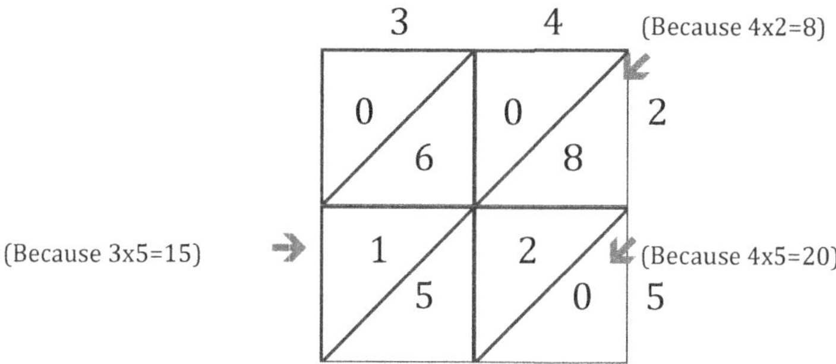

To get the answer, we add up the numbers in each diagonal stripe, beginning with the right-hand side. If we end up with more than 10, we "carry the one," just like in regular addition, into the next column. Put the answers underneath each stripe like this:

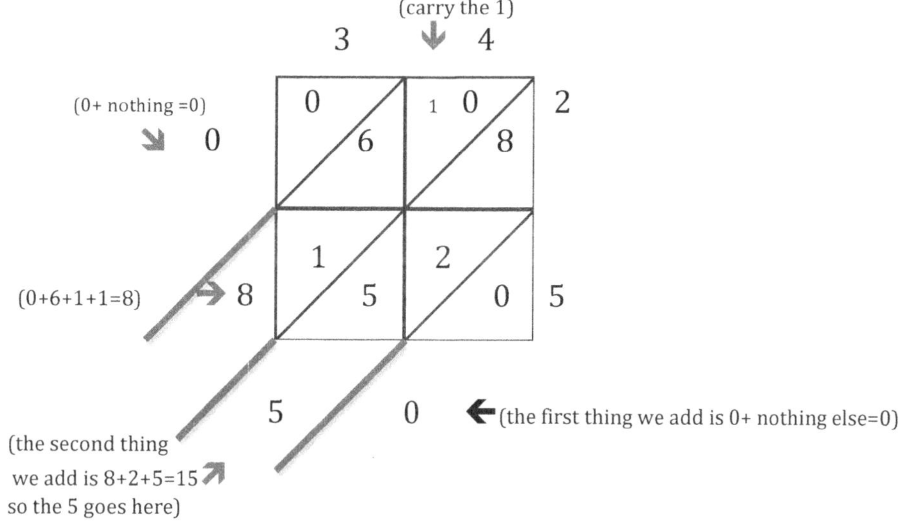

Your answer is read from top left to bottom right. In this case: 0850 or 850.

 #214 Steps for Partial Quotients

Partial Quotients is a method some elementary teachers use to introduce long division to young children. In this method, kids don't have to know exactly how many times one number goes into another. They can use easy multiples that they know to begin, and narrow the number down from there. Here is how you do it!

Take, for example: $164 \div 6 =$

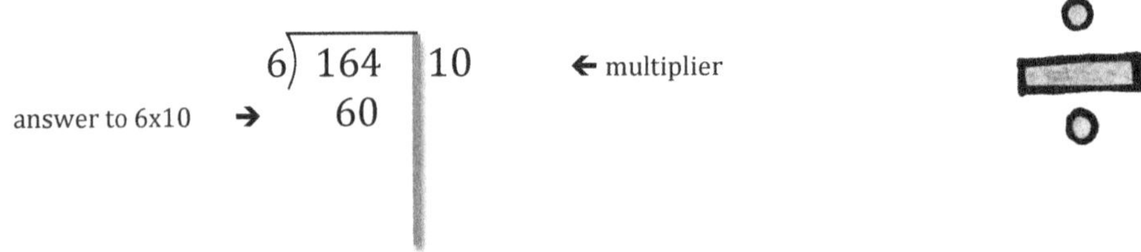

1. First, ask yourself how many 6s are in 164. Think about easy multiples of 6 like 6x 100= 600 and 6x10= 60. Obviously, 600 is much too big. So let's begin with 60. It would look like this:

$$6\overline{)164} \quad 10 \quad \leftarrow \text{multiplier}$$

answer to 6x10 → 60

2. Subtract to see how much you have left. 164-60= 104. Now repeat the steps, but this time see how may 6s go into 104. Think about multiples you know well. It can be anything, as long as it is under 104. Let's try 11. 11x 6= 66 so we will subtract 66 from the 104 we had left. Now we only have 38 left.

$$6\overline{)164} \quad 10$$

leftover → 104 11 ← new multiplier used

answer to 6x11 → - 66

leftover → 38

3. Continue on until you are left with a number smaller than 6. (This ends up being your remainder.) Add up the numbers along the right-hand side. This is your answer!

    For this example the answer is 27 R 2.

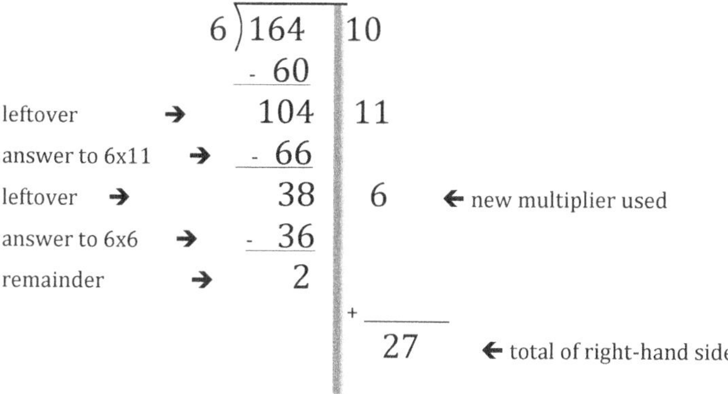

Other Books by Cindy McKinley and Patti Trombly

One Smile. McKinley & Byrne (Illumination Arts Publishing)

One Voice. McKinley & Byrne (Illumination Arts Publishing)

Workbook for 365 Teacher Secrets for Parents; A Collection of Additional Materials to Compliment the Text. McKinley & Trombly (found at www.365TeacherSecrets.com)

Other Books by MSI Press

A Believer-in-Waiting's First Encounters with God

Blest Atheist

Forget the Goal, The Journey Counts...71 Jobs Later

Joshuanism

Losing My Voice and Finding Another

Mommy Poisoned Our House Guest

Road to Damascus

Syrian Folktales

The Gospel of Damascus

The Marriage Whisperer

The Rise and Fall of Muslim Civil Society

The Rose and The Sword

The Seven Wisdoms of Life

Thoughts without a Title

Understanding the People Around You

When You're Shoved from the Right, Look to Your Left

Widow: A Survival Guide for the First Year